American Poetry and Culture
1945–1980

American Poetry and Culture 1945–1980

Robert von Hallberg

Harvard University Press
Cambridge, Massachusetts, and London, England   1985

Publication of this book has been aided by a grant from the
Andrew W. Mellon Foundation.

This book is printed on acid-free paper, and its binding
materials have been chosen for strength and durability.

Library of Congress Cataloging in Publication Data

Von Hallberg, Robert, 1946–
   American poetry and culture, 1945–1980.

   Bibliography: p.
   Includes index.
1.   American poetry—20th century—History and criticism.
2.   Literature and society—United States.
3.   Creeley, Robert, 1926–   —Criticism and interpretation.
4.   Merrill, James Ingram, 1926–   —Criticism and interpretation.
5.   Lowell, Robert, 1917–1977—Criticism and interpretation.
6.   Dorn, Edward, 1929–   —Criticism and interpretation.
I.   Title.
PS379.V58   1985   811′.54′09   84-22387
ISBN 0-674-03011-7

Pages 267–269 are an extension of the copyright page.

*In memory of my parents
Erin McGinnity and
Richard von Hallberg*

· Contents

We were wise indeed, could we discern truly the signs of our own time; and by knowledge of its wants and advantages, wisely adjust our own position in it.

Thomas Carlyle, "Signs of the Times" (1829)

· Introduction: Centers

Several friends have admitted to me that, however firmly literature or other arts may bear on their lives, the poetry of their contemporaries is almost entirely unknown to them. This situation, perhaps unremarkable, is sometimes thought to reflect on poets themselves, as though they had removed their art from the mainstream of American culture. The belief that the most serious, demanding art maintains an adversarial relationship to the culture at large is now so widely held that poetry is claimed to be permanently and properly off to the side of the nation's thought and expression; those poets whose rhetoric insists on this sideline position commonly seem the most genuine poets. My intention is to show that in the last thirty-five years a number of excellent poets have written well about what they have taken to be the range of thought and experience most central to American life. The place of poetry in the culture seems to me now secure and, measured against the recent past, mildly encouraging—despite all one hears of the death of poetry—largely because I see abundant evidence that many of the best recent poets have written with fascination about the spirit of their time. In order to make this case convincingly, I have focused on one sort of poetry.

In 1959 Karl Shapiro distinguished between "culture poetry and just *poetry*":

> the first type is that which attempts to explain culture. It can do this in the manner of the Metaphysical poets, who were troubled by scientific knowledge and who wished to compete with science; by rewriting history according to a plan; by tracing the rise and fall of a particular belief, and so forth. Culture

poetry is always didactic, as indeed most modern poetry is. It is a means to an end, not an end, like art. Culture poetry is poetry in reverse; it dives back into the historical situation, into culture, instead of flowering from it. And there it remains to enrich the ground for criticism.[1]

Critic that I am, my subject is culture poetry, and I know well what that excludes from attention here: Robert Lowell's "Will Not Come Back," Elizabeth Bishop's "One Art," Edgar Bowers' "An Elegy: December 1970," Robert Hass's "Against Botticelli." Many of the poems that I read to friends, upon the slightest pretext, will finally be crucial to a just assessment of recent American poetry, but they do not relate directly to my subject. What is left to me are some poems that obviously involve recent cultural history—inauthentic poems, Shapiro would claim.

My own view is that the years since World War II have been especially good for this culture poetry and that, far from deserving the stigma of inauthenticity, these poems honor the loftiest ambitions poets and critics have traditionally voiced for the art. On my side of this disagreement, I can claim Matthew Arnold as an ally:

The grand work of literary genius is a work of synthesis and exposition, not of analysis and discovery; its gift lies in the faculty of being happily inspired by a certain intellectual and spiritual atmosphere, by a certain order of ideas, when it finds itself in them; of dealing divinely with these ideas, presenting them in the most effective and attractive combinations,—making beautiful works with them, in short.[2]

Arnold had in mind Homer, Sophocles, Shakespeare, and Goethe; they set the highest standard of poetic achievement by incorporating their milieux intelligently, critically, and above all comprehensively. In 1795 Goethe vigorously defended contemporary German writing against one of its critics, "whose destructive work might only make productive writers disheartened, the sympathetic public listless, and the onlookers distrustful and indifferent."[3] His definition of a "classical national author"—exactly what he wanted to be—is worth attending to now:

He must, in the first place, be born in a great commonwealth, which after a series of great and historic events has become a happy and unified nation. He must find in his countrymen loftiness of disposition, depth of feeling, and vigor and consistency of action. He must be thoroughly pervaded with the national spirit, and through his innate genius feel capable of sympathizing with the past as well as the present. He must find his nation in a high state of civilization, so that he will have no difficulty in obtaining for himself a high degree of culture. He must find much material already collected and ready for his use, and a large number of more or less perfect attempts made by his predecessors. And finally, there must be such a happy conjuncture of outer and inner circumstances that he will not have to pay dearly for his mistakes, but that in the prime of his life he may be able to see the possibilities of a great theme and to develop it according to some uniform plan into a well-arranged and well-constructed literary work.[4]

No one would argue that recent American writers have commonly felt "a happy conjuncture of outer and inner circumstances"; post-Romantic poets, anyway, could admit to no such conjuncture. Yet never before have so many American poets registered bold claims to being a classical national author. Charles Olson, Allen Ginsberg, Robert Lowell, Edward Dorn, and A. R. Ammons have certainly attempted the synthetic culture poetry Goethe and Arnold describe, and the list could be extended. At the end of World War II, Americans were extraordinarily united. The national spirit had every reason to be high, for America had come out of severe economic depression to accomplish what the Europeans had plainly failed to achieve—the defeat of fascism. Traditionally, Europeans had figured in American thought as guardians of the past; after the war America took over the military guardianship of Europe, and with it came a challenge: could Americans measure up culturally as well as they had militarily? We answered this challenge by assuming the outward signs of European tradition, the way one might undertake the administration of a museum—vigorously, ambitiously. Americans suddenly recognized a new relationship not just to their own past but to the entire history of the West. As we saw ourselves after the war, the conditions for the production of a national classic set down by Goethe were almost fully met. Judging from the many attempts at long synthetic poems, American writers are still inspired by the power and scope of American culture.

Once we realize that the past thirty-five years have been conducive to culture poetry, the task of defining what makes for excellence in this

kind of writing remains. For Arnold, it is the business of poets to occupy themselves with the center of ideas in their time.[5] To Arnold's
notion of fresh, true, and timely ideas, I would add that the best culture poetry engages as well the feelings, experiences, and difficulties
that are considered the irreducible center of public life. And what
Americans think of as central to their lives, it has to be said, is especially compelling in the years following World War II, for, as Edward
Shils put it, "By the end of the 1940s, America had become the center
of the world. The increasing number of American intellectuals—academic and literary—who went abroad, thanks to the largesse of their
government and the private philanthropic foundations, were made
aware of this."[6]

This is the Roman feeling, and its basis is firm. One historian of the
postwar era begins his account with the observation that in 1938 the
American army consisted of 185,000 men and officers, none of whom
was stationed in a foreign country, and was supported by a budget
of $500 million. The United States had no military alliances then. A
generation later the United States had alliances with 48 nations and
1,517,000 soldiers and sailors stationed in 119 countries.[7] Americans
had every reason, if not right, to think that their experience was central to world history, but how to write about that experience is a tricky
matter.

Hearty patriotism promotes rhetoric, and by 1945 American poets
knew to be suspicious of Pindar's bass drum, as Pound called it. The
difficulty for poets was to hold on to the center, to profit from its energy, power, and consequence, but retain an ironic, sophisticated attitude that would save them from the facile jingoism for which
Americans abroad are infamous. An ironic tone may have been the
strictly literary inheritance of Eliot and Auden, but it served a larger
cultural office, too, for the last thing a Roman can afford is innocence.
If Eliot and Auden had not been the ironic predecessors whose tone
could be incorporated by postwar poets, they would have been invented. Worldliness and sophistication were the very qualities that
Americans had strong political reasons to display during the years
when the Pax Americana was being settled.[8]

Arnold knew that the center consists not only of ideas but also of
social institutions. Poets who wish to speak from the center must accept a measure of responsibility for established institutions whose acts
are far beyond the control of any single writer. Centrist poets, that is,
must live with their complicity, fully aware that moments of shame go
along with access to the cultural authority of a centralized culture.
Arnold wrote about four faces of the institutional center of England.

From 1851 to 1886 he served as a school inspector. Much of his prose—*The Popular Education of France* (1860), *The Twice-Revised Code* (1862), *A French Eton* (1863), and *Schools and Universities on the Continent* (1868)—was devoted to urging the British to undertake a more democratic and uniform approach to publicly supported education. Throughout his most famous book, *Culture and Anarchy* (1869), he chastises the institutions of Protestant dissent, partly because of their influence upon education but also because of their sectarian stubbornness, as he saw it, in resisting absorption in the national Church of England. He advocated liberalizing Church of England doctrine so that it could absorb into one unified religious community all of the Protestant sects of the latter nineteenth century. Then, too, he spoke of "our grand centre of life" as London, its streets and buildings ("its unutterable external hideousness") and its organ of civic communication ("the *Daily Telegraph!*"). All of these institutions, schools, universities, church, chapel, city, buildings, and newspapers could be subsumed under one head—the State. "Well, then," Arnold asked, "what if we tried to rise above the idea of class to the idea of the whole community, *the State,* and to find our centre of light and authority there?"[9]

More than a century later, this is an entirely different question. Arnold had no way of knowing what horrors could come of a state's taking too much responsibility unto itself; for him the problem was that the British government would not shoulder enough responsibility. But he had one advantage over us on this score: he could see more plainly, and discuss with greater honesty, the advantages that a centralized culture bears to a poet. Arnold spoke of these advantages in terms of style.

> The provincial spirit, again, exaggerates the value of its ideas for want of a high standard at hand by which to try them. Or rather, for want of such a standard, it gives one idea too much prominence at the expense of others; it orders its ideas amiss; it is hurried away by fancies; it likes and dislikes too passionately, too exclusively. Its admiration weeps hysterical tears, and its disapprobation foams at the mouth. We get the *eruptive* and the *aggressive* manner in literature; the former prevails most in our criticism, the latter in our newspapers. For, not having the lucidity of a large and centrally placed intelligence, the provincial spirit has not its graciousness; it does not persuade, it makes war; it has not urbanity, the tone of the city, of the centre, the tone which always aims at a spiritual and intellec-

tual effect, and not excluding the use of banter, never disjoins banter itself from politeness, from felicity. But the provincial tone is more violent, and seems to aim rather at an effect upon the blood and senses than upon the spirit and intellect; it loves hard-hitting rather than persuading.[10]

Arnold is not directly concerned here with poetic style; his interest is rather in those institutions, critical reviews and newspapers, which form the taste that poets address. Critics and journalists set the tone of what we call cultural discourse. Poets who catch that tone easily are the most likely to be well received. In 1864, when Arnold lectured at Oxford on "The Influence of Academies on National Spirit and Literature," he certainly thought that British culture suffered from its provinciality and that as a poet he suffered from the corrupted taste of his time. For a poet who does not wish to address an extravagant, promiscuous taste, the absence of a central academy is a genuine loss. An academy establishes correct literary opinion by upholding standards of clarity and a sense of propriety, without which the *"journeyman-work* of literature"—translation, philology, lexicography—will not be excellently accomplished.[11] The tone of the center is calm, confident, self-controlled, and temperate because the reason of the audience can be taken for granted. Fine shadings and distinctions are properly made because the audience is expected to make its own choices. Savage critics and poets alike overpower their readers, but civilized writers presume that their readers think and decide, after considering alternatives.

The two most commonly invoked evaluative principles in literary criticism are exactly opposed to each other. The best known rests on a notion of universality. In 1765 Samuel Johnson praised Shakespeare for having outlived his century; the timeliness of his writing, once past, left Shakespeare's poetry none the worse.[12] In 1800 Wordsworth said that the truth of poetry is "not individual and local, but general."[13] This criterion is too familiar to require explanation here; it is written into textbooks still. When Arnold in 1880 quoted Homer, Dante, Shakespeare, and Milton and spoke of their seriousness, he meant to be developing the tradition whereby the value of poetry does not change from century to century.[14] And Arnold's earliest piece of critical prose, the preface to his *Poems* (1853), follows in the line of the great poet-critics Johnson and Wordsworth. Arnold clearly holds that a writer most properly engages "the eternal objects of poetry, among all nations, and at all times." The poet, he asserts, should "escape the danger of producing poetical works conceived in the spirit of the passing time, and which partake of its transitoriness." His preface was written with the keen sense of a powerful adversary in mind—the reviewers and readers who were disinclined toward "any subjects but modern ones."[15] He knew his antagonists well: J. A. Froude, J. D. Coleridge, and his best friend Arthur Hugh Clough—all of whom criticized his poems for their antique subjects. Arnold's defense of himself is one of his strongest essays—his best ever, George Saintsbury thought.[16] Less than three years later he won the Oxford chair of poetry partly on the basis of this essay.

And yet, as I have suggested, Arnold has in fact set the terms for the countervailing argument: poetry should be evaluated more in terms of its contemporaneity than its universality. In 1869 he said that he who "has risen to the comprehension of his age: he who communicates that point of view to his age, he who interprets to it that spectacle [of a vast multitude of present facts], is one of his age's intellectual deliverers." In order to "interpret the activity of his age" a poet must in fact be in sympathy with it, Arnold says.[17] But sympathy is not enough: the hard task is to harmonize the ideas of the present, to set the religious, political, literary, and economic ideas of the time together.[18] To see the relation of one idea to another, to inquire into the *"rationale* of things," as he put it—this, not nay-saying, is what he meant by being critical.[19] Poets who manage this synthesis achieve something grand, exactly to the extent that their times are momentous. Arnold knew that he was living through an "epoch of expansion," as we are now: "the essence of an epoch of expansion is a movement of ideas, and the one salvation of an epoch of expansion is a harmony of ideas."[20] In 1869 England was a thriving empire. Queen Victoria was proclaimed Empress of India in 1876. A poet who could bring harmony to the ideas of the time would provide a cultural service, as the French did by bringing the Napoleonic code to their colonies.[21] Arnold was honest in admitting that this was in fact a thrilling prospect.

In one sense, contemporaneity is a humble standard for evaluating poetry. It entails the surrender of absolute criteria in favor of historical relativism. At one moment "the world's progress" may depend more upon fire and strength than upon sweetness and light; the climate of historiographical thought in nineteenth-century England made it relatively easy for Arnold to accept this viewpoint. Part of what he holds against the Hebraic habit of mind is the belief that Judaism provides "a sufficient basis for the whole of their life fixed and certain for ever."

Sticking to one's single standard of judgment, however high, was not Arnold's idea of civilization: "the being in contact with the main stream of human life is of more moment for a man's total spiritual growth, and for his bringing to perfection the gifts committed to him, which is his business on earth, than any speculative opinion which he may hold or think he holds."[22]

He customarily praised particular poets or poems by singling out certain qualities for approval: sanity, adequacy, serenity, cheerfulness, or seriousness.[23] The help he offers now, though, has little to do with whether poems display these qualities or whether they are sufficiently fortifying. Much of Arnold's criticism is limitedly Victorian. The overall argument for contemporaneity is, as I have said, relativistic. "Literary criticism's most important function," he said, "is to try books as to the influence which they are calculated to have upon the general culture of single nations or of the world at large."[24] In 1970, the expression of sanity may have been just that rare thing most deserving of esteem, but fifteen years earlier poetry may have had too much sanity. "The critic of poetry," according to Arnold, "should have the finest tact, the nicest moderation, the most free, flexible, and elastic spirit imaginable; he should be indeed the 'ondoyant et divers,' the *undulating and diverse* being of Montaigne."[25] At the risk of being *un peu trop ondoyant,* and with no hope of being genuinely comprehensive, I have selected for extended commentary a group of poets (Robert Creeley, John Ashbery, James Merrill, Robert Lowell, Edward Dorn, Mona Van Duyn, Robert Pinsky, and James McMichael) who are not all read by the same audience, and not all of whom care deeply about each other's work. More important, I have tried to allow the poets themselves their own flexibility, by not limiting my discussion to poets who strike any one particular attitude toward what they take to be the center of the culture. Arnold's greatest critic argued eloquently that writers properly "judge and condemn" the mainstream culture, though Trilling himself came to be appalled once this notion of an adversary culture hardened into a dogma for a generation of Americans who had no convincing claim even to being intellectuals.[26] All of the poets I write about have shown marked curiosity about the dominant American culture. Some have judged and praised, celebrated and questioned the center—as much by their styles as by their statements. These are the poets, it seems to me, whose flexibility and candor most deserve praise.

Although this book is intended to be synthetic in the sense of ranging over a lot of ground, I have not tried to exhaust the subject indicated by my title. I preferred to find my own way through this territory and have in fact taken satisfaction in avoiding some of the ways of exploring my subject (Allen Ginsberg as a political poet, for example) that might occur to many of my readers. Most of the poets whose writing appears in the quasi-political anthologies of gay poetry, women's poetry, or black, Chicano, and Amerasian poetry are not discussed here. Although this sort of decentralization of American literary life would be a major topic in a full history of American poetry and culture since 1945, my special interest here is in poetry written with an eye on the center. The justification for my inclusions and omissions is simply that the poems I do discuss lend the strongest support to the claim that the poetry of the last thirty-five years is unusually distinguished, especially when taken in large samplings. In order to strike a balance between historical argument and the advocacy of particular poets, I have organized the chapters in pairs: the odd-numbered chapters set out a broad context, and the even-numbered ones take up in detail the work of individual poets whose work seems exemplary in the larger context of their contemporaries' work. I have not tried to draw point-by-point connections between the contextual chapters and those on single poets. The main connections will be plain enough, and the poets I have singled out all deserve to have their writing discussed in their own terms—insofar as those are ever accessible.

1 · Audience, Canon

"Apostate, illaureate, and doomed to outlawry the modern poets may be"—Ransom believed that modernism put poets in this sorry position, and much of current literary opinion is on his side still.[1] In "The Decline of Anglo-American Poetry," Christopher Clausen argues that the influence of Eliot and modernism has brought about a disaster: "the decline in the American poetic audience that seems to have been most rapid between the 1920's and 1950's" has signaled "the disappearance of poetry as a major cultural force." Eliot believed that in order to represent the variety and complexity of modern civilization, "the poet must become more and more comprehensive, more allusive, more indirect, in order to force, to dislocate if necessary, language into his meaning."[2] Eliot presumed the worth of exactly what Clausen challenges: the poet's effort to render into poems (to interpret, Arnold would say) the thought and temper of the present. "It is highly probable," Clausen claims,

> that serious poetry has alienated its audience in large part because some traditional ideas about its forms and functions have, to put it mildly, gone out of fashion with 20th-century poets—that it should illuminate rather than simply mirror experience; that it should discriminate those aspects of experience which are important from those which are trivial or transient; that while it may be difficult, it ought not to be pedantic or obscurely private; and that its language and structure are more formal than those of prose.[3]

Many influential critics and poets share some of these beliefs. James Atlas, now an editor of *Atlantic Monthly*, has referred to the "distressing loss of an audience" for poetry. Herbert Leibowitz, editor of the poetry review *Parnassus,* has spoken of poetry readers as "phantom consumers." Joseph Epstein, editor of *American Scholar,* remarked in *Commentary* that "Never have writers seemed so much to be writing for themselves." Charles Molesworth, a contributing editor of *Salmagundi,* agrees with Epstein: "Though there are over seven hundred manuscripts submitted each year to the Yale Younger Poets competition, scarcely any first book by an American poet will sell that many copies." Wendell Berry has complained that poetry is now so specialized an art that "poets have very nearly become their own audience." Delmore Schwartz agreed and said that "it is more and more true that less and less people read serious poetry." Karl Shapiro imagined the audience for contemporary poetry as "a grim little army of poet-critics grinding out mean little stanzas under the gooseneck lamp."[4] These different writers often disagree among themselves about the causes of the situation they deplore, and most of them have one or another specific antidote to promote. The particular solution Clausen proposes is that poets not try so hard to keep up with their times, that they return to the heightened idioms of earlier poetry and to metrical verse.

Despite so much agreement about the absence of an audience for poetry, this is more a contention, or article of faith, than a report of facts. From 1925 until his death, Eliot made his living in publishing; distributing poetry was his business. In 1944 he observed that "there is, in fact, a considerable public for contemporary poetry: there is, perhaps, more curiosity, and more expectation, about contemporary poetry than there was a generation ago."[5] Eliot was attentive to a relative measure of the poetry audience, its alleged attrition or growth. The poetry audience is certainly smaller than for any of the other arts. But Eliot went on to point out in 1945 that what matters most is that a poet have "the right, small audience in his own time"; the poetry audience is properly an elite, a vanguard for a developing culture. Eliot's sense that the poetry audience properly prefigures the coming shape of the culture would meet with approval among most poets and critics today. This optimistic, avant-gardist sense of the proper role of poetry deepens the current malaise, for many contemporary writers and readers agree with Clausen that the poetry audience is now too small even to support an avant-garde.

With few exceptions (only Byron, Browning, and Tennyson come to mind), fiction has enjoyed an audience much greater than that of poetry. And poets have felt the anguish of comparison. Shelley remarked: "Nothing is more difficult and unwelcome as to write without a confidence of finding readers."[6] That poets have only small audiences in relation to other literary audiences is not even yesterday's news. It may be true, however, that in America poets command a smaller share of the national literary audience than in other countries, such as England.[7] Yet what is misleading about recent literary opinion is the assertion that poets now have a distressingly smaller audience than those of earlier American poets, and that poets themselves are to blame for this decline. Even poets, who have reason to know better, cringe guiltily when this finger is pointed their way.

The Waste Land, above all other poems, has been taken to represent the temper of Eliot's time, though he himself said that it was not written with such an objective in mind. The poem first appeared in America in 1922, in the pages of *The Dial,* which a few years later claimed a surprisingly large readership of 30,000, and was an instant cause celèbre.[8] In December Boni and Liveright brought out a hardcover edition of 1000 copies, and within months a second edition of 1000 copies was released. Those 2000 copies were enough to satisfy American readers for the next decade. In 1932 Eliot's *Poems, 1909–1929,* which included *The Waste Land,* was printed in a large edition of over 4000 copies. It took, then, about ten years after the initial publication of the poem for Eliot to be absorbed by American culture in a way reflected by the sale of his books.

The sales of other poets during the 1920s and 1930s were even less encouraging. Not until 1933, for instance, could *il miglior fabbro* find an American publisher for the *Cantos,* though they had been appearing in magazines since 1917. Wallace Stevens had established a distinguished reputation for himself after nine years of publishing in small magazines before his first book appeared on September 7, 1923; *Harmonium* is probably the most remarkable first book of American poems to appear since *Leaves of Grass.* The book had a printing of 1500, but in its first year fewer than 100 copies were sold. Stevens' royalties for the first half of 1924 amounted to $6.70. He wrote to Harriet Monroe: "I shall have to charter a boat and take my friends around the world."[9] The book was remaindered by Knopf, and Stevens, depressed by this reception, wrote no poetry for the next eight years. He was less content than Eliot and Pound to remain an avant-garde poet. About the same time that *Harmonium* appeared, Stevens' friend William Carlos Williams published *Spring and All,* containing two or three of what would become his most famous poems. This book was published in Paris in an edition of 300. Most of the copies sent to the United States for distribution were lost on the docks of New York; any books from Paris were then held up there as suspect. As for reviews, *Spring and All* received only two, both of them in *Poetry* magazine (the second was a reaction to the first).

These figures indicate that the poetry now regarded as most profoundly representative of this century was, during its time, taken to be far from the center of American life. The intelligent reviewers, like Mark Van Doren and Louis Untermeyer, rightly noted with alarm that this poetry was not trying to be popular, for scorn of popularity was an important part of modernist poetry. When these poets (Stevens is an exception here) wrote about history as if from the outside (as Eliot and Pound did in "Gerontion" and "Hugh Selwyn Mauberley," for instance), they were honestly reflecting their position in the culture of the 1920s: they were outsiders, expatriates. From outsiders, one does not expect what Arnold called "the tone of the centre," the moderation that comes from sympathy and complicity. The civic virtues are not the responsibility of the avant-garde. What America got from these outsiders was, in the main, poetry on the attack, a genuinely avant-garde poetry.

The generation born in the 1920s, when Eliot, Pound, and others were publishing the major modernist poems—poets such as Robert Creeley (b. 1926), Allen Ginsberg (b. 1926), Robert Bly (b. 1926), John Ashbery (b. 1927), and Edward Dorn (b. 1929)—knew their own avant-garde decade, the 1950s. While the major literary journals seemed to specialize in metrical poems about foreign cities, some of these poets were establishing tiny magazines and presses. *Origin,* which first appeared in the spring of 1951, was one of the first of these ventures. Later the *Black Mountain Review* was published by Creeley in Mallorca, where printing was cheap. Five hundred to 750 copies of each issue were printed, but Creeley could usually manage to distribute only about 200.[10] His own publishing history during this time tells the rest of the story. Between 1952 and 1959, he published seven books and pamphlets of his own poetry. Six of the seven appeared in editions running from 200 to 600 copies. In 1959 Jonathan Williams, Creeley's poet-publisher, evidently sensed a change in the market: he published *A Form of Women* in a printing of 2000. Three years later Scribner's brought out *For Love,* a collection of the poems published in those first seven books and pamphlets; the first printing was over 6000. Within ten years there would be 39,000 copies of this book in circulation.

Beginning in 1960 the poetic avant-garde was drawn into the mainstream of American literary life; since then there has been no avant-garde, though there have been poseurs. The causes of this change were various. A weakening political consensus helped make a change of literary taste seem increasingly appropriate during the 1960s.[11] The two literary events that contributed most to the lionizing of the avant-garde were the publication of Allen Ginsberg's *Howl* (1956) and Donald Allen's anthology, *The New American Poetry* (1960). The anthology, which deliberately set out to publicize the avant-garde, was remarkably successful: by the mid-1960s it had gone through eight printings for a total of 40,000 copies. Ginsberg's *Howl* is legendary: to date there are 315,000 copies in print. It is customary to think of the 1950s as a dull time for poets and of the 1960s as a culturally lively one for all. However, the popularity of Charles Olson, Robert Creeley, Allen Ginsberg, Gary Snyder, and others in the 1960s was mainly—though unwittingly—nostalgic: their styles were formed more in the 1950s, when they were writing their best poems, than in the 1960s, when they were popular.[12]

After 1960, as a result of this publicity, most of the avant-garde poets of the 1950s had little trouble finding trade presses to publish their books in printings they could only have dreamt about ten years earlier. Furthermore, the audience for all serious poetry, established as well as avant-garde, grew during the early 1960s. In one year, between 1963 and 1964, the total distribution of *Poetry* magazine jumped by almost 50 percent to just under 10,000. And no one needs to be reminded just how many small poetry magazines have appeared in the last twenty years; my university library subscribes to more than 80 American magazines devoted chiefly or exclusively to the publication of new poetry. One of the consequences of this growth of po-biz was that a young poet starting out in the 1960s stood a good chance of selling as many copies of his or her first book as T. S. Eliot had sold, forty years earlier, of *The Waste Land*. During the early 1960s Edward Dorn was known to readers of Donald Allen's *New American Poetry* and Donald Hall's *Contemporary American Poetry*, but otherwise his work was little known; his books were seldom reviewed. Since the appearance of *Gunslinger* he has achieved a much wider following, though even now several of the most influential critics of contemporary poetry—Helen Vendler, Harold Bloom, Richard Howard, Robert Pinsky—have taken no notice of his writing. His second book, *Hands Up!*, appeared in 1964; 1700 copies were printed. Five years later 2000 additional copies were issued. Even though this book has received very little acclaim, in the decade following its publication 3700 copies were in circulation; only about half as many copies of *The Waste Land* were available in America between 1922 and 1932.

Several forces combined to increase the poetry audience. During

the 1960s the federal government gave support to libraries, and their
purchases generally increased after World War II. But libraries today
rarely purchase more than a total of about 400 copies of the average
book of poems; some books do a little better, or worse, depending upon
prizes and reviews in the *Library Journal* or Kirkus. Changes in the
material production of books also have to be taken into account. Type-
setting has become much more expensive over the last thirty years.
Unless print runs were increased, the unit price of each individual volume would have increased stunningly. During the same period trade
publishing houses grew into or were absorbed by large corporations.
In order to justify the activation of a large, often cumbersome apparatus of editing, marketing, and distribution such as Knopf, Viking, and
Houghton Mifflin maintain, a respectable print run is needed. These
houses routinely print 4000 copies of a new poetry book on their current lists, even for poets who have had little time to establish a following. The consequences of these changes in the publishing business
(and there have been others too, such as the proliferation of small
presses) has been to increase pressure on salesmen and bookdealers
to find an audience for poetry.[13]

And that has been done. There now is a stable poetry audience, still
minuscule but not so small as it was a half-century ago. It is a national
audience, though it is not spread evenly across the country. It is also
coherent and even possesses some independence of taste. If its taste
were not somewhat independent, only books that received the national
prizes and notices in the large literary journals would enjoy large sales.
Certainly, when a book receives the famous prizes, people who do not
follow contemporary poetry will buy and read the book. Ashbery's *Self-
Portrait in a Convex Mirror* (1975) is one example. That book swept
the awards: the National Book Critics Circle Award, the National Book
Award, and the Pulitzer Prize. Well over 20,000 copies are now in
print. This post-prize rush indicates that the poetry audience is expandable, when the authority of prize panels can be rallied behind a
single volume, as it can only too easily. The other big prize-winning
poet of our time is James Merrill, who has two National Book Awards,
one Bollingen, and one Pulitzer Prize to his credit. His first prize-winning book, *Nights and Days* (1966), which got the National Book
Award, did the best so far: 8500 copies are in circulation. Edward Dorn
has received none of these prizes; to my knowledge, he has never received a Guggenheim or an NEA fellowship. All the same, his *Slinger*
(1975), which was well reviewed by Marjorie Perloff in *The New Republic*, but ignored by *Poetry, Sewanee, Hudson, Georgia, Partisan*,
the *New Yorker*, and the *New York Review of Books*, has independently

found its own audience of about 8500, much to the credit of the audience for new poetry.[14]

The poetry audience has a special coherence. The large trade presses specialize in what can be termed an incoherent audience. Poets sometimes think that these houses have doors to a large readership and national acclaim that small presses cannot offer. The large concerns do routinely advertise in journals, such as *The New Republic* and the *New York Review of Books,* that have readerships of over 100,000; probably books from these houses also stand a better chance of receiving reviews than those appearing from Sand Dollar, Greywolf, Four Seasons, Wingbow, Sun, or even Black Sparrow. Still, the judgment of very few critics has an important influence on the reception of poetry. To give a sense of the indifference to poetry in the national intellectual journals, I should mention that in 1979 the *New York Review* reviewed a total of five books of recent poetry; one was a new book of poems by Derek Walcott, one the *Collected Poems* of Stanley Kunitz; the others were translations and books by European poets. *The New Republic,* published weekly, managed to review ten books: five by American poets; one translation; two by European poets; and two anthologies—one of women poets, one of American light verse. These journals are far from representing the poetic segment of the national culture; they want their literary taste to be thought of as global, or at least European.

The real difference between large and small presses has to do with distribution. Knopf and the other big houses have direct access to the chain bookdealers, such as Walden and Dalton, with outlets in the suburban shopping centers; their distribution network can reach an inclusive readership that displays no very definite characteristics of taste. The fact that Wingbow, which published six books in 1979, can find 8500 people who want to read *Slinger* and that Atheneum, whose 1979 list included 222 books and is owned by Scribner's, which carried another 325, can find only 8500 readers for Merrill's *Nights and Days,* even after the National Book Award, suggests that, first, the influence of awards is limited and, more important, that the distribution machinery of the large houses has no particular effect with poetry. Access to Walden and Dalton bookshops means nothing to poets. The audience for poetry is dispersed across the country, but it is concentrated in urban centers and particularly in college and university towns. Small presses and poetry distributors, such as Bookpeople, know how to reach this audience efficiently. A book from Wingbow can sell as many copies as one from Atheneum, and the Wingbow book will cost less because the smaller press operates with lower overhead.[15]

Large publishing houses, however, are not discouraged by their limited ability to sell poetry. They can live with those limits; the publishing of high-culture writing brings prestige (a huge photo of a jubilant Saul Bellow hangs on the lobby wall of the New York office of Penguin-Viking), prestige brings diverse authors, and many authors bring money to their publishers. Nevertheless, the prestige syllogism is not powerful enough to create interest from scratch. Editors at the houses I mentioned promote poetry because they are personally interested in it, and they make most editorial decisions on the acquisition of manuscripts by themselves. The editors at Knopf and Houghton Mifflin have undertaken new poetry series. They can increase the number of poetry volumes published only because a stable audience of about 2000 or more readers can be reached for most books. About $10,000 to $12,000 of capital is tied up in the production of an average book of poems. Editors know that they can recover most of this with each book they publish, and some volumes will bring in a little more. Because an audience is there, the risk with any one book seldom amounts to more than a few thousand dollars. If it now appears that too much poetry is published, that there is a "creative glut," in Karl Shapiro's phrase, that is due largely to the existence of a small but reliable group of people who are curious enough to want to look into most of what is published and distributed nationally.[16]

A stable audience that reads a lot of poetry has rather sophisticated, if trendy, tastes. Even limited exposure to the verse of the 22 percent of all Americans who write poems or stories shows how selective the poetry audience is. Books published by national presses seldom reveal much influence of the dominant strains of naive poetry: the sentimental and the didactic-inspirational. Editors weed out such verse quickly because it does not meet the standards of the national audience. There are of course more refined measures of sophistication. A set of distinct ideas about what constitutes the poetic quality of writing prevails in this audience, so distinct that one can identify the characteristics of certain period-styles that reflect as well as stabilize poetic taste; this stabilizing effect is sometimes enforced by institutions. The Bare Style is the most easily recognized and widely employed; Robert Pinsky has analyzed it brilliantly, and Paul Breslin later showed its relation to popularized depth psychology.[17] W. S. Merwin more or less invented the style; Merwin, Mark Strand, and Philip Levine practice it artfully. Their epigones are too many to name. The three masters of the Bare Style are all published by Atheneum. The style has been diffused to young poets partly through the Iowa Writers' Workshop, partly through particular journals such as *Field*. Marvin Bell, who oversees the poetry program at Iowa, also publishes through Atheneum. The Cosmopolitan Style, whose influence is now far less than that of the dominant period-style, was started by James Merrill. Anthony Hecht, John Hollander, and Turner Cassity are all masters of this manner of writing, and Alfred Corn is the brightest young poet working in it. Merrill and Hecht are also published by Atheneum (the Atheneum list had closed before Corn circulated his first book).[18] While Daryl Hine edited *Poetry* magazine (1969–1977), Cassity and Corn each received two of the magazine's prizes. Other, now less influential, period-styles, such as the one forged by Robert Creeley, persist as well. What matters here is that such period-styles exist at all, and that the range of tested options for poets is broad enough to allow the formation of several conventional styles. Few periods maintain simultaneously several period-styles, in which distinguished work proceeds.

Some characteristics of current poetic style are so conventional that even poets writing in thoroughly different styles share them, and one of these traits shows pointedly where the main audience for poetry lies. In the Preface to *Lyrical Ballads* Wordsworth says that a verse-writer "makes a formal engagement that he will gratify certain known habits of association, that he not only thus apprizes the Reader that certain classes of ideas and expressions will be found in his book, but that others will be carefully excluded."[19] Exactly because words carry with them "known habits of association," a poet's diction is a sure sign of how a poet imagines his audience. Poetic diction consists not only of terms that are frequently used but, more important, of words employed in such a way as to show that their habits of association are so well known that they can be taken for granted. In every period there are a small number of words by means of which poets can invoke habits of feeling or thinking without stipulating just why those habits are justified in a particular passage. The terms of poetic diction are the overly taxed words, those expected to do a great deal of work without much help from the poet. They are found most often at the beginnings and ends of lines, where they have the greatest chance of setting a tone. Also they are commonly found in odd combination with more usual words that are meant to be overpowered by the aura-bearing term of poetic diction. Young poets who are concerned to establish their own authority are the ones most likely to become addicted to the words that come to suggest, for a short while, bona fide poetry.

I have assembled a small anthology of passages exemplifying the use of terms that comprise a poetic diction common in American poetry over the past thirty-five years. These words belong to no one school or style of poetry.

> A womb of celluloid already
> contains my dotage and my total absence   *Adrienne Rich*

> Empowered now by absence, blessed with tireless ease
>   *Richard Wilbur*

> . . . I was there, and yet with a sort of absence . . .
>   *Richard Howard*

.   .   .

> Let's fly to the famous Asian cities,
> Stealing our maps from dark museums,
>   Ancient, inaccurate maps
>   With curly-headed winds.   *Henri Coulette*

> Surely the plainest thug who read them
> Would cluck with the ancient pity.   *James Wright*

> It was the toothless murmuring
>   Of ancient willows, who . . .   *John Ashbery*

> Ancient cadences return . . .   *John Hollander*

> I am happy in this ancient place . . .   *Robert Bly*

.   .   .

> As solid-seeming as antiquity,
> you frown above
> the *New York Sunday Times*   *Adrienne Rich*

> Day dwindles, drowning, and at length is gone
> I the wide and antique eyes . . .   *Richard Wilbur*

.   .   .

> Who will unhorse this rider
> and free him from between
> the walls of iron, the emblems
> crushing his chest with their weight?   *Adrienne Rich*

... They are fit to be taken for signs, these emblems
Royally sane ...   *Richard Wilbur*

... O annual, grand
Tourist: Watch all the arch, old emblems fall ...   *John Hollander*

.   .   .

Or, like a sunbather, whose lids retain
A greenish, gemmed impression of the sun
In lively, fluctuant geometries,
you sometimes contemplate a single image,
Utterly silent, utterly at rest.   *Anthony Hecht*

                    Today the
light gives less geometric shapes   *John Hollander*

.   .   .

... in nature too there is a history ...   *Howard Nemerov*

But how to draw the history
Of things that matter most ...   *John Hollander*

... the cars
... Echo like history
Down walled avenues ...   *George Oppen*

They fell to stroking their shyest histories   *W. S. Merwin*

.   .   .

... you
alert to presence and entrance
man your pick and hammer   *A. R. Ammons*

Presences were everything.   *Richard Howard*

This is the presence of things present ...   *Henri Coulette*

Absence as presence; where, in skies not ours,
An empty flagstaff seeks the zenith still.   *Turner Cassity*

.   .   .

What is it that one sells, the self? *Howard Nemerov*

. . . Self cries to self. *Charles Gullans*

. . . self to self shall roar
Till, deaf and blind to all,
I shall be self no more. *Richard Wilbur*

Yet I cannot escape the picture
Of my small self in that bank of flowers . . . *John Ashbery*

. . . my self,
voluble in the dark side of hills . . . *A. R. Ammons*

Essential arrogance become the perfect self . . . *Turner Cassity*

The self has agreed to lecture
before a psychoanalytic group. *Robert Hass* .

Alphabetically, then: Absence, Ancient, Antique, Emblem, Geometry, History, Presence, and Self. These words resonate for a particular sector of the reading public. Although some of them (Absence, Geometry) are trendier than others (Ancient, Emblem), they are all common in educated circles, more particularly in academic literary criticism.

"The Female Presence in the Novels of Virginia Woolf and Colette"

"The Vortex: Five Essays on Symbolic Form and the Geometry of Aesthetic Vision"

"Beyond the Meaning of History: The Quest for a Southern Myth in Faulkner's Characters"

"Beyond the Imprisoning Self: Mystical Influences on Singer, Bellow and Malamud"

"The Presence of Absence: Studies in the Theory of Tragic Structure"

These titles come, rather obviously, from recent volumes of *Dissertation Abstracts*. The eight words I have listed are firmly institution-

alized. Literary scholars and poets seem to agree that they signify inherently interesting notions, that rather little needs to be done in a
poem to suggest the powerful feelings attached to them. These words
are easily promoted from the literal to the figurative level—easily and
without justification. But the truth is that, as these words are debased
by loose usage, a poet must in fact work all the harder to give them
exactness and justness.

A number of conclusions follow from the fact that the audience for
contemporary poetry can be identified to a considerable extent with
one particular set of social institutions: colleges and universities. Most
important, literary critics can ask whether poets are addressing the
subjects that are most consequential to its audience. For surely one
way of evaluating "culture poetry" is to ask if its engagement of common experiences is ambitious, farsighted, critical. Only poor poets
flatter their audience interminably; only negligible ones play always to
the reader's prejudices. In the forty years since the end of World War
II, American intellectuals have been studied thoroughly. A critic now
has a great deal of help from historians and social scientists in defining
the crucial issues facing the intellectual and academic communities of
this country. One can reasonably measure the degree to which various
poets either flatter or question the beliefs of their audience, and this
measurement ought properly to bear on a just estimation of the value
of recent poetry.

At present minor poetry (most of the writing in these conventional
styles is certainly that) is especially encouraged and also accomplished. This is no backhanded praise of contemporary poetry. In
Canto 81, Pound wrote: "What counts is the cultural level." Quoting
Villon from a prison in Pisa, he asked, "où sont les heurs of that year."
He was remembering, among others, some of the minor writers—Victor Plarr, John Henry Newbolt, Edgar Jepson—who had once formed
a milieu in London. In Canto 80 he addressed his daughter, Mary de
Rachewiltz:

> Quand vous serez bien vieille
>   remember that I have remembered,
>   mia pargoletta,
>   and pass on the tradition
> there can be honesty of mind
>   without overwhelming talent
> I have perhaps seen a waning of that tradition[20]

Pound knew that the strength of minor poetry is one of the more reliable indices of the cultural level of a nation. When accomplished writ-

ing is possible without extraordinary talent, the language itself (not a particular genius) is upholding the possibilities of meaning and communication. There is no reason to think that the proliferation of minor poetry in any way impedes the progress of a major poet. Nor should literary critics or poets want to see the circulation of poetry, which upholds minimal standards of taste, in any way lessened; its circulation is a vital sign of the culture. Minor poetry requires sustenance, access to publishing outlets, and a stable, appreciative audience. American academic institutions provide much of this institutional support. Major poets will come on their own—some say they are born.

The distinction between major and minor poetry is one of those few basic issues upon which the project of literary criticism has traditionally rested. One must be able to distinguish clearly between major and minor poets in order to form a canon. By the term "canon" I mean to refer to a consensus of literary critics, historians, and readers on a list of poets and poems representing the best; more particularly, I am interested in the formation of a national-historical canon that would include recent American poetry. In order to have a canon one need not have unanimity, but the areas of disagreement must be acknowledged as reasonably disputable. There is a canon, for example, of English Romantic poetry, though the place of Byron (and *Don Juan* in particular) is one of those subjects about which historians and critics agree to disagree, without endangering the overall consensus. Consensus shades off into greater uncertainty when the names of Landor and Crabbe come up. Robert Bridges and T. Sturge Moore, or Landor and Crabbe, may be considered by some to be excellent minor poets; a canon can be large enough to include some poets who will be read only by an ardent few. But when critics, such as Yvor Winters or Ezra Pound, profess that Landor, Crabbe, Bridges, and Moore are unrecognized major poets, the canon is in jeopardy.

The touchiest question in canon formation is not that of inclusion. A literary canon is more expandable than legal or theological canons because literary canons are not expected to be doctrinally homogeneous, though the critical standards upon which the canon rests are expected to account for all entries on the accepted list. Frank Kermode has recently argued persuasively that literary canons change more by accommodation than by the elimination of contenders, exactly because literary institutions (college and university humanities divisions, editorial boards, and the like) are notably weak by comparison with other social institutions.[21] The easiest way to accommodate contenders is to issue minor-poet standing liberally. But when hierarchi-

cal relations arise between canonized poets—differences between
major and minor poets—accommodation is difficult: the standards
that would provide Landor with major status might well subordinate
Wordsworth to minor standing. Over demotions there is serious fighting, since the institutional consequences of canonical status are material for critics, historians, and even for poets, who emulate models.

Pound seemed to think that minor poets are "Good writers without
salient qualities. Men who are fortunate enough to be born when the
literature of a given country is in good working order."[22] Eliot was
more delicate: "whatever a minor poet may be, a major poet is one the
whole of whose work we ought to read, in order fully to appreciate any
part of it: but we have somewhat qualified this extreme assertion already by admitting [to major status] any poet who has written even
one long poem which combines enough variety in unity." Having introduced the troublesome matter of the long poem, he then takes back
some ground:

> The difference between major and minor poets has nothing to
> do with whether they wrote long poems, or only short poems—
> though the *very* greatest poets, who are few in number, have all
> had something to say which could only be said in a long poem.
> The important difference is whether a knowledge of the whole,
> or at least of a very large part, of a poet's work, makes one enjoy
> more, because it makes one understand better, any one of his
> poems. That implies a significant unity in his whole work.[23]

Eliot rightly focuses on the oeuvre rather than the single poem. His
remarks serve as reminder that major status has little to do with the
production of any one poem, a "masterpiece." The production of a
masterpiece has traditionally served to validate only technical skill and
journeyman standing, admission to the guild of qualified craftsmen.[24]
Furthermore, the production of an acknowledged masterpiece depends upon a consensus with regard to the demands of a genre. By
Eliot's time, generic conventions had lost force; the critical term
"masterpiece" consequently lacked importance and currency. Eliot
prefers to recognize as major the most ambitious poets, whose entire
careers bear witness to a wide range and diversity of subject or style.
By Eliot's standard, one minor poet might well be a better craftsman
than some major poet. Auden saw the difficulty clearly: "Only a minor
talent can be a perfect gentleman; a major talent is always more than a
bit of a cad. Hence the importance of minor writers—as teachers of
good manners. Now and again, an exquisite minor work can make a

master feel thoroughly ashamed of himself."[25] But then a major work leaves a minor poet feeling trivial.

The attempt at a long poem in itself does not assure major standing (otherwise, Kenneth Koch would be our major major poet). Yet a poet whose career displays diversity may well include an effort at a long poem, since longer forms often extend range of subject and style. If a long poem is an utter failure, the attempt matters little; only an achieved extension of range in a long poem would help readers to appreciate better the other work of that poet. In sum, a major poet displays throughout the oeuvre a diversity of either subject or style (Eliot does not favor either side of the dichotomy); a major poet cannot be properly evaluated by reference to a single poem, even if it is called a masterpiece.

The difference between major and minor poets is rarely pressed with reference to the poetry of the last forty years—which is one reason why it is not possible to refer to a canon of postwar poetry. Reviewers and blurbists often call Ashbery (or even someone else) a major poet, but the label is meaningless so long as no effort is made to define the term. A recent ad in the *American Poetry Review* described "The Great Living Poets Institute" at the University of Maine; Basil Bunting, Robert Creeley, Archibald MacLeish, Stephen Spender, May Sarton, and Constance Hunting were the presiding dignitaries. Although such statements give evidence of a desire for a canon, they have little to do with genuine canon formation because they arise from a void rather than a consensus. (Who *is* Constance Hunting?[26])

One obvious explanation why recent poetry appears little affected by the institutions of criticism is that too little time has passed for substantial agreement to be attained. To some degree, contemporary literature must be noncanonical. In the future, agreement will be reached, breached, and reached again; intermittently, a consensus as to the poets and poems of 1945–1980 most deserving of commentary and preservation will prevail. Patience is plainly to the point, but more than time must pass before agreement can be achieved. Some progress toward agreement on evaluative standards is necessary too. In 1955 a consensus did exist on a list of many of the major and minor poets of the preceding thirty-five years: Eliot, Frost, Stevens, and Moore were all recognized masters. Tate, Ransom, and Jarrell were understood to be lesser figures. Pound, Crane, and Williams were in a limbo of acknowledged dispute.

It might be thought that in 1955 there was a greater interest in poetry than there is now (surely there was somewhat closer agreement on evaluative criteria). A canon may seem worth constructing only when poetry is understood to be articulating the priorities of a culture. The mundane form of a canon counts most: textbooks and anthologies serve as the basis of literary education. The growth in the audience for contemporary poetry, however, is one sign of considerable interest in poetry today, and evidence of this interest mounts (though the spirit sinks) as one tallies up the anthologies of contemporary poetry that have appeared in the last forty years. Few anthologists directly address the absence of a canon. Instead they hedge their bets by taking on all comers, as though we might be living in the Age of Ashbery, or of Ginsberg, Creeley, Wakoski, Howard, Hollander, or Hecht—who knows? The dimmest prospect is that this may turn out to be the Age of the Anthology, when only errant sampling can reflect the worth of poetry, even though in such uncertainty anthologies lack their use as reflections of the cultural coherence of an age.

Eliot argued that major poets are least well served by an anthology; they can be fairly measured only after extensive reading of their work. A minor poet, he believed, sits comfortably in the pages of an anthology. The many editors of recent eclectic anthologies imply that now is simply a time of minor poetry, and even some poets are convinced. In 1965 Irvin Ehrenpreis proclaimed the Age of Lowell, but the poet himself asked only for a place "on the minor slopes of Parnassus." "The anthology," Lowell said, "holds up without us."[27] In 1979 *Poetry* ran this note:

> Believing that "there are not two or three towering poets whose careers indicate the poetic shape of the past twenty-five or thirty years" and that "The real poetic achievement of the period would be shown by the thirty or forty best *poems,*" Robert Schultz and A. R. Ammons are planning an anthology of such poems.[28]

And they invite suggestions. Ammons is giving up on the notion that this may be the Age of Lowell, Berryman, Olson, Ashbery, Ginsberg, or, of course, Ammons. In Eliot's terms, he is relinquishing the possibility of a major poet for our time, which in itself is a criticism of the quality of contemporary culture, though there can be no question about all six of the poets named laying claim to the kind of attention Eliot thought due to a major poet. Only one who dared to be measured as a major poet would entitle a book *History, The Maximus Poems,* or *The Fall of America.* American culture seems automatically to foster poets who deliberately try to be major. The question is whether critics and historians, driven by the conviction that the construction of a canon may well serve the highest interests of the literary culture, will set about the task of earnestly measuring achievement against aspiration.

In literary criticism, the term "canon" is partly figurative; critics hold no church councils to sanction a particular list.[29] The word helps to vest authority in literary opinion, which is often loose and unauthoritative in itself. The figurative dimension of the term indicates the ambitions of literary culture, and these deserve to be spelled out. In Latin *canon* refers to a rule, and this is to the point, for the idea of a literary canon has something to do with Rome. Canonical poetry reflects, and thus reinforces, a rule or law; it meets the demands a culture has of its past. When historians attempt to define the sensibilities of an age, one of their main resources is the prevailing canon, for it represents the tastes and manners of the time. The most ambitious literary critics, who know they can help mold ideology, set themselves the task of constructing a canon. Samuel Johnson in the *Lives of the Poets,* Arnold, Eliot, Pound, and Winters all attempted this. In the last decade, Harold Bloom's efforts on behalf of Geoffrey Hill, A. R. Ammons, Mark Strand, and others had this objective; surely it is what Hugh Kenner had in mind as well, when he urged the readers of the *New York Times Book Review* to pay attention to Louis Zukofsky or when he designated the first half of this century the Pound Era.[30] The complaint is often heard that these critics want to limit matters unnecessarily. Why did Winters not simply celebrate the virtues of Robert Bridges, T. Sturge Moore, Fulke Greville, and Barnabe Googe, without attacking Yeats and Donne? Most of us hope for the time to read them all. Time, however, was not the issue—taste was. Critics who build canons deliberately fight not for a list of poets only, but for a proper audience whose taste is formed correctly rather than eclectically. For Wordsworth, literary taste was not easily separable from "our moral feelings." Canonists worry about what will enable a community of readers to distinguish first- from second-rate thought and expression. A national canon stands as proof that such distinctions can be made so as to command assent; that the nation asks from its writers support for its policies, at the very least its educational policies; that one national objective is to preserve, by education, a hold on the past and a claim on the future.

The institution of the canon has medieval and authoritarian roots. E. R. Curtius said that "Canon formation in literature must always proceed to a selection of classics," and Frank Kermode has shown how the idea of a literary classic—Vergil is the type—depends upon one or another variety of imperialism.[31] This is not to say that only empires have an interest in forming canons. Liberal and totalitarian, insular and cosmopolitan cultures have all set canons. But canon formation has a particular function in an empire. When critics have as an objective the formation of a canon and the selection of classic texts, they tacitly presume or deliberately construct a culture with a strong authoritative center, a metropolitan culture. A canon demonstrates not only the quality of a culture but also its coherence, especially in terms of quality. The nations that most need to demonstrate coherence are those that are most open to diverse influences and are yet striving to assert hegemony, which is the situation of a colonizer. A culture that is spread over the globe needs to demonstrate its ideological integrity, and not just for moral reasons. An extended culture has an interest in showing that it is not overextended and vulnerable in its diffuseness; it must display the coherence to confront aliens and hold its own.

Empires are not made or broken by poems, but through poetry they are remembered and somehow even justified. During the decade after the war, and since, there has been a demand in America for those signs of cultural coherence that help to ratify imperium. The authority of contemporary writers is far from indispensable to the survival of an American economic empire; there is no reason to exaggerate the utility of poetry now (aside from the perennial desire of litterateurs to feel important), but neither should it be underestimated. The nation has a use for a canon, for classics and for worthy contemporary poems: to validate in one not altogether abstruse way its right to global superiority. Madison Avenue understands this sort of need, which is why it produced the television commercial about the appeal of American popular music to people all over the world—that bit of cultural enthusiasm is meant to make it *right* to drink Coca-Cola. American mass culture has successfully met the needs generated by expansion. If only the mass-level culture answers this need, the national interest may be ill served because television series, rock music, and other cultural exports often plainly express barbarous and shallow tastes. The sanctions of high culture are needed too, just to show that the culture is vital and coherent at multiple levels. Eliot referred to this particular function of poetry as the aesthetic sanction: "any way or view of life which gives rise to great art is for us more plausible than one which gives rise to inferior art or to none."[32] My point is not only that, as Eliot says, high culture has its own sanction to dispense, but also that when a culture shows vitality on the levels of high and mass culture, the impression of cultural coherence is the special dividend—one that an expansive culture particularly wants to receive.

In the 1980s there are good reasons to doubt whether one can accurately speak of a center in American culture, and this is an old uncertainty in American thought.[33] As recently as the 1950s, however, the center was in less question. Those years are customarily regarded as a time when strain and contention were repressed—in family life, in national politics, in letters. But the evidence in poetry suggests that this was an ambitious, complicated, and exciting decade. And New York was then the acknowledged cultural center. David Riesman and Nathan Glazer could plausibly remark in 1955 that "new ideas have their headquarters in New York."[34]

In the 1950s Americans were not just aware of being a centrist society; they were vigorously proud of their concentration. Senator Fulbright introduced a bill in the spring of 1958 to establish the National Cultural Center that later became the Kennedy Center for the Performing Arts. The debate surrounding the bill concerned only the selection of a site and the financing of the building; no one thought it a bad idea. There might have been disagreement about Washington as the proper location of a national cultural center, had the federal government not committed finances three years earlier to the plans for Lincoln Center in New York. In 1871 Whitman was commissioned to write "Song of the Exposition" for a fundraising drive to underwrite a cultural and science center in New York.

> Come Muse migrate from Greece and Ionia
> Cross out please those immensely overpaid accounts,
> That matter of Troy and Achilles' wrath, and Æneas',
>   Odysseus' wanderings,
> Placard "Removed" and "To Let" on the rocks of your
>   snowy Parnassus . . .[35]

Whitman got $100 for the poem, but New York had to wait for its center. In the spring of 1959 Eisenhower himself went to the true cultural center to toss the first shovelful of earth for Lincoln Center:

> Here in the heart of our greatest metropolitan center men of vision are executing a redevelopment of purpose, utility and taste . . . The beneficial influence of this great cultural adventure will not be limited to our borders. Here will occur a true interchange of the fruits of national cultures. From this will develop a growth that will spread to the corners of the earth, bringing with it the kind of human message that only individuals, not governments, can transmit.[36]

While speeches were made about the New York center, the debate about financing the Washington Center continued, with even poets joining in. A week after Eisenhower went to New York, Robert Frost proposed to State Department officials that a Department of Arts be established with a Secretary of cabinet rank. That Secretary should be a poet, of course, "because poets are spokesmen while other arts are silent." The following spring Frost returned, to testify before the Senate on behalf of a bill to create a National Academy of Culture (Arnold would have smiled): "Everyone comes down to Washington to get equal with someone else. I want our poets to be declared equal to— what shall I say?—the scientists. No, to big business."[37]

In American poetry of the 1950s there was a tone of the center. The poet who best maintained that tone, and who long insisted on its connection to New York, is John Hollander (though now even he has left the city for New Haven). In "New York" (1970) he defends the city life against the suburban lure by claiming for New Yorkers virtues that are mainly social—good sense, civilized conversation, and an environment that, with a decent plainness, exhibits the tears in the social fabric. He forthrightly accepts the commitment to consensus politics that logically accompanies Augustan love of the metropolis:

> Ed Koch, my congressman, can represent me
> Because there is about as much good sense
> Concentrated in his constituents
> As there is anywhere; my children go
> To un-selfconscious school at home, and so
> They feel at home in school—good luck, it's true.
> But whether in China or, indeed, Peru,
> In small towns, the well-favored and the wretch,
> Haven't much room in which their luck can stretch.[38]

The test of Hollander's position, so far as poetry is concerned, is whether the tone of the center is sufficiently flexible to render a rich variety of subject matter intelligently. One of the best poems in his first book, "For Both of You, the Divorce Being Final" (1958), is an occasional poem—itself an expressly civilized sort of writing—about divorce. At the end of a masterful first strophe, stretching an elaborate rhetorical syntax over almost fifteen lines, Hollander flatly laments his inability to respond fittingly to what is an only too common urban experience, the divorce of friends: "what we lack are rituals adequate/To things like this."[39] (Hollander would years later write movingly about his own divorce in "The Dying Friend" and "The Park."[40]) His claim here is the commonplace that we no longer live within archaically sanctioned social forms, that we are somewhat at sea socially. But then the poem takes its real direction.

> We tell some anxious friends
> *"Basta!* They know what they are doing"; others
> Whom we dislike and who, like queens, betray
> Never a trace of uneasiness, we play with:
> "No, it could never work, my dears, from the start.
> We all knew that. Yes, there's the boy to think of,"
> And so on. Everyone makes us nervous. Then,
> For a dark instant, as in your unlit foyer
> At sundown, bringing a parcel, we see you both
> And stifle the awkward question: "What, are *you* here?"
> Not because it has been asked before
> By Others meeting Underground, but simply
> Because we cannot now know which of you
> Should answer, or even which of you we asked.
> We wait for something to happen in the brown
> Shadows around us. Surely there is missing
> A tinkle of cymbals to strike up the dirge
> And some kind of sounding brass to follow it,
> Some hideous and embarrassing gimmick which
> Would help us all behave less civilly and
> More gently, who mistook civility
> So long for lack of gentleness.

Hollander is trying out a light, deft style on a serious subject; the question is what the urbane manner can include. The first lines of this strophe keep attention focused on social propriety, on urbanity itself. What matters is not so much the severing of friends, their pain, failure, or loss, as the management of this change in social encounters. And management is another word for style. Hollander feigns Italian impatience on one set of friends, gay campiness on another. Different circumstances, different tropes—"And so on." The adjustment of personality to setting can go on indefinitely. When the mask slips for a moment—"Everyone makes us nervous"—the personal feeling revealed is social. The social dimension of experience is stretched to accommodate, if it can, even the moral judgment that the visionary Dante displayed. The line from the *Inferno* (and from *Little Gidding*) expresses Dante's astonishment at the scope of evil, but for Hollander it signals only social discomfort: not who should be damned but who should get the apartment. The tone of the poem is not seriously challenged by the entry of Dante; Dante yields ground to Hollander, not Hollander to Dante. Dante's words are gobbled up by Hollander's style, as are "Basta," "queens," "my dears," "dark instant," "gimmick." Hollander does not so much move from one level of diction to

another; he pulls different idioms onto his level, the insistently urbane. Yet at the farthest reach of this omnivorous style is a moral. In
the last three lines, with a bit of contortion, he asks for deliverance
from all this civility into a gentler way of speaking with his friends. His
trouble, he says, is theirs too: they have all wrongly formed their sensibilities around the presumption that civility and gentleness (originally a term of social status) are at odds. But having made that
mistake long ago, the only way to behave more gently now is to surrender some civility. In that last clause, Hollander anticipates the ending
of the poem: "whatever / Has happened to all of us, it is too late / For
something else ever to happen now." Historical change, emotional
confinement, faulty expression, misunderstanding, loss—these must
be lived with.

A style that can represent the sadness of its own failures cannot be
taken lightly, nor can a poet who writes so vigorously and humanly
about his difficulties in composing a poem fit for friends. Hollander is a
master of urbane style. He speaks as humanely as anyone from the literary center. For just this reason, his failures indicate the binding limitations of metropolitan poetry. This poem is weakest just where he
would like to pull his strength together, in the last strophe:

> Along the river
> The sky is purpling and signs flash out
> And on, to beckon the darkness: THE TIME IS NOW . . .
> (What time, what time?) Who stops to look in time
> Ever, ever? We can do nothing again
> For both of you together. And if I burn
> An epithalamium six years old to prove
> That what we learn is in some way a function
> Of what we forget, I know that I should never
> Mention it to anyone. When men
> Do in the sunny Plaza what they did
> Only in dusky corners before, the sunset
> Comes as no benison, the assuring license
> Of the June night goes unobserved . . .

As he looks west across the Hudson, Hollander is pained by the simple
fact that when there might have been time to help his friends, he
failed to notice their need. At just this point, where the subject is least
social, most moral, the style falters badly. There was a popular song
lyric that later sounded the lugubrious note Hollander gets here:
"Does anybody really know what time it is? Does anybody really

care?" When Hollander becomes ethical here, he loses deftness, tact; the writing becomes ponderous ("What time, what time?" "Ever, ever?"). He picks the poem up momentarily by resuming, with remarks about burning an epithalamium and the wisdom of reticence, the smart tone—only to lose it again in the bitter acknowledgment of the blatancy of homosexual rendezvous now that words like "benison" are strictly literary. The urbane style will not accommodate an earnest or an ethical tone gracefully; its emotional range is limited. His is the tone of the center in that on the one side is the extreme lightness of the other New York poets—O'Hara, Ashbery, Koch—and on the other the earnest didacticism of Olson, Dorn, and even Creeley. Hollander was flanked on both sides by the avant-garde. The poetic style that best approximates the cultural center in America is still rather specialized, however impressive it is within its range.

The idea of a cultural, even a specifically literary, center cannot be altogether separated from a more inclusive, coherent ideology. A consensus about the state of literary life means most when it rests on a larger sense of where letters fit into a nation's understanding of the world—political, social, economic. In the 1950s there was such deep-rooted agreement, but it was recently won and lasted less than a decade. While Charles Olson was living in Washington, just after resigning from the Office of War Information, Ezra Pound was brought to St. Elizabeth's Hospital. Olson visited Pound frequently in 1946, often several times a week, and constantly felt thrown back on his heels. Pound, as a fascist, knew his political, economic, and literary principles and objectives. As an ardent New Dealer in 1946, after the death of Roosevelt, Olson felt no such assurance. The liberal ideology that commanded his loyalty (his last political effort was in the Claude Pepper campaign of 1948) was not settled on its objectives—it lacked not effective political power but intellectual coherence.[41] Olson withdrew from Washington to Yucatan and then Black Mountain College, giving up all hope for the political center. In 1949 another Harvard-educated New Dealer, Arthur Schlesinger, Jr., published *The Vital Center,* claiming with passion that "The center is vital; the center must hold." He felt, as Olson did, that liberalism was threatened by the extremes of both the right and the left. His optimism was greater than Olson's, but his assessment of the endangered consensus in the late 1940s was the same as the poet's: once the war ended, the center was in trouble; the challenge facing liberal activists was "to restore the center, to reunite individual and community."[42] In 1951 the editors of *Fortune* attempted to meet that challenge head on. Their February issue (immediately reprinted in book form) began with the widely held premise that America has a crucial role to play in world affairs. "But the unhappy fact is that just at this juncture in world affairs the American goals are not clear. Almost nothing in the way of a goal has emerged from current thinking beyond the purely negative *objective* (which is something less than a goal) of 'containing' the U.S.S.R. and 'stopping' the red Communism."[43] What followed was a 250-page effort to put into middle-brow terms the nation's proper objectives. The strained rhetoric of this book alone makes it clear that the malaise Olson sensed in 1946 lasted until 1951. But it passed soon after that.

In 1950 Eisenhower—then president of Columbia University—founded the American Assembly at his university. As president of the United States he later commissioned that "nonpartisan educational institution" to formulate a national policy document that would define American objectives for the 1960s. In 1960 the Assembly released a 372-page book, *Goals for Americans,* a national ideology articulated by a committee of academics, public officials, editors, businessmen, and labor leaders under the auspices of New York's most distinguished university. This document is variously fascinating, but what is most striking now is its simple existence. Eisenhower had reason to believe that a national consensus could be not only achieved but actually spelled out in print on a wide variety of domestic and international issues.[44] He knew that the institution best qualified to produce such a document was the university and that the policy discussion leading to the document ought to be centered in New York City. By comparison with the similar effort of the editors of *Fortune* in 1951, the tone of this book is eminently self-assured. The postwar ideological uncertainty was long gone by 1960. *Goals for Americans* is only one of several well-known monuments to the 1950s consensus. What is important to literary history is not only that this consensus existed but that its maintenance and definition depended somehow upon academic institutions and upon New York as its center. As Godfrey Hodgson puts it, "for the first time, the academic world seemed thoroughly integrated into the life and purposes of the nation."[45]

What then of the charge that poetry of the 1950s was narrowly academic? To the extent that poets looked to universities for an audience, they were addressing an audience with an explicit commitment to the most consequential ideas of the time. Another way of putting this is to say that such poets—Richard Wilbur, John Hollander, W. S. Merwin, Anthony Hecht—were in the honorable tradition of addressing the audience that felt greatest responsibility for the refinement of taste and the preservation of a national culture. The mainstream was clear: New York was its main channel, and branches flowed to New Haven, Cambridge, Ann Arbor, Madison, Berkeley. The Eisenhower report is plain about this: "These academic communities, with their museums and libraries, their theatres and auditoriums, are the essence in embryo of true cultural centers, not artificially imposed upon a society, but alive and growing from within."[46] Only because the ideological center was firm, and the cultural center effective at dominating cultural institutions, could a genuine avant-garde form in the 1950s. Olson, Creeley, Dorn, and Duncan were at an outré college in North Carolina; Ashbery left New York for Paris and hacked for the *New York Herald Tribune;* Ginsberg, Snyder, and Rexroth were in San Francisco. So long as the center was identifiable, poets knew what sort of exploration was called for at the peripheries.

In the 1980s New York can no longer be spoken of as the literary center of the country; nor can one imagine a committee, even a university committee, undertaking now to spell out the terms of an ideological consensus. I began this chapter with a discussion of the place of poetry in the national culture of the last thirty-five years. The shape of that culture is more open to dispute today, and so is the place of poetry. Were the culture more assured about its own configuration, poetry might well assume its proper place without much fretting. The attempt to formulate a canon, to designate the major and minor poets of the recent past—this is what critics can do to help poetry occupy its appropriate place in the culture. There is no necessary dichotomy between contemporary and canonical poetry. A canon in fact is a claim on the present and the future as much as it is a hold on the past: it provides models for young poets, showing them what the culture at its best approves, setting standards of emulation, and assuring some poets a receptive audience by training readers to appreciate a designated range of the art's possibilities.

2 · Robert Creeley and John Ashbery: Systems

The two most self-conscious statements of the 1950s consensus rest on a single point: the value of the individual is preeminent among other allegiances.[1] This is the traditional first term on a liberal list of avowals. Yet a competing premise was in the air then. In 1950 Peter Drucker claimed, "It is organization rather than the individual which is productive in an industrial system." "The proper study of mankind," he said, "is organization." From this hypothesis about business management, Drucker drew the conclusion that "The world revolution of our time is 'made in U.S.A.,' " since America is the country where systematic arrangement of all sorts has been given most consideration. Henry Ford, the systematizer of production, was, for Drucker, the greatest revolutionary of all time.[2]

Heady predictions of the epoch-making consequences of systematization have been more or less constant since the postwar years. In 1966 Gregory Bateson, for instance, told an audience of college students: "I think that cybernetics is the biggest bite out of the fruit of the Tree of Knowledge that mankind has taken in the last 2000 years."[3] In 1949, shortly after reading one of the pioneering books on systems analysis, Norbert Wiener's *Cybernetics*, Charles Olson wrote "The Kingfishers," the poem for which he is best known still. "The light is in the east. Yes. And we must rise, act": the enthusiasm got to Olson. "The present age," Wiener wrote, "is as truly the age of servomechanisms as the nineteenth century was the age of the steam engine or the eighteenth century the age of the clock."[4] In the months just before Olson wrote "The Kingfishers," Mao Tse-tung had come to power in China, and Olson saw Mao as a new representative of "the will to change." About Marxism or peasant revolutions, Olson cared not at all. The particular beliefs and objectives that motivated Mao and his supporters do not enter the poem, or Olson's thinking. Quoting Wiener, Olson rises to a level of rarefied abstraction on just this matter of ideology:

And what is the message? The message is
a discrete or continuous sequence of measurable
events distributed in time[5]

For those who were developing the principles of systems analysis in sociology, political theory, or international relations during these years, particular beliefs were immaterial. Specific ideologies were said to be exhausted.[6] Even particular identities were coming to count for rather little; Talcott Parsons wanted to counter "the long tradition that a society is 'composed' or 'made up' of 'individuals.' "[7] For the systems analyst, an individual is known only through his or her role. By 1970 it had become common to hear that electronic communications, cybernetics, and the use of computers were rendering obsolete nothing less than the boundaries between nations.[8] The systems approach is designed "to single out purely relational isomorphisms that are abstracted from content."[9] The implication of systems analysis, as Parsons says, is that "neither personalities nor social systems have direct contact with the ultimate objects of reference."[10] Perception and communication occur through mediating systems. Significance derives from that mediation.

The particular understanding that systems analysis offered to Olson and his contemporaries in various fields was rightly thought to be, however abstract, impressively comprehensive. Norbert Wiener tells of having

dreamed for years of an institution of independent scientists, working together in one of these backwoods of science [the border area between scientific fields], not as subordinates of some great executive officer, but joined by the desire, indeed by the spiritual necessity, to understand the region as a whole, and to lend one another the strength of that understanding.[11]

As an intellectual movement, systems analysis bears the signs of its moment. It is a dramatically expansionist approach to knowledge, for its advocates propose to explain and manage vast fields of inquiry, from electronics to political theory and social policy, and to accomplish this largely by rearranging intellectual jurisdictions. Intellectuals with new claims to expertise would exercise sufficient authority to restructure social institutions and intellectual disciplines for greater efficiency. That this ambitious call for change should be heard at the end of the war, when political, military, and economic jurisdictions were rapidly shifting in America's favor, seems appropriate. Indeed, the movement owes its inception somewhat directly to the war effort itself.

For nearly a decade starting in the mid-1930s Wiener participated in an informal group of scientists who met monthly to discuss scientific method, but the breakthrough in his own work came during World War II, after the group had broken up. He collaborated with other scientists to develop effective antiaircraft artillery that could be used in England against the Luftwaffe. Their problem was to predict accurately the course of an aircraft guided by a pilot who might well attempt a diversionary maneuver in order to avoid antiaircraft fire. Wiener conceived of the pilot's variation of course as "feedback," which is negative in the sense that it opposes to some degree the established course of the plane. The degree of variation was the issue, for feedback operates within predictable limits; Wiener used an electronic computing machine, the differential analyzer, to compute rapidly the probabilities for the plane's change of course. Out of this experience came his notion of cybernetics, a method of steering, the goal of which is to control uncertainty by manipulation of information.[12] Having won the war more with machines than with soldiers, the time was right for American intellectuals to think that a new technical expertise might bring order and plenty to nearly all areas of human endeavor.

This notion of systematic organization had its greatest appeal not to those poets who felt closest to the consensus of the 1950s—quite the reverse. Only among the avant-garde (Olson, Robert Creeley, John Ashbery, Gary Snyder) was the notion of system subjected to scrutiny in verse. And they tended to be most attentive to just how so abstract a notion might affect the most stable, permanent aspects of life—love, marriage, maturation—where the themes of poetry are traditionally found. The poems by Creeley and Ashbery that I will discuss in this chapter would not have struck Karl Shapiro as culture poetry, but that is just the point. These poets were able to sense connections between the ideas and figures current among intellectuals and the most traditional subjects of poetry. Their poems show how even two intensely personal, introspective writers were drawn toward the terms of public discourse. Creeley, I think, pursued this subject most thoughtfully and produced the best poems on the theme. He tested this idea of system by pitting against it those odd particularities that are difficult to encompass within a single set of terms, and ultimately by subjecting his own art to the aleatory antagonist of system: randomness. Beyond the pleasure of individual poems, one can see how even a poet whose ambition looks insistently small on the page—an apparently deliberate minor poet—was in fact responsive to one of the most wide-ranging intellectual currents of his time.

Charles Olson, Robert Duncan, Allen Ginsberg—these are some of the poets Robert Creeley has associated himself with during the past thirty years, and they are dwarfing company for a poet like Creeley. These three figures, like Whitman before them, are seldom at a loss for an encompassing proposition. They are poets with systems who, one feels, given time and opportunity, could confidently find a place for anyone or anything in their writing. But Creeley? "Well, I've always been embarrassed for a so-called larger view. I've been given to write about that which has the most intimate presence for me, and I've always felt very, very edgy those few times when I have tried to gain a larger view. I've never felt right. I am given as a man to work with what is most intimate to me—these senses of relationship among people. I think, for myself at least, the world is most evident and most intense in those relationships."[13] That embarrassment "for a so-called larger view" has periodically returned to Creeley, sometimes in the form of a desire to escape his own precedents and specializations— "Short intensive poems. Short intensive stories" (CP 164).[14] Between 1967 and 1969 he resolved to try the high road of his three friends: *Pieces* is his first attempt to make chronological time serve the inclusive ends of a system of belief. More than twenty years of short poems, some of them wonderful, led to that deliberate shift away from his poetic past.

The poems of his that I return to most eagerly come from these first twenty years, but they bear a curious relation to this matter of a larger view. Many of the best of these poems reinforce—sometimes by teasing—the assumption that human experience is intelligibly ordered within definable spheres, and the more ambitious assumption that the world at large is intelligibly ordered. This is to say that Creeley has always, in an important though unusual sense, been a systematic poet. He presumes that people conduct their affairs in orderly fashion and that a poet's task is to reveal the order behind human behavior as a delicately articulated but binding system of understanding. In this regard Creeley is an empirical poet: whereas Olson, Duncan, and Ginsberg *constructed* systems in order both to write poetry and to answer questions about history, Creeley *discovers* systematic behavior in the people he observes or imagines.[15]

It is easy for Creeley to assume that personal experience is intelligibly ordered; convention quietly weaves the lines of personal relationship into a dense, fine fabric. But the relationships between classes and institutions, these Creeley approaches obliquely—at times, through another poet's vision. Here is "After Lorca," which first appeared in 1952:

> The church is a business, and the rich
> are the business men.
> When they pull on the bells, the
> poor come piling in and when a poor man dies, he has a wooden
> cross, and they rush through the ceremony.
>
> But when a rich man dies, they
> drag out the Sacrament
> and a golden Cross, and go *doucement, doucement*
> to the cemetery.
>
> And the poor love it
> and think its crazy.   (FL 27)

The intelligibility of social relationships is posited as directly by the manner of the first two lines as by any proposition the poem advances: before *Pieces* Creeley's poems characteristically open with an assertion; the definitive copula is still his staple predicate. His manner, like Olson's and Dorn's, is discursive; this is appropriate for poets who proceed on the assumption that life is explainable by general laws. The first two strophes nicely elaborate the sort of class analysis common in political verse and oratory, but Creeley's poem really lies in the concluding lines. That the church and businessmen routinely force the prerogatives of class structure on the community's worship could surprise no one. That these prerogatives arouse bemusement rather than resentment among the poor is more startling. The poor understand the class system perfectly, and they delight in its misplaced discriminations. To see clearly a system's symmetries disarms its oppressive significance; systems analysis and good humor supplant politics.

Political questions do not engage Creeley. The social relationships he deftly analyzes fall within the province of manners. "The Lover," published in 1953–54, takes it for granted that rules routinely govern social behavior:

What should the young
man say, because he is buying
Modess? Should he

blush or not. Or
turn coyly, his head, to
one side, as if in

the exactitude of his emotion he
were not offended? Were
proud? Of what? To buy

a thing like that.   (FL 41)

Routine is no more interesting than the dull hum of an electric clock, but at the edges of convention, where a system is ill known (as here) or under strain (as in "Hello" [W 401]), its delicate workings slip into place as astonishingly as in high art. Through these angular lines, Creeley uncertainly pursues the young man's options. Postured "exactitude" would be one possibility, but the analysis produces a more instructive conclusion—signaled chiefly by a period where one more question mark might have inverted the sense of the poem: to buy Modess is, for the generic young man, a rite of passage, one of those points at which the social system escalates its terms.

Creeley is especially interested in rites of passage; they are social junctures which momentarily seem to be hiatuses rather than turning-points: the young man gropes for the determinacy of a predictable imperative, for what he *should* do. Creeley's best poem about these apparent hiatuses is "The Business" (1955):

To be in love is like going outside to see what kind of day

it is. Do not
mistake me. If you love

her how prove she
loves also, except that it

occurs, a remote chance on
which you stake

yourself? But barter for
the Indian was a means of sustenance.

There are records.   (FL 44)

Creeley is testing the apparatus of intellectual analysis on the theme of love. He begins with the syntax of a universal proposition; apparently he is about to define the nature of love when the poet's tool ("like") comes to the aid of the sanguine analyst. But it is awkward aid: the simile attempts to illustrate a state by referring to an action, and the analyst resolves to try again (lines 3–4). This time he draws out the apparatus not of definition but of validation ("how prove she / loves also"). Yet the syntax of validation is no more complete than that of definition; in place of an "unless you" clause completing the conditional syntax comes a clause that dissolves the possibilities of validation: "except that it occurs." The point behind Creeley's dissolution of syntactic structures seems to be the obvious one that love is beyond the eager, assured reach of discursive understanding; in James Merrill's phrase, love "is everyone's blind spot."[16]

Love is apparently where systems end; change is another word for lawlessness, or indeterminacy. And yet this surrender to contingency ("going out- / side to see what kind of day / it is") is only a disguised and rudimentary form of organized behavior: barter. Creeley suggests that although, in the absence of general laws, the requital of love seems only "a remote chance," the power of barter is such that requital "occurs." Love offered is taken; love taken, returned. That archaic circle of exchange shows that love seems chancy chiefly because it involves a part of the social system which we naively think we have surpassed.

Manners, the code of acceptable social behavior, are not easily surpassed and can only briefly be interrupted. Human nature is a delicate thing and cannot take its experience raw. There is a fine poem on just this subject, "Something," written in 1963:

> I approach with such
> a careful tremor, always
> I feel the finally foolish
>
> question of how it is,
> then, supposed to be felt,
> and by whom. I remember
>
> once in a rented room on
> 27th street, the woman I loved
> then, literally, after we
>
> had made love on the large
> bed sitting across from
> a basin with two faucets, she

had to pee but was nervous,
embarrassed I suppose I
would watch her who had but

a moment ago been completely
open to me, naked, on
the same bed. Squatting, her

head reflected in the mirror,
the hair dark there, the
full of her face, the shoulders,

sat spread-legged, turned on
one faucet and shyly pissed. What
love might learn from such a sight.   (W 35)

Creeley nicely frames this anecdote with invitations to interpretation; the title, "Something," shows how little he is willing to say about "What / love might learn from such a sight." Among the notions covered by that one word "something" is the awareness of how time measures and places even intimate experiences. "A moment ago" she had been completely open to him; but he cannot complain, for she is that woman he "loved / then." She had carefully placed their intimacy in the immediate past; Creeley forcefully assigns his love of her to the now distant past. Love might learn that people need and cherish the relieving distance that comes with even small increments of time. In the opening sentence of the poem, Creeley expresses the onerous burden of intimacy, for intimacy sets one in the interstices of the system of manners, scrambling, like the young man in "The Lover," to deduce proprieties. In this awkward moment, when the sink must serve as a toilet, she needs the screening sound of water running, just as the poet, in order to capture her delicacy, needs that euphemism "to pee." And in her shy distance she is engagingly beautiful as ever: "the hair dark there, the / full of her face, the shoulders." What love might learn is the care people take with themselves and require of one another.

But why is Creeley so taken by systematic behavior? Why is a poet who is unwilling to formulate "a so-called larger view" consistently engaged by the *idea* of a larger view? One might answer with the claim that the explain-all has long been a national resource. The following passage shows Creeley tapping this resource in the customary way:

It is all a rhythm,
from the shutting
door, to the window
opening.

the seasons, the sun's
light, the moon,
the oceans, the
growing of things,

the mind in men
personal, recurring
in them again,
thinking the end

is not the end, the
time returning,
themselves dead but
someone else coming.

(W 19)

These lines from "The Rhythm," written in 1961, open *Words;* after the first stanza they show Creeley following Whitman and Emerson in tracing the concentric circles of cosmic cycles. But this poem has too much of the generalized credo about it to be characteristic of Creeley at his best. He seldom declares his faith in such centralizing systems; he prefers to uncover order in commonly overlooked corners of experience. This poem, "Midnight," was written in 1959:

When the rain stops
and the cat drops
out of the tree
to walk

away, when the rain stops,
when the others come home, when
the phone stops,
the drip of water, the

potential of a caller
any Sunday afternoon.

(FL 111)

Creeley's sense of system is vaguer than Whitman's or Emerson's—less cosmic, more ordinary, more amiable. His images suggest the completion of a number of small processes and activities—the rain, the cat taking shelter in a tree, the expedition of "the others," the phone ringing. These completions reinstate stability, "the drop of water." Yet for Creeley stability, in the inclusive system of simply observable phenomena, is a context for novelty: "the / potential of a caller / any Sunday afternoon." For as surely as the repetitive, insistently rhymed "when" clauses, after momentarily devolving on the cat's four-line exit, create the expectation of a resolving predicate (which never comes), so the steady drip of water in a quiet house full of its occupants leaves one awaiting disturbance—as though people, weather, and plumbing obeyed a set of laws as abstract and predictable as those of English syntax. Abstractness seems to be exactly Creeley's point. The particular significations of a system are seldom his focus; relations are more binding. Specific signification sometimes seems a source of oppression in Creeley's poetry.

Although it is hard to say why Creeley is lured by the idea of a system—hard, that is, to ascribe a single cause to his systematic imagination—one can locate the first systematic moment in his poetry. And this poem, "Return," which opens his collection of early poems, suggests that Creeley's systematic bent once expressed a response to the political climate of the mid-forties:

> Quiet as is proper for such places;
> The street, subdued, half-snow, half-rain,
> Endless, but ending in the darkened doors.
> Inside, they who will be there always,
> Quiet as is proper for such people—
> Enough for now to be here, and
> To know my door is one of these.   (CH 3)

Creeley's poems generally seem timeless in a simple sense: when they refer to a context, it is often so personal as to be beyond reach. "Return," however, is an exception. It was written in the winter of 1945–46, when Creeley came back to Harvard after driving an ambulance at the Burma-India front. Thematically, it belongs with poems like Lowell's "Exile's Return" and Wilbur's "Mined Fields"—poems about how to return after the war. Creeley's strategy for return: to discover in domestic Cambridge an order clean of the taint of ideological combat. The people of Cambridge are silently, permanently governed by laws whose simple propriety is reassuring. Creeley will not push the subject too far: the genesis of that domestic order, the relation between domestic and other, larger and smaller, systems of order, the claims and obligations of domestic order—he will not broach these matters.

> Enough for now to be here, and
> To know my door is one of these.

Why that satisfaction? Such self-restraint here means staying on a plane of abstraction where questions of genesis and consequence are not allowed to arise. Creeley has explained that during these postwar years he felt distrustful of analysis:

> I wanted to get out of that awful assumption that thinking is the world. I was thinking of how things have shifted, literally, in my experience of the world from that time of the forties when mind was thought of as the primary agent of having place in the world. I think that came probably from that sense of getting out of the whole nightmare of the Depression by being able to think your way out. And isn't that characteristic of Roosevelt's administration that there enters into American government in political circumstance a sense of expertise—the ability to think your way out of dilemmas; that is, to deal with the national economy by thinking of a way out. I mean, even the Second World War was a mind game. You confront one agency—isn't Hitler, for example, thinking the world is one thing; and then there are those obviously involved thinking it another.   (CP 166)

Like any number of his contemporaries, after the war Creeley tried to locate his writing beyond ideology.[17] He avoids the iron reference of particular ideologies by turning to the subject of manners with the abstract delicacy of an anthropologist's attention. After the spectacle of World War II, he wanted no part of the proud construction of systems of belief; no part either of that postwar intellectual ambition that powered the development of systems analysis. Yet the poems show, one by one, that this very ambition made itself felt in the best of his work through the 1950s and early 1960s. His own taste for order would be satisfied by discovering the operation of systems of behavior that make no claim to historical meaning.[18]

Increasingly in the sixties, however, the systems that engaged Creeley were constructed rather than discovered by the human mind. On occasion this sense of the mind as a spidery weaver of systems led to anxiety, as in "I Keep to Myself Such Measures" (1963), because mental systems, in their abstractness, can deprive one of the world (W 52). More typically, though, the notion that systems are constructed leads the poetry to playfulness and humility. The play is clear in "Numbers" (1968): Creeley meditates on the psychological valences of an arbitrary construct, the decimal system (P 21). He is interested in the way feelings have accrued to a purely formal set of conventions; the feelings have nothing to do with the signification permitted by the system, only with its structure. His humility in this regard is clear in this first section of a meditation on death:

> We'll die
> soon enough,
> and be dead—
>
> whence the whole
> system
> will fade from my head—
>
> "but why the
> tort-
> ure . . ." as if
>
> another circumstance
> were forever
> at hand.   (DB 70)

Mortality, the loss of consciousness, is referred to austerely as a "circumstance"—as neutral and uneventful as the light around us. Yet mortality lies behind the system Creeley likes to imagine; the mind, under the pressure of its own dissolution, constructs a system as an elaborate way of giving ground before the inevitable.

> We resolve to think of ourselves,
> insofar as one of us can so speak
>
> of the other, as involved with
> a necessary system, of age and its
>
> factors.   (DB 102)

The "necessary system" is not just biological: by the power of collective resolution people invent other dimensions for the system. Mortality is the mother of necessity, and what are known as manners are finally the "factors" of age. All delicacy follows from the fact of impending death. *A Day Book,* written between 1968 and 1971, expresses a deeper perception of systematic behavior than the earlier volumes did. In this book Creeley elaborates an elegiac perspective on human conventions.

Creeley's sense of style is consistent with his interest in systematic order. I have observed that his manner is characteristically discursive; his poems commonly begin with a definition or a proposition and then proceed to qualify and illustrate that proposition. (In addition to "The Business," quoted above, some distinguished examples of this type of poem are: "The Immoral Proposition" [FL 31], "Air: 'The Love of a Woman' " [FL 142], and "On Vacation" [DB 112].) This is not to say that his poems are verse-essays but rather that, like Williams, Creeley intends his poems to display "all the complexity of a way of thinking" (CP 16). Creeley's many attempts to disclaim a discursive motive (QG 54, 57, 72, 207; CP 91, 127) or to assign that motive to the distant past (CH xi) should not go ignored—especially since, in verse, he has wittily undone the discursive ambition:

> Do you know what
> the truth is,
> what's rightly
> or wrongly said,
>
> what is wiseness,
> or rightness, what
> wrong, or well-
> done if it is,
>
> or is not, done.
> I thought.
> I thought and
> thought and thought.
>
> In a place
> I was sitting,
> and there
> it was, a little
>
> faint thing
> hardly felt, a
> kind of small
> nothing.   (W 87)

Those last five lines show how small is his esteem of the Big Questions addressed by poets with systems, poets like Olson, Duncan, and Ginsberg. Yet, as I have shown, Creeley often tries to relate his poems to a general system. "Had I lived some years ago, I think I would have been a moralist, i.e., one who lays down, so to speak, rules of behavior with no small amount of self-satisfaction" (QG 3).

On the level of style, one can speak of Creeley as a systemic poet with less qualification. In 1951 he wrote "Le Fou," a gentle parody of the Olson manner:

> who plots, then, the lines
> talking, taking, always the beat from
> the breath
>   (moving slowly at first
> the breath
>   which is slow—
>
> I mean, graces come slowly,
> it is that way.
>
> So slowly (they are waving
> We are moving
>   away from   (the trees
>   the usual   (go by
> which is slower than this, is
>   (we are moving!
> goodbye   (FL 17)

The style here is grammatical in that it advances by reference to antecedent phrases and clauses. Both Olson and Creeley make their poems move with constant reference to the rules governing English usage. Their styles are systemic in the sense that by underlining the grammatical grid behind the clauses and by favoring the small systemic, nonspecific words—prepositions, conjunctions, pronouns— these poets declare at nearly every turn that poems are generated as much by the systemic properties of language as by individual temperaments. This poem opens with a subordinate clause so that its first words refer back to a preceding term (the title, "Le Fou," or the dedication, "for Charles") which can preside over this syntax. The many pauses punctuating the poem mark off the boundaries of grammatical units (phrases and clauses), the terms of the system of utterance.

There are a number of ways in which the poem is made to seem a

web of internal relationships: each of the nine pronouns in these fifteen lines dispatches attention to the rear, as if words were generated
by antecedent words or statements. And they are: in the second line,
"taking" clearly issues from a phonological resemblance to the preceding word, "talking"; the tenth line—"we are moving"—is born out
of the syntactic analogue ending the ninth line—"they are waving."
Still more obviously, out of one word in the fourth line, "slowly," come
at least the following five lines; that single word keeps bobbing up, apparently compelling the poet to the brink of inarticulateness: "I mean,
graces come slowly, / it is that way." Yet, of course, this is not fully
Creeley's style; it is, as the title suggests, more an acute but playful
parody of Olson's.

Creeley knows, though, that his own style also leans on the systemic symmetries of language. In 1957 in *The Whip* he placed this
poem, "A Song," on the page facing "Le Fou":

> I had wanted a quiet testament
> and I had wanted, among other things,
> a song.
> That was to be
> of a like monotony.
> (A grace
>
> Simply. Very very quiet.
> A murmur of some lost
> thrush, though I have never seen one.
>
> Which was you then. Sitting
> and so, at peace, so very much now this same quiet.
>
> A song.
>
> And of you the sign now, surely, of a gross
> perpetuity
> (which is not reluctant, or if it is,
> it is no longer important.
>
> A song.
>
> Which one sings, if he sings it,
> with care.   (FL 18)

Like Olson, Creeley uses simple repetition ("I had wanted . . . / and I
had wanted") and subordinate clauses branching out of pronouns
("Which was you then"; "which is not reluctant"; "Which one
sings") to keep the poem going. But his tone is so different from

Olson's that the comparison will not hold for long. This poem seems at several points (lines 9–10, 12–13, 17–18) about to conclude or expire when it draws another shallow breath; its small fitful movements are part of Creeley's design. For the poem should seem to have been written almost inadvertently: his reluctance to write the "quiet testament" for his first wife is overcome or forgotten ("it is no longer important") in the course of talking about the poem he once wanted to write. This fiction about the poem's genesis depends upon a literary convention Olson never invoked: sincerity—the convention to end conventions—which Creeley understands, after Pound's Confucius, as *"Man standing by his word"* (CP 188). That steadfastness, Creeley claims, may gain "a political term of responsibility" (CP 83). In a time when political immoralities are conducted by means of linguistic contortion, the sincere use of language may imply a political challenge to step free of the predictable deceptions of ideology.

Creeley's use of the literary convention of sincerity is tricky, though. His claims to sincerity are convincing enough to allow him outrageous liberties: here, not just the artlessness of simple repetition, but also the use of three "very"s—two of them back to back—in the course of nineteen lines. But the first words indicate a counterpressure: "I had wanted." The past perfect tense stands for a characteristic distance. Though regularly claiming sincerity, Creeley customarily tries to indicate some measure of alienation from his own avowals. Those throwaway clauses—"among other things"; "though I have never seen one"; "or if it is, / it is no longer important"—cool down the tone, as if the poem commanded no more than the surface of Creeley's attention. He often looks back on his creations with a measure of disgust: "the sign now, surely, of a gross / perpetuity." Similarly, his diction is seldom so homogeneous that it might, in some context, be spoken of as "natural." The polysyllables, "testament," "monotony," "perpetuity," glare out from the page as though they might, among so many "low" words, require footnotes to the dictionary. Speech, for Creeley, is an idea more than a method.

His method is, instead, to set at odds a personal subject matter and an abstract, generalized manner of treatment: that tension represents Creeley's attempt at impersonality. This abstract manner is the stylistic expression of Creeley's systematic imagination; it offers the discipline of distance from the emotions behind the poem. Yet "The Operation," written in 1953, shows Creeley's suspicion of his technique of tension:

> By Saturday I said you would be better on Sunday.
> The insistence was a part of a reconciliation.

> Your eyes bulged, the grey
> light hung on you, you were hideous.
>
> My involvement is just an old
> habitual relationship.
>
> Cruel, cruel to describe
> what there is no reason to describe.   (FL 34)

The occasion of the poem was apparently Creeley's seeing his first wife immediately after her surgery (this moment is narrated in *The Island*). Creeley submits the anxiety of the occasion to the defusing cool of his impersonal diction: "The insistence was a part of a reconciliation." That, evidently, is Creeley's mannered way of saying that his desire to patch up differences with his wife made him express the hope for her recovery. He himself cannot swallow the antiseptic impersonality of this contrived manner. In the last two lines, he reproaches himself for the abstract meanness of the poem, and especially of the preceding couplet. Sincerity, then, recovers control of the poem in time to dash it to a close: self-exposure is filtered through the screen of an impersonal style. Creeley acknowledges, in these final lines, that this abstract style deals with other people no more civilly than a predator does. Yet he never dismisses the impersonal manner completely, for

> In the narcotic and act
> of omniscience
>
> a gain, of the formal,
> is possible.   (CH 56)

That gain will always lure Creeley; without the sometimes histrionic "act" of omniscience, some of his poems would not achieve form of any kind.

Creeley's poetry, then, is intimate and disembodied at the same time, like a late-night phone call. He moves back and forth between the convention of sincerity and the discipline of systematic abstraction. His work can be underestimated if either term of this relationship between sincerity and systematic abstractness is taken as the last word. In recent years he has tended to move away from his discursive mode; the didactic form that has come to interest him, beginning with *Pieces* (1969), is the epigram. He has written some short poems that seem, in isolation, naively sincere; but fairness to Creeley demands that they not be taken in isolation. Behind even so slight a poem as "One Day"

> One day after another—
> perfect.
> They all fit. (TT 67)

there lies more than twenty years of pressing the pieces of experience for systematic meaning. Creeley is a minimalist only in the sense that he needs little to work with. The ends of his art are perhaps as far-reaching as those of Olson, Duncan, and Ginsberg. Like them, he has his own way—abstract, unspecific, empirical—of responding to political history, and he too, sometimes just by his style, urges understanding of a "larger view"; he allows for no isolated detail.

> It
> all drops into
> place. (W 38)

Among his contemporaries, Creeley may well seem the least likely poet to invoke the terms and figures of systems-analysis writers of the postwar years. His writing has always seemed insistently personal, claustral, small. Yet who but a securely minor poet can engage with impunity the grandest, often grandiose, claims of explainers? Although he did not take up, as Olson did, particular concepts put forward by cyberneticists, their larger categories and figures provide a backdrop for some of Creeley's writing—to his best poems, I think. That a poet raising chickens in New Hampshire, or writing tiny, jagged poems in Aix-en-Provence, Mallorca, or North Carolina, should show a kind of attention that some of his most ambitious contemporaries were developing in various fields is evidence not only of how pervasive the influence of the postwar American intellectual milieu could be, but also of the enthusiasm and vitality of years that have been too easily dismissed as gray.

In 1975 John Ashbery came to the University of Chicago to receive one of the less prestigious awards he would win that year for *Self-Portrait in a Convex Mirror*. He was especially pleased to learn that Robert Creeley had been one of the judges for the Harriet Monroe Prize (John Hollander had been another). He had long been an admirer of Creeley's poetry, he said, and was glad (even a little surprised) to hear that the appreciation was mutual.[19] Creeley was born in Massachusetts and, like Ashbery, educated at Harvard; since 1966 he has taught regularly in Buffalo. Nevertheless, he has become associated with the west coast contingent of old avant-gardists—so these two poets from distant camps are not expected to like one another's work greatly. Yet the affinity makes sense because they both write poems whose difficulties derive mainly from the effort to render accurately, though often inelegantly, the ways a meditating mind actually moves through confusions, distractions, and banalities. More particularly, they both write about the orders that silently prevail over hardly noticed details of daily life, and about where those orders begin to dissolve.

I began this chapter by saying that, in regard to the publicly avowed individualism of 1950s liberals, systems-analysis writers stood against the explicit statements of political and social consensus. More generally, though, it was appropriate for poets during a period of express political agreement to notice conformity to rules in those areas of life that are not apparently political. Both Ashbery and Creeley inquire into what has been settled, and how firmly. They each ask what consolation can be derived from these patterns that hold so much of our lives in tacit order. Ashbery's poems of the late 1960s and 1970s show how the intellectual climate changed once the consensus began to crumble. Creeley took pleasure in the discovery of systematic behavior, admiring how much had been quietly settled. Ashbery rather determinedly undoes systematic arrangements. The chance elements of his poems are intended to unsettle expectations, even at the expense of the form of his own poems. Although he is only a year younger than Creeley, in this sense he is much the "later" poet, not because Creeley did not try as well to bring aleatory elements into his writing but because Ashbery has been so much more successful with this sort of program.

One of the recurrent motifs in Ashbery's poems is a long look back over his life only to discover its boring predictability. Here is a well-known passage from "Soonest Mended" (1969):

> These then were some hazards of the course,
> Yet though we knew the course *was* hazards and nothing else
> It was still a shock when, almost a quarter of a century later,
> The clarity of the rules dawned on you for the first time.
> *They* were the players, and we who had struggled at the game
> Were merely spectators, though subject to its vicissitudes
> And moving with it out of the tearful stadium, borne on
>   shoulders, at last.[20]

All those "kisses, heroic acts" that are supposed to reveal character were in fact merely part of some program from the start, a program set elsewhere:

> Weren't we rather acting this out
> For someone else's benefit, thoughts in a mind
> With room enough and to spare for our little problems (so they
>   began to seem),
> Our daily quandary about food and the rent and bills to be
>   paid?
> To reduce all this to a small variant,
> To step free at last, minuscule on the gigantic plateau—
> This was our ambition: to be small and clear and free.

But this is a complicated ambition. For to reduce the daily variety of life to a manageable variant is to submit rather thoroughly to a system; once submission is comprehensive, freedom can only come by means of transcendence, a breaking away. And that seems unlikely, for the very language of the poem is lethargic, anything but free: "With room enough and to spare"—the idiom of a car commercial. The poem instead ends characteristically by trying to draw consolation from very small divergences from the predictable roles into which we are cast—"sowing the seeds crooked in the furrow."

One traditional way of imagining a life governed by principles or rules sets great weight on certain events or decisions, "kisses, heroic acts," in the lives of individuals: one may choose to act well or poorly in some key situation, and the consequences make themselves felt thereafter. Ashbery's "Song" (1967) is a dark love poem about the stunning force of consequences. The terror of what he describes is that there may be no key circumstances, nor even a way of knowing that a decision is being made—let alone how to measure or predict its outcome. So long as all events are stitched one to another in some systematic web, none can be dismissed as merely local or trivial. To a lover trying to understand how an affair has changed, or how to assign responsibility for failure, this sense of system is especially dispiriting. "Song" begins with a memory of how one relationship was formerly sweet and composed, like a flower arrangement, and innocent of those acts that seem to determine an everafter of resentment: "things merely ended when they ended." But

> Later
>
> Some movement is reversed and the urgent masks
> Speed toward a totally unexpected end

> Like clocks out of control. Is this the gesture
> That was meant, long ago, the curving in
>
> Of frustrated denials, like jungle foliage   (DD 30)

Perhaps some movement as slight as a wave of the hand indicated reversal of the relationship; some gesture that was more deliberate than he realized turned the affair around, as though it were a mechanism, all of whose parts count. "Feedback," Norbert Wiener might say, but a lover speaks of frustrations, denials, which determine relentlessly the changes that come to an affair. And not just to lovers:

> Sooner or later,
> The cars lament, the whole business will be hurled down.
> Meanwhile we sit, scarcely daring to speak,
> To breathe, as though this closeness cost us life.

This vision of the nadir is spread out over "the whole business," as if the structure of a love affair and the entire social order were isomorphic. Here the poem turns, apparently with a lover's faith, toward a vision of the world matured to correspond with the tempered strength of old lovers:

> The pretensions of a past will some day
> Make it over into progress, a growing up,
> As beautiful as a new history book
> With uncut pages, unseen illustrations,
>
> And the purpose of the many stops and starts will
>   be made clear . . .

This hope is very old: that the world will one day be shown to be meaningful in all its parts, that the new era will stand free of the failures of the old. In the meantime, though, he can write only this song to celebrate a love neither fully expressed nor altogether accepted. The poem's last sentence: "A dumb love."

Yet this is one of Ashbery's strongest themes, how ideas of order surround our loves. "Fragment" (1968) is the most searching and obscure treatment of this subject. Ashbery seems darkest and most confusing just when he is most poignant. The poem opens with a grid laid over the daily contingencies of life: the last block on a bescribbled calendar page for April is filled in.[21] All movements for this early spring are accounted for, or all but one: his lover has left, "And in doing so open[ed] out / New passages of being among the correctness/ Of familiar patterns" (DD 78). The little blocks in May may bring some surprises. At the outset, though, these new possibilities hold out so little consolation that Ashbery can only wish for his lover to return:

> Not forgetting either the chance that you
> Might want to revise this version of what is
> The only real one, it might be that
> No real relation exists between my wish for you
> To return and the movements of your arms and legs.
> But my inability to accept this fact
> Annihilates it. (DD 79)

From this antiseptic view, his lost lover is like a mechanism gone beyond the reach of its controller.

The accuracy of "Fragment," the sense in which this difficult poem is genuinely moving, derives from Ashbery's ability to write about the cool terror of a life without the structure of a love affair. "Seen from inside," he says, "all is / Abruptness." Suddenly, when the lover goes, the unnoticed details of the world come a little closer:

> Just one step
> Takes you into so much outside, the candor
> Of what had been going on makes you pause momentarily . . . (DD 85)

In that pause is the pain of the present and some hope for an unforeseen future. Since as early as 1949, Ashbery has represented this sometimes encouraging neutrality of the external world as simply trees:

> Treetops whose mysterious hegemony concerns
> Merely, by opening around factors of accident
> So as to install miscellaneous control. (DD 79)

The trees reach outward without any program for the future, merely taking in light, air, and water; yet, as he once said, "their merely being there / Means something."[22] They indicate that most of the world is uninvolved in one's grief, that a life exists beyond loss:

> This was the first day
> Of the new experience. The familiar brown trees
> Stirred indifferent at their roots, deeply transformed. DD 86–87)

Beyond that indifferent openness to contingency is one more plan for the future. But this new one will incorporate what had been ruled out of the old one.

> People were delighted getting up in the morning
> With the density that for once seemed the promise
> Of everything forgotten, and the well-being
> Grew, at the expense of whoever lay dying
> In a small room watched only by the progression
> Of hours in the tight new agreement.   (DD 93)

And those old folks left to die? They are the casualties of the new regime, too settled in the past to make the crossing.

Well before Ashbery published *Three Poems* in 1972, the word *system* took on a narrowly ideological sense. The central section of this book is entitled "The System," and that is the way the term arose most often in the late 1960s and early 1970s: the System, the Establishment, and so on. Ashbery wrote then from a sense of being painfully uneasy but also excited in the midst of social change. "The System" opens with these then timely words:

> The system was breaking down. The one who had wandered
> alone past so many happenings and events began to feel, back-
> ing up along the primal vein that led to his center, the begin-
> ning of a hiccup that would, if left to gather, explode the center
> to the extremities of life, the suburbs through which one
> makes one's way to where the country is.   (TP 53)

That the social system was collapsing under strain of severe political dissent was not news, nor was the sense that the danger of deterioration went far beyond the stability of social institutions. Yet the common sense was that the collapse began with particular political and social forces. The liberal consensus forged in the 1950s was recognized as the source of the foreign policy whose failures took Lyndon Johnson out of the 1968 presidential campaign, and the social order of the fifteen years following World War II was just what had been undermined by the civil rights movement. Ashbery wondered:

> Is it possible that the desires of one might not conflict with the
> desires of all the others, and vice versa, or is it precisely this im-
> broglio of defeated desires that is coming up now, a sort of

Thirty Years' War of the human will, terrible in its destructive surging that threatens to completely annihilate the life which it so ebulliently manifests?   (TP 44)

It was that vivacity so evident in the marches of the late 1960s that attracted many intellectuals of Ashbery's generation away from any lingering dream of political and social consensus ("that the desires of one might not conflict with the desires of all the others").

The change that had occurred, as Ashbery also saw it, began with the erosion of consensus, but it did not stop there. Apparently remembering the stability of the 1950s in terms of *The Wealth of Nations,* he wrote: "it began to seem as though some permanent way of life had installed itself, a stability immune to the fluctuations of other eras: the pendulum that throughout eternity has swung successively toward joy and grief had been stilled by a magic hand" (TP 60). The hand of the marketplace, of prosperity. But in the late 1960s no one felt that calm because so much then seemed unsettled, unaccounted for: "Outside, can't you hear it, the traffic, the trees, everything getting nearer" (TP 5). Ashbery speaks eloquently of the way that objects or the wind itself can seem suddenly unfamiliar and demanding of attention, once the mental structures that hold the trees, the traffic, and our futures at a distance begin to dissolve; a social revolution or the breakup of a love affair can make the plainest objects before one's eyes look startlingly novel, as if they had just arrived on the scene. "How to deal with the new situations that arise each day in bunches or clusters, and which resist categorization to the point where any rational attempt to deal with them is doomed from the start?" (TP 87) In "Soonest Mended" Happy Hooligan intrudes on the scene of Ingres' "Roger Rescues Angelica" like a gate crasher from another time zone. This anachronistic, apparently gratuitous, configuration gives a sense not so much of dramatic tension between raw experience and the mental structures designed to hold it in place as of simply a poor fit. His similes and metaphors are typically inauspicious, more arbitrary than apt: "None of us ever graduates from college, / For time is an emulsion." This image and phrase maker who so often seems to be putting left shoes on right feet has fashioned a discursive style that cannot be suspected of any irritable reaching after reason.

Yet the goal of his writing, he says, is "some kind of rational beauty" (TP 26).

> This kind of beauty is almost too abstract to be experienced as beauty, and yet we must realize that it is not an abstract notion, that it really can happen at times and that life at these times

seems marvelous. Indeed this is truly what we were brought
into creation for, if not to experience it, at least to have the
knowledge of it as an ideal toward which the whole universe
tends and which therefore confers a shape on the random
movements outside us—these are all straining in the same direction, toward the same goal, though it is certain that few if
any of those we see now will attain it.   (TP 72–73)

Is it just corny for a poet to try to say "what we were brought into
creation for"? The phrases themselves force that question upon
one—"life at these times seems marvelous." Yet Ashbery's point is
that those moments when the disarray of apparently random movements slips into a rational, intelligible order are indeed marvels, and
these are the words that have kept faith with the ordinary perception
of that order. No fiery wheels or gyres, no figures of elation or transcendence—merely the well-worn words of common vision. What
allows Ashbery to write so plainly about such elementary subjects is
not literary populism but techniques that seem to display indifference,
as though one phrase or figure would do as well as the next:

as the discourse continues and you think you are not getting
anything out of it, as you yawn and rub your eyes and pick your
nose or scratch your head, or nudge your neighbor on the hard
wooden bench, this knowledge is getting through to you, and
taking just the forms it needs to impress itself upon you, the
forms of your inattention and incapacity or unwillingness to
understand.   (TP 80)

Creeley's achievement can be seen plainly in a handful of short
poems; the anthologies can be fair to him in a way that they cannot to
Ashbery. Although Ashbery has a number of unusually compelling
poems to his credit, his work will be justly assessed, I think, by reference to an artistic ambition that has troubled several generations of
American poets. Yvor Winters spoke of the notion that a poem's form
should mime its subject as the fallacy of imitative form. All the same,
one American poet after another tries to write in a style that does not
betray the feel of those confusing experiences that sometimes generate poems.[23] Ashbery's style always claims that the most banal and
chancy of urban experiences can in fact support the intense scrutiny
associated with meditative poetry. Baudelaire said that "Chance has
no more place in art than in mechanics," and Mallarmé believed that
"No successful poem can be written by Chance."[24] Ashbery, perhaps

humbler than these French poets, or less in need of writing only successful poems, has set himself against this line of thought, in order to speak for those areas of daily experience that are least susceptible to the shapeliness of art. Especially in his longer efforts, like "Grand Galop," "Fragment," and *Three Poems,* where he is able to go back and forth between genuine insight and the drone of distraction, he has staked out for poetry some rather little-examined mental terrain. Despite the ostensible humility of this project, paradoxically Ashbery is the sort of poet who will doubtless be evaluated by the measure of his own intention.

What impact, then, did the development of systems analysis make on poetry? First, it encouraged one of the several traditional offices of poetry: the search for patterns of coherence, order, and meaning where none are commonly recognized. Ashbery and Creeley, in doing just this, are writing poems in the line of Donne, Frost, or Stevens. Yet they are exploring this traditional role with the curiosity of their contemporaries who had learned that such patterns, once discerned, stated as principles, and put to use, render broad regions of knowledge newly fruitful. The optimism of systems analysis derives from a belief that much of what appears disordered is in fact complexly ordered, and that the conflicts inherent in economic, political, and social activity can be reduced by the proper coordination of competing factors. This kind of optimism is characteristically American in seeing a way around political and ideological confrontation. When Ashbery and Creeley engage the figures of systems analysis, they are testing this strain of American social thought and, it must be admitted, suggesting how the easily parodied American trust in understanding, planning, and ingenuity provides terms and figures sufficiently rich to illuminate our experiences of loneliness, maturation, love, and the coming of spring. That Norbert Wiener's methods of computing variations in the flights of bomber planes should have any bearing on these entirely traditional subjects of poetry is one of the odd quirks of recent literary history—and a sign too of how the poems speak, curiously and skeptically, to much more than what is taken as the literary province of American culture.

3 · Tourists

In 1951 Charles Olson left the nation's capital, where he had worked since 1942 in the government and the Democratic Party, for a year in the Yucatan, and that was about half-typical. Many of Olson's contemporaries traveled in the decade following the war, but not many explored North America. In 1949 W. S. Merwin left America to live in France. A year later Robert Lowell took his first trip to Europe and stayed for three years. Elizabeth Bishop had been traveling since the mid-1930s; in 1951 she settled in Petropolis, near Rio de Janeiro. Anthony Hecht won the Prix de Rome Fellowship that year, and James Merrill was living in Rome then too. In 1952 James Wright took a Fulbright to Vienna, Richard Howard went to study at the Sorbonne, and Adrienne Rich had a Guggenheim year in Europe. The following year Charles Gullans went to England on a Fulbright, and Olson's friend Robert Creeley moved to Mallorca. Then in 1954 Richard Wilbur won the Prix de Rome Fellowship. And in 1955 John Ashbery left New York to study in Paris on a Fulbright, not to return for a decade.

Of course poems were spun off these centrifugal circuits. In fact, three conventional poetic subjects dominated the decade: animals (almost always referred to by the more evocative biblical term "beasts"), the fine arts (mainly this meant poems on past European painters and sculptors), and travel. Olson was severely critical of poets who stayed within those conventions. W. S. Merwin was obviously accomplished in just these terms; his second book was entitled *The Dancing Bears* (1954), the third, *Green with Beasts* (1956). Olson insisted that Merwin's poetry showed none of the force and scope of American culture of the early 1950s.[1] Like William Carlos Williams, he felt that poets writing about English gardens, French boulevards, and Italian piazzas were begging off the challenge of a dramatically expanding American culture. In this respect he was quite wrong, though thoroughly American.

The disapproval of travel writing, even of travel, was not new to American thought. Olson's puritanical censure of travel poetry had little to do with the strictly literary merits of such writing. Rather, his complaint was that a nobler subject—"the Americanization of the world"—was waiting in the wings, and not being called. Travel poems were just not serious enough. And he had a point. Henry James, no mean travel writer, said, "Our observation in any foreign land is extremely superficial."[2] Emerson was especially strenuous on this score: "For the most part, only the light characters travel."[3] Melville, a vigorous advocate of American travel, claimed that to travel well one must be "a good lounger," "care-free."[4] American writers are slow to defend lightness; earnestness is more their game. Travelers are first struck by what is different, new, or odd. Melville understood that the experience of such differences in itself has a liberalizing effect on the sensibility. But for a writer, American or not, this subject has a special danger. Travel is the most difficult subject, Auden said, because it restricts freedom of invention while it offers the lure of journalism, of superficial "typewriter-thumping." All that a journalist requires to create interest is "the new, the extraordinary, the comic, the shocking"; travel supplies these in abundance. The danger is that the serious writer, whose work is not done until the meaning of new experiences has been suggested, will, like a reporter, be too quickly satisfied.[5]

Most of the tourist poems of the 1950s work the traditional themes and concerns of travel poems, English and American; not all of them seem timely. This uneasiness about superficiality, for instance, shows up without surprise when poets approach the moral fringes, the lustiness of tourists, say. John Hollander is simply playful about all of this:

> O for the perfumes that arise
> From all those extra-specialty shops
>   In Copenhagen!
> O for the welcome looks from eyes
> Like blue, unbuyable lollipops
>   In Copenhagen!
>
> *"Non Sum Qualis Eram Bona in Urbe Nordica Illa"* (1960)[6]

But this is admittedly light verse and barely counts. More commonly, American poets grow rather serious when they consider the freedom of a tourist; "Nothing in transit need be done by thirds," Anthony

Hecht once remarked.[7] Adrienne Rich is rather melancholy and *per-due* about a traveler's promiscuity:

> You will perhaps make love to me this evening,
> Dancing among the circular green tables
> Or where the clockwork tinkle of the fountain
> Sounds in the garden's primly pebbled arbors.
> Reality is no stronger than a waltz,
> A painted lake stippled with boats and swans,
> A glass of gold-brown beer, a phrase in German
> Or French, or any language but our own.
> Reason would call us less than friends,
> And therefore more adept at making love.
>
> *"The Kursaal at Interlaken" (1951)*[8]

American travelers fear tawdriness and decadence. Speaking a foreign language, dancing with an almost-stranger, giving free rein to circumstance ("perhaps")—these are the things that make American poets sense duplicity, even if they consent to it for the moment. Charles Gullans consents, but with tight-lipped self-reproach:

> The fugitive acquires enduring shape,
> The resonance of all that it might be:
> The freedom of assault, the blow, the rape,
> For this is without responsibility.
>
> *"The Traveler in the Hotel Bar" (1962)*[9]

Gullans writes as one trapped and ashamed by transient desire. Along with Edgar Bowers and Turner Cassity, Gullans helped this traveler's theme, the degradation of eros, to evolve into a subgenre, the barroom poem of jaundiced courting.[10] And James Merrill, in "The Thousand and Second Night," wrote a masterpiece on this tourist's subject.

A great many tourist poems have been written by American poets who were simply glad for the chance to write descriptive poetry—poems that are traditionally supposed to be superficial. These are easy to identify, and the motive comes naturally to a stranger in a new place. Every tourist knows that feeling of greater intimacy with the flowers, pavement, and air of a foreign city than with its natives, one's fellow souls. These poems express a loneliness that has more to do with uncertainty and an attendant quick exuberance than with sadness.

I went out at daybreak and stood on Primrose Hill.
It was April: a white haze over the hills of Surrey
Over the green haze of the hills above the dark green
Of the park trees, and over it all the light came up clear,
The sky like deep porcelain paling and paling,
With everywhere under it the faces of the buildings
Where the city slept, gleaming white and quiet,
St Paul's and the water tower taking the gentle gold.
And from the hill chestnuts and the park trees
There was such a clamour rose as the birds woke,
Such uncontainable tempest of whirled
Singing flung upward and upward into the new light,
Increasing still as the birds themselves rose
From the black trees and whirled in a rising cloud,
Flakes and water-spouts and hurled seas and continents of
    them
Rising, dissolving, streamering out, always
Louder and louder singing, shrieking, laughing.

                W. S. Merwin, "Birds Waking" (1956)[11]

The sharpest criticism of this sort of exercise in elaborate description is Ashbery's mock-tourist poem, "The Instruction Manual" (1956):

Around stand the flower girls, handing out rose- and lemon-
    colored flowers,
Each attractive in her rose-and-blue striped dress (Oh! such
    shades of rose and blue),
And nearby is the little white booth where women in green
    serve you green and yellow fruit.
The couples are parading; everyone is in a holiday mood.[12]

Those bright colors glare a bit desperately, as though all that Merwin or Ashbery can see should be registered, almost labeled, since what cannot be understood looms so large for a tourist. Merwin strains a bit ("streamering"!) for his joy. He draws the poem to a close by asking that the world explode, perhaps even atomically ("Explosion of our own devising"), right now when the birdsong is at its highest pitch.

It can be tricky to end a poem that is motivated only by a desire to describe, because description often does not lead to a take-home message. American poets, writing in a tradition that disapproves of superficiality, sometimes have guilty consciences over such things. After giving himself over to seven elaborate stanzas describing the fauns in a Roman fountain, Richard Wilbur draws himself up short to ask, "Yet since this all / Is pleasure, flash, and waterfall, / Must it not be too simple?" This is the moralist's question, though Wilbur is enough of a poet to know how to escape:

> Are we not
>
> More intricately expressed
> In the plain fountains that Maderna set
> Before St. Peter's— . . .
>
> *"A Baroque Wall-Fountain in the Villa Sciarra" (1955)* [13]

Then follow seven more elaborate stanzas on the fountains at St. Peter's. That time Wilbur got away from the puritanical conscience, but few of his contemporaries did and even he is nabbed badly when, at the end of a poem in which he figuratively consumes, with the zest of a connoisseur, an entire landscape, he reflects morosely:

> And we knew we had eaten not the manna of heaven
> But our own reflected light,
> And we were the only part of the night that we
> Couldn't believe.
>
> *"The Terrace" (1950)* [14]

However urgent the impulse just to describe all that is strange, the sanctions of an earnest literary tradition, the wagging finger of Emerson, has its way almost every time. The best descriptive tourist poems take sides with that tradition.

Easy joy is only a small part of the tourist's life. Those flashy surfaces seem sometimes to stretch without end. In "Waiting for Ada" (1970), Richard Howard writes about sitting out a rainy day in the lobby of "Rimini's Grand Hotel du Miroir," eager to get beyond the "panoramas and preconceptions" and back home to the deeper pleasure of reading Nabokov's *Ada*. [15] Wilbur and Merwin may usually feel jubilant, but others testify that the interminable spectacle of foreign details—the smaller, the odder—is powerfully unsettling. When tourist-poets begin to elaborate figures, emblems, and allegory, or parable, they are simply wielding the traditional tools for getting the words off the plane of mere circumstance. Gullans writes, with obvious pleasure, about simply walking across a moor:

> The drying goarse, the heather, and the bracken
> Move with a brisk confusion, and the sound
> Will sometimes deepen and will sometimes slacken.
>
> *"The Moor, Haworth" (1957)* [16]

A tourist hears the buzz of insects, and only someone uncertain of his footing, as a tourist often is, notices that this sound is not addressed to him:

> Though all about me voices seem to spring,
> They are not any voices that I know.

Those are not just the voices of insects, of course, but all "The other and the alien tongues" that leave a "brisk confusion" around even simple acts, like walking across a field or staring at a brick.

> Neutral and dull, the bricks that serve as shores
> Enforce their color on the channeled water;
> And if a distant movement, as of oars,
> Has made that mirrored brick, its mortar scatter,
> Now, as the soon abated force goes slack,
> A leveling inertia lays them back.
>
> *Turner Cassity, "A Somewhat Static Barcarolle" (1966)* [17]

"Neutral," "dull," "inertia"—these too are the tourist's terms, and it takes effort and style to get beyond them. Cassity wrote his barcarolle (a gondolier song) in bourgeois Amsterdam, where the power is oil not oars. The small disappointment of a tourist (that Amsterdam is not Venice, that the boats are motored not rowed, that the shore is merely unpicturesque brick) is dispelled by hard concentration on nothing more than the old pun in the word "reflection": the surface of the brick, its image reflected in the water, and in the mind only intermittently, during calm. With the last stanza, that concentration, as tough but supple as the rhythm, brings surface and reflection, these foreign surfaces and this mind bordering on torpor, together in a quasi-parable (and another pun, on "sense"), where Venice and Amsterdam are joined (and the last line picks up the gondolier's tread).

> As if our shadows, lengthening below,
> Received us bodily to calm, to vision,
> Always to rock with lifted oars; where, low
> Beside the mirror, sense and its precision

> Give to the arching sky, the dormered town,
> A motion one brick up and one brick down.

For Howard, Gullans, and Cassity, none of them descriptive poets, worries about superficiality are troublesome only momentarily and never really challenge their poetry in general. But for Elizabeth Bishop, a traveler and descriptive poet always, the challenge held high stakes—and led to the best poem on this subject. Here are the opening lines of "Questions of Travel" (1956):

> There are too many waterfalls here; the crowded streams
> hurry too rapidly down to the sea,
> and the pressure of so many clouds on the mountaintops
> makes them spill over the sides in soft slow-motion,
> turning to waterfalls under our very eyes.
> —For if those streaks, those mile-long, shiny, tearstains,
> aren't waterfalls yet,
> in a quick age or so, as ages go here,
> they probably will be.
> But if the streams and clouds keep travelling, travelling,
> the mountains look like the hulls of capsized ships,
> slime-hung and barnacled.

> Think of the long trip home.[18]

Bishop knows her most artful moves well, even—as here—to the point of weariness. Those figures, tearstains and hulls, seem to come easily to her, and so does that bird's-eye view, as though from an airplane. Too easily, for the Emersonian: "Where should we be today?" The play of spirit that brightens tourist poems is dazzling but cheap, like sequins. Readers of the *New Yorker,* who first came across this and many of Bishop's poems, might be impressed, but who would be moved? Always to be going on, or over, like the streams and clouds, may only corrupt the soul ("Is it right to be watching strangers in a play/in this strangest of theatres?") and leave a poet stranded like those barnacled ships.

Streams and clouds can be made to stand for travelers, beached ships for dry poets: figures hold the Emersonian at bay with the claim that nothing is merely literal or light. But here that is a debater's defense. Bishop is more a literalist than a fabler; she cannot afford to give away the prerogatives of the descriptive poet.

> But surely it would have been a pity
> not to have seen the trees along this road,

really exaggerated in their beauty,
not to have seen them gesturing
like noble pantomimists, robed in pink.
—Not to have had to stop for gas and heard
the sad, two-noted, wooden tune
of disparate wooden clogs
carelessly clacking over
a grease-stained filling-station floor.
(In another country the clogs would all be tested.
Each pair there would have identical pitch.)
—A pity not to have heard
the other, less primitive music of the fat brown bird
who sings above the broken gasoline pump
in a bamboo church of Jesuit baroque:
three towers, five silver crosses.

The first three lines of this strophe, with those homely words that a poet types with terror ("it would have been a pity," "really," "their beauty"), are nothing if not candid. Description and simile (not fable) she needs, even when the language is only amusing, like pantomimists. There are times when a close eye can find the human spirit even on the unfamiliar facets of a tropical gas station. That the music of the clogs is made against the greasy work floor is not exactly an emblematic detail, though that kind of interpretation could be made to work from time to time; it is wonderfully fresh description, with only a restrained hint of some metaphysical fit. The interpretation that counts for more here is the cultural one suggested parenthetically by the contrast between Northern European tidiness and South American baroque. One thing a tourist-poet can do naturally is to scrutinize the interfaces of cultures, where the Jesuits meet the jungle.

The imagination that finds "history in/the weak calligraphy of song-birds' cages" is illuminating rather than light. Bishop has set the poem up for a firm, cogent answer to the skeptical charge that travel (and travel writing) is frivolous. All is in place:

> *Continent, city, country, society:*
> *the choice is never wide and never free.*
> *And here, or there . . . No. Should we have stayed at home,*
> *wherever that may be?*

What makes the poem genuinely moving is that the well-made argument dissolves into the ellipsis. Differences between continents do in fact count for a great deal, and Bishop is genuinely American whether she chose her nationality freely or not. There can be no relish for the ways that culture shines through bamboo birdcages without the tourist's or expatriate's feeling of estrangement. If the Brazilian character shows in those local details, and if she has faith in the life of those details, why has she given up the physical proximity to American details? This question of travel goes unanswered at the end, which is what makes the poem deadly serious and finally sad.

Bishop asks herself why she is always traveling, traveling, and writing stunning poems about odd details. The question can be put more broadly to a generation of poets. Why in the 1950s was such intense concentration brought to this particular genre? Was this just a time, as Olson and James Dickey suggest, of light poetry? No, but it was a traveling time. In the 1950s airfares seemed low and the exchange rate favorable to Americans. More Americans traveled to Europe in that decade than ever before. Poets were addressing a subject that had great pertinence to the time: many Americans were going abroad for the first time, and many of them were the first in their families to conceive of a vacation as a tour of Europe. These travelers can be identified more particularly because the international tourist industry has gone to considerable trouble to locate the spenders. They are spoken of as middle-class, with annual incomes of over $15,000 for the most part, and predominantly white.[19] Poets were giving form to a new cultural experience, or rather to a newly diffused one. They were writing about the class of Americans who conceived of themselves as the center of American social, political, and economic life: these were the Americans whose interests were comprehended within the political consensus of the 1950s.

There is more to it, though. With the end of World War II, the United States expressly took on military responsibility for the security of Western Europe. And American economic interests moved into those markets that had formerly been held by French and British firms. After 1945 the United States set about the job of becoming a global power in short order. Exactly when American foreign policy was first directed by the imperialist urge is open to disagreement, but there is no question that the years following the war saw a rapid and immense extension of American power around the world. Most of this was done, it should be remembered, with the encouragement of the then withdrawing Western European imperial powers. England, France, and the United States continued after the war to see their interests as allied. Americans had the military and economic strength needed to keep England and France's former political and economic colonies open to western development. So Americans had to take the lead.[20]

Militarily and economically, they were prepared to assume that responsibility: the American army and the major industries were stronger right after the war than they had ever been, though all the other belligerents had been hurt in just those terms by the war.[21] There was a chink, however, in the cultural armor. American artists did not think of themselves as well prepared to assume western leadership in the arts. Many twentieth-century artists, poets most conspicuously, had expatriated, in large measure because America lacked a vital artistic center. Marianne Moore, William Carlos Williams, Georgia O'Keeffe, and many other artists stayed in America, some of them fiercely defending the vigor of the national culture; they were part of an American tradition that reaches back to the first years of nationhood. Noah Webster told schoolchildren, in his *Speller* (1783), that "America must be as independent in *literature* as she is in *politics.*" Most of the post-World War II poets who wrote tourist poems, however, were not obviously of either camp—neither expatriates nor principled nativists—for the terms of the problem had suddenly shifted with the resolution of the war. The question in the early 1950s was no longer whether American culture was fecund enough to produce a world-class literature; that challenge had been plainly met. But could Americans assume the custodianship of European cultural traditions as adroitly as military and economic responsibility was being shouldered?

Even the generals knew that this question would arise. In 1944 Eisenhower warned Patton, Bradley, and other military commanders to move cautiously around the "monuments and cultural centers which symbolize to the world all that we are fighting to preserve."[22] Again and again in the next two decades, Americans would show how eager they were not to proceed too bullishly. In 1956 the largest restoration in the Athenian agora (the Stoa of Attalos, now a museum) was completed by the American School of Classical Studies. Tourists trying to find the narrow pass at Thermopylae, a difficult search after water and earth shifted, are helped by a marker-monument erected by American Friends of the Spartans. American poets proceeded in a similar fashion. Although poets traveled widely, the poems tend to gather, like pigeons and hawkers, around the sights and monuments: Richard Wilbur on the "Marché aux Oiseaux" (1949), "Wellfleet: The House" (1948), "Piazza di Spagna, Early Morning" (1955), and "A Baroque Wall-Fountain in the Villa Sciarra" (1955); James Merrill on the recovered bronze statue "The Charioteer of Delphi" (1950) and, at Versailles, "In the Hall of Mirrors" (1957); Anthony Hecht at "Ostia Antica" (1967), at the Palazzo Farnese, in "A Hill" (1964), in "The Gardens of the Villa d'Este" (1953); Charles Gullans at "St. John's, Hampstead" (1958); X. J. Kennedy in the "Theater of Dionysus" (1953); Randall Jarrell on "The Orient Express" (1950); W. S. Merwin on "A Sparrow Sheltering under a Column of the British Museum" (1955); John Hollander in "Late August on the Lido" (1958) and on a restored Polish palace, "Lazienka" (1962); Edgar Bowers at St. Mark's, "To Accompany an Italian Guide-Book, 2" (1954); Adrienne Rich at "Versailles (*Petit Trianon*)" (1953), at the "Villa Adriana" (1955), and on "A View of Merton College" (1955); and Paul Blackburn at the Place Dauphine in "La Vieille Belle" (1957). They were all self-conscious tourists, with a mission. By fountain, statue, palazzo and piazza, the poets were demonstrating their ability to write intelligently, tastefully about the outward signs of the cultural heritage America was taking over after the war. These poems—and most of them are certainly intelligent, tasteful, and worthy of continued attention—are part of America's cultural claim to global hegemony.

Although American poets did not speak about tourist poems in these terms, the ways they wrote about monuments suggest that the poets were somehow aware of the American need for such credentials then. When Keats looked at the Elgin Marbles in the British Museum in 1817, he felt "Like a sick eagle looking at the sky"; he acknowledged that he stood in the "shadow of a magnitude."[23] Rilke, in front of the archaic torso of Apollo in the Louvre in 1908, also felt the sting of comparison: "Du musst dein Leben ändern" (You must change your life).[24] European poets could better afford admissions of inferiority.

American poets customarily maintain equanimity in these circumstances, as though the contemplation of a monument were a test of strength and a flinch could cost the game. American writers (and some tourists too) are painfully aware of the need to prove themselves culturally. In 1959 Allen Tate wrote to the U.S. State Department: "Mr. Lowell is the kind of a man I think we should send abroad more and more in order to eliminate some false impressions that foreigners seem to have about the qualifications of Americans to participate in international cultural life on equal terms with them."[25] Some poems by Americans show tourists reduced by their proximity to the monuments, as when the departing couple Merrill observes in the Hall of Mirrors leaves no trace on the glass.[26] (American poets often establish their own refinement against the background, it must be admitted, of garish compatriots.) More commonly, though, poets overcome distance between themselves and the icons of Europe, though there is little question but that they begin their travels a bit estranged. "Ease is what we lack," Adrienne Rich says ("At Hertford House" [1955]). This is why the poets look around them for some sign of comfort.[27]

> [the sparrow] knows simply that this stone
>
> Shelters, rising into the native air,
> And that, though perhaps cold, he is at home there.
>
> *Merwin, "A Sparrow Sheltering under*
> *a Column of the British Museum" (1955)*[28]

> One is at home here. Nowhere in ocean's reach
> Can time have any foreignness or fears.
>
> *Wilbur, "Wellfleet: The House" (1948)*[29]

These poems aim at that sweet conclusion, of course, because a lack of comfort is the obvious burden the American poet carries through Europe: for the poets, this is as much a test as a vacation. They need to appropriate Europe:

> —The light has changed
> Before we can make it ours. We have no choice:
> We are only tourists under the blue sky . . .
>
> *Adrienne Rich, "The Tourist and the Town" (1955)*[30]

Rich's poem ends with that appropriation achieved, only because she has received a painful letter from home that leaves her feeling common emotions there in San Miniato al Monte, like a normal person more concerned with her own state than with the streets and buildings around her. Anthony Hecht's "A Hill" is a less discursive and more powerful poem on a similar experience. In both poems, memories of American "bitter origins," as Rich puts it, leave the poet with a profound bond to the European landscape. Hecht stands before the Palazzo Farnese transfixed by a vivid boyhood memory of a wintry hill in Poughkeepsie. When the Palazzo becomes that hill, for a moment, it is Hecht's—and Renaissance Rome is his too.

Appropriation occurs in poem after poem, in subtler, more interesting ways. Poets have special methods of establishing their authority over a subject. Often only a few lines setting a tone will do the job, as when Wilbur refers to "a faun-ménage and their familiar goose" in "A Baroque Wall-Fountain in the Villa Sciarra."[31] His ability to be lightly ironic asserts firm self-possession and knowledgeability; here, sophistication is power. These lines from Merrill's "The Cruise" (1954) give a sense of the larger dimensions of this procedure:

> Mild faces turned aside to let us fondle
> Monsters in crystal, tame and small, fawning
> On lengths of ocean-green brocade.
> 'These once were nightmares,' the Professor said,
> 'That set aswirl the mind of China. Now
> They are belittled, to whom craftsmen fed
> The drug of Form, their fingers cold with dread,
> Famine and Pestilence, into souvenirs.'
> 'Well I'm *still* famished,' said a woman in red
> From Philadelphia. I wondered then:
> Are we less monstrous when our motive slumbers
> Drugged by a perfection of our form?
> The bargain struck . . .[32]

That woman from Philadelphia could do with some drugging; a little civility would take her a long way. Artistic and social form tend to come together. These Chinese monsters, manageable now, have had their power reduced by being given artistic form. Social form does something similar for the base human drives. A poet's power is form: a subject caught (Europe, say) is tamed. Without the poems, without social manners, mere power is barbaric. The rapid buildup of the American military and the proliferation of defense treaties after 1941 gave this equation particular force in American thought. To prove to others, and perhaps to ourselves too, that this phenomenal power was not monstrously raw and vulnerable to wit and sophistication, monuments had to be restored and written about—preferably with wit and sophistication.

Nearly all the poets who responded to that need by writing tourist poems were conservative in terms of poetic technique. Merrill, Wilbur, Howard, Hecht, Hollander, Rich, Cassity, Gullans, Merwin, Bishop—for most of these poets, Frost, Stevens, Auden, and, a bit anomalously, Eliot were the great masters, not Pound, certainly not Williams. One reason they were better prepared than their avant-garde contemporaries (Ashbery, Olson, Creeley, Duncan) to demonstrate the refinement and sophistication of American culture is simply technical. These are the poets who were obviously competent writers within the inherited body of poetic technique. That they wrote metrical poems was part of their display of competence, but only part. Although Stevens never left the United States, and Eliot and Auden were seasoned travelers, those poets were all international in their sense of the history of art and especially of poetry. Frost is the odd master in this sense. Why should these cosmopolitan young poets take the homespun Yankee as their mentor? (And it is Frost whose influence may be deepest on these poets.) The answer is technical. Of course Frost kept his meters, but more important he wrote in traditional figurative language: unlike the modernists, he wrote parables. Merrill's "The Cruise" and "The Charioteer of Delphi" are both parables, and so too is Cassity's barcarolle. Wilbur explicitly likens human nature to the fountains at the Villa Sciarra and at St. Peter's. In "The Gardens of the Villa d'Este," Hecht claims that a horticultural

> style can teach us how
> To know the world in little where the weed
> Has license, where by dint of force
> D'Estes have set their seal.[33]

Charles Gullans reads a cemetery in the same fashion:

> For church and tombs and landscape all define
> A style of calm and dignified restraint
> As cautious as their faith; unbroken line,
> The spacious order that their lives maintained.
>
> *"St. John's, Hampstead" (1962)*[34]

Adrienne Rich concludes her poem about the Petit Trianon with this moral:

> O children, next year, children, you will play
> With only half your hearts; be wild today.
> And lovers, take one long and fast embrace
> Before the sun that tarnished queens goes down,
> And evening finds you in a restless town
> Where each has back his old restricted face.
>
> *"Versailles" (1955)*[35]

This is an early poem, not one of her best. Still, how confident all these poets are of their mastery of the sights and monuments before them! They seem to understand it all. Poets using monuments to write parables or extract a lesson are secure in their authority; this way of writing does not easily admit uncertainty or faintness of voice. The monuments are subordinated somehow, as instances of the poets' general truths. Frost, it should be said, did write mysterious parables that pointed to his own incomplete understanding of particular experiences. These younger poets took to heart the part of Frost that encouraged a more confident "reading" of experience for analogies to the moral life of the individual.

The richest of these poems taking lessons from monuments is John Hollander's "Lazienka" (1962).

> Ruins are what we make of them, and wrecked
> Imaginations could want to do so little
> With any real rubble. Acres of crumbled bricks,
> Painful, cracked chunks of stucco, even, can be
> Reused with the right kind of patience, fitted
>   Back into a fairly free
> Orderliness again. If broken Doric
> Columns look less like finished sculptures now
> Than twisted piles of rusty scrap, all stuck
> About with dreadful bits of plaster do,
> It's not because our own junked age is over
> Yet, but that our young sculptors are so clever.[36]

Hollander's subject is the corruption of a culture's imagination, indicated here by paltry misreading of ruins. The reach of the poem can be suggested by noting that responsibility for this sort of failure belongs not only with Poland but with Germany, America, and with the culture too of those people (including Hollander) who, along with various national allegiances, feel loyalty to those lost in the Holocaust. Acres of crumbled brick can be found in the South Bronx, but these are not the ruins that capture the imaginations of Americans. Even the Doric columns are too simple and rudimentary in use and design to fire the imagination of Hollander's overly clever contemporaries. For them, Berlin's Gedächtniskirche is a real ruin because it is properly framed by glittering postwar buildings that stand, really, for a deplorable complacency. Lazienka, the restored palace with its Greek ruins and amphitheater on the water, is as fake a ruin as the Gedächtniskirche: the Polish government uses this monument to proclaim its reverence for history, for those who have served in the past. But the lost Jews of Warsaw are ill remembered, "With no great love." The poem is not strictly a complaint about antisemitism. The ruin that commands attention lies closer to home:

> Ruination is the ordure
> Of violence: a burned-out mattress, still
> Stinking of scorch; smashed glass; or the broiled ooze
> Of something organic on a plate of dull
> Metal. The calyx of no blasted rose,
> No shard with a red shape on it, resembles
> These portions of a way of life in shambles.

That mattress comes from New York, not Warsaw. Urban rubble is the great neglected ruin of Hollander's time—neglected despite polite, abstract talk of the Death of Cities. Hollander acknowledges that he too is caught up in this failure of imagination. He feels "No flaming pains" for the "burnt race" from which he is descended; all he can do is compose "rusty ironies,"

> Never quite forgetting that every city
> Will one day flower in a burning instead of beauty.

No other monument poem is more assured in tone than "Lazienka": the utterance—to call it a "speech" would be misleading—is extraordinarily well composed. Within this twelve-line stanza, Hollander moves his syntax freely over the line breaks so that each pentameter or tetrameter gets a fresh grip on the flow of speech. Hollander is the most accomplished stanzaic craftsman of his generation. The diction is comparably various and free: "Orderliness," "Ruination," "ooze," and "plaster do." Freedom is just the point. The poem is firmly didactic and utterly convincing because the poet shows in his lines that he abides by his own precepts, fitting all sorts of words into a fairly free orderliness, and suffers by his own judgments. For this, after all, is one more American poem on a picturesque and remote monument; this particular New Yorker knows that his attention belongs less in Warsaw than in the South Bronx. The variety of diction and the play of syntax against the grid of the stanza are responsible for the sense that a full person is speaking freely; however earnest and at times formal the poem becomes, the poet seems never to be contriving to speak through a role. Hollander's contemporaries have often tried to tap the Holocaust for images—Sylvia Plath, W. D. Snodgrass, and William Heyen are well-known instances—but their efforts do not always escape the taint of presumption that this subject brings with it.[37] Although "Lazienka" is written in a confident and at times elevated style, Hollander reveals no pride in his ability to address his subject, to write of monuments.

Some of the poets writing about sights and monuments are explicit

about the appropriation of icons, though most often the subject is just
below the surface, as when Rich ("A View of Merton College") and
Hecht ("Rome" [1977]) cannot help seeing Europe figuratively as a
museum.[38] Just who the custodians of this museum are must be evident by now. In 1950 construction of the Rome Termini was completed, and Richard Wilbur commemorated the achievement a few
years later:

> Those who said God is praised
> By hurt pillars, who loved to see our brazen lust
> Lie down in rubble, and our vaunting arches
> Conduce to dust . . .
>
> *"For the New Railway Station in Rome"* (1955)

Wilbur, who comes from New York, has written no comparably civic
poem on an American subject; American poets seldom sing the praises
of train stations (Allen Ginsberg's "In the Baggage Room at Grey-
hound" [1956] is something quite different). In fact, American poets
seldom take up the civic laurels at all, but for an American to serve,
momentarily, as Rome's civic laureate has a special appeal. For a moment, Wilbur could play at being a Roman and speak on behalf of its
traditions: those first-person plural pronouns could be said to rest on
the sense that all westerners have a claim to representation in the
Foro Romano, and for a moment it seems that bella Roma is Wilbur's,
and he, hers. There are times, though, when poets wanting to speak
similarly for monuments build up their own authority by snooty ges-
tures toward others. When Richard Howard's traveling companion
asks, "Richard, What's That Noise?"—wondering about the nightingales at the Pozzo di San Patrizio—Howard is quick, and proud, to answer only half-facetiously: "Noise! The natural history of nightingales
/ comes down to that! and from this: / 'No bird hath so sweet a voice
among all silvan / musicians . . .' Sundays, / Milton, Keats to Hollander's / Philomel, nightingales sing with no intermission, / but
now, only now, tonight in Umbria, a *noise.*"[39] In a poem about the
Roman spot most crowded, inch for inch, with American tourists, Wilbur likens a young girl, implausibly pirouetting down 137 steps, to a
leaf floating over the lip of a fountain, "Perfectly beautiful, perfectly ignorant of it [the falls] " ("Piazza di Spagna, Early Morning" [1955]).
The poets are eager to distinguish themselves, as who would not be,
from all those other tourists, ignorant of the ground they tread. The
guards at the Palatine doze in amnesia (Hecht, "A Roman Holiday"
[1954]), and only an American poet attends to the ritual significance

of St. Paul's bells (Wilbur, "Bell Speech" [1947]). The real custodians of all this are of course those responsible for the Pax Americana, or so some would have it.[40]

Many of the poets I have discussed sense a connection between tourism and imperialism, partly because the monuments they write of derive from particular empires. In the 1950s, America seemed to be just beginning its reign, as France, England, and Germany retreated. The rise and fall of empires is a subject that comes up often in these poems. John Hollander's "Late August on the Lido" (1958), for instance, is about the end of the Venice season, when the bathers at the Lido cross the Grand Canal and leave for the year. Here is the last stanza:

> All this is over until, perhaps, next spring;
> This last afternoon must be pleasing.
> Europe, Europe is over, but they lie here still,
> While the wind, increasing,
> Sands teeth, sands eyes, sands taste, sands everything.[41]

Hollander expresses no hope for what is to come, only disgust at what is being lost. The last thing the wind erodes, before everything is lost, is taste. The European sense of value, discrimination, propriety—in short, civilization—is passing. Europe is already only a bathing beach. In Merrill's "Three Sketches for Europa" (1954–55) Henry Adams' aunt explains to her departing nephew, "The Tourist," that Europa,

> Poor soul, she's peevish now, an invalid,
> Has lost her beauty, gets things wrong.
> Go now. But do not stay too long.[42]

The Americans are taking over. "All her [Europa's] radiant passage known," Merrill says, "Lamely as Time by some she dreamt not of." Part of what had passed, poets had a stake in believing, was imaginative vision, just what they might provide for American culture. Rich remarks in "Villa Adriana" (1955) of the Roman emperor and poet Hadrian (bound to her in name), who planned rooms of his villa to reproduce some of the exotic places he had seen as a traveler:

> Dying in discontent, he must have known
> How, once mere consciousness had turned its back,

> The frescoes of his appetite would crumble,
> The fountains of his longing yawn and crack.[43]

Consciousness, more than brick and mortar, built the great villa; the remaining ruins are "artifacts of thought." Poets are not only, as Rich suggests, the archaeologists of thought, they are, like Hadrian, its architects too. For them, empires and the flow of weath offer opportunities, commissions, subjects.

Not that opportunities are innocent. When Edgar Bowers looked at St. Mark's and the gondolas crossing from the Lido, he was reminded of how

> The Slavic fleet crept toward it from the sea
> With muffled oars, concealed by mist and rain
> And early morning darkness, silently,
>
> Past Arsenal and *dromi* anchored near,
> Feeding their pirate cunning on the rich
> Shadow of treasure glimmering in the air,
> And waiting for the drag of hull on beach.
>
> *"To Accompany an Italian Guide-Book" (1954)*[44]

In the seventeenth century, Slavs from the Dalmatian coast periodically raided Venice with encouragement from the Austrian empire. In 1954 Bowers sees an analogy between those raiders and the American tourists of his own party. (And, of course, the irony that the Venetian treasures themselves were stolen from Constantinople is also part of the circle.) Strangers all come to take what they can carry away, Venetians, Slavs, and Americans alike, pirates and poets.

Empires run on rapine, and poets follow empires—the plunder sometimes being imaginative. Elizabeth Bishop's *Questions of Travel* (1965) opens with "Arrival at Santos," dated January 1952, about her own disembarkation in South America. Next comes "Brazil, January 1, 1502," about the Portuguese colonization of Brazil. Bishop focuses on the way that the Portuguese projected onto this foreign landscape the imaginative structures of their belief. Birds were seen as symbolic, lizards as dragons, or simply "Sin, / and moss looked like hell-green flames."

> Just so the Christians, hard as nails,
> tiny as nails, and glinting,
> in creaking armor, came and found it all,
> not unfamiliar:

no lovers' walks, no bowers,
no cherries to be picked, no lute music,
but corresponding, nevertheless,
to an old dream of wealth and luxury
already out of style when they left home—
wealth, plus a brand-new pleasure.
Directly after Mass, humming perhaps
L'Homme armé or some such tune,
they ripped away into the hanging fabric,
each out to catch an Indian for himself—
those maddening little women who kept calling,
calling to each other (or had the birds waked up?)
and retreating, always retreating, behind it.

Originally in New Yorker, *2 January 1960*[45]

The connections among Christianity, empire, and Brazil are there in the area's first name: Vera Cruz, the true cross. In the sixteenth century, the Portuguese community that controlled the port of Santos was based in São Paulo; the *paulistas* were pathfinders to the interior, and they were slavers too. Many of them had children by the captive Indian women, but an offshoot of this community, the *bandeirantes,* lived in free union with the Indian women, or married them, though the *bandeirantes* were specialists in seizing slaves. Jesuit missions were established along the Amazon in the seventeenth century, which were then raided by *paulistas* looking for slaves, as well as gold and precious stones. The slave traffic survived until 1853. Bishop attends to the way that the Christian framework was brought down on the backs of the South American Indians. Brazil was an Eden for the Portuguese. They could play at being Adam, while taking those "maddening little women" whose calls seemed as provocative as the erect tail of the female lizard. This is mainly an ugly business, the way the imagination can disguise rape and plunder, but for a poet from a Christian country it is perfectly understandable. The poem's first words point to what she can understand, a fresh landscape: "Januaries, Nature greets our eyes / exactly as she must have greeted theirs." Setting up these two poems, "Arrival at Santos" and "Brazil, January 1, 1502," as the coordinates of Brazilian history is meant to implicate Bishop herself in the appropriation of that territory. She comes out of a culture that reaches right back to those Christian imperialists. Horrifying as their actions were (the poem captures that), she can understand their way of seeing. An empire does rest, as Rich suggested in "Villa Adriana," on lively imagination.

As poets follow the rise of empire, so too they sink with its decline, and the dark fate of empires is a wonderful subject for poets. Perhaps Bishop's best tourist poem, "Over 2000 Illustrations and a Complete Concordance" (1948), raises just this point, in an oblique, desperate fashion.

> Thus should have been our travels:
> serious, engravable.
> The Seven Wonders of the World are tired
> and a touch familiar, but the other scenes,
> innumerable, though equally sad and still,
> are foreign. Often the squatting Arab,
> or group of Arabs, plotting, probably,
> against our Christian Empire,
> while one apart, with outstretched arm and hand
> points to the Tomb, the Pit, the Sepulcher.[46]

Bishop seems to be writing playfully about a nineteenth-century Book of the World ornamented by predictably postured illustrations. She describes the black-and-white engravings until they ignite into color-ful memories of her own travels in the West Indies, Rome, Mexico, and French Morocco. The poem begins to pull toward its close when these two tours coalesce in one scene:

> It was somewhere near there
> I saw what frightened me most of all:
> A holy grave, not looking particularly holy,
> one of a group under a keyhole-arched stone baldaquin
> open to every wind from the pink desert.
>
> An open, gritty, marble trough, carved solid
> with exhortation, yellowed
> as scattered cattle-teeth;
> half filled with dust, not even the dust
> of the poor prophet paynim who once lay there.
> In a smart burnoose Khadour looked on amused.

These lines, recalling an actual experience, are a color version of the first engraving ("Arabs, plotting, probably, / against our Christian Empire"). Bishop imagines a death (a prophet's, her Christian em-pire's, her own) that leaves the cultural stranger, the Muslim, amused as he stands near the Tomb, even the tomb of a muslim prophet; for the faithful, death avails not. (Khadour, or al-Khadir, is an Islamic figure of immortality who was the protector of mariners and river travelers. In an Urdu poem [1924] by Muhammed Iqbal, he is the Guide who asks the most serious questions of travel and has the answers.) The last strophe begins: "Everything only connected by 'and' and 'and.' " The engravings, her memories of travel, and death are all arranged paratactically. Her original, facetious reference to the plotting Arabs seems merely frivolous now that these passages come together—the tone of the poem has changed drastically. In a sense the Arabs were plotting: they stand against lightness, no matter how sophisticated, bound by a faith so absolute that mortality means little, and the threat of a foreign empire is of only passing interest. Bishop does not articulate the pieces of the poem. It ends with her opening the book ceremoniously, as if it were holy, and wishing that when the time had been right she could have been captivated by her culture's claim to authority, a fresh beginning, the Nativity scene. Instead, she or, better, some faithless "we" (she insists on the plural, from the first to the last line) are tourists among our own culture's deepest sanctions: God's fingerprint is a mere engraver's etching; St. John is the name of an island; at St. Peter's the "purposeful" Cardinals seem only, to our eyes, antlike specks on a pale ground; volcanoes are all we can understand of resurrection. The poem is obviously personal—about the fear of death without faith—but two kinds of culture, secular and sacred, are also compared; when East and West face each other, in this poem, the West blinks, in empty terror.

In the 1950s few American poets wrote with a sense of imperial doom (only Bishop and Lowell come to mind); then there was mainly earnest optimism among intellectuals about the expansion of American industry and the obvious accomplishment of the military. Bishop did not criticize her government; she rather wrote of an intuition that those cultures regarded as weak may stand amused before what causes the rich and strong to quake. A couple of years after his 1962 visit to the Netherlands, Turner Cassity published a remarkable poem on this theme.

> Hotel des Indes
> (*The Hague*)
>
> The bell-pull summons, toward my ease,
> Mnemosyne as Javanese.
>
> Inscrutable from sole to head,
> Two chambermaids turn down the bed;

While, pyramiding in my eye,
The contoured ricefields siege the sky,

And where their stepped horizon ends,
An even sugar reascends.

Forever, by those porches, leaves
Extend the shade of tilted eaves,

As if, in our pajamaed noon,
Inherent night, through form undone,

By shadow particled, were stayed;
As though event were so betrayed,

And those who with a Dutch wife lie
Embrace there immortality.

Bowing double, the maid retreats.
It rains till midnight, then it sleets.[47]

This leisured, pajamaed poet gets inspiration with a bell-pull. His Mnemosyne is plainly the mother of Clio: without words, she embodies the history of Dutch empire. Java was colonized at the end of the eighteenth century. In 1942 the Japanese occupied it, and they were followed by the British. From 1945 to 1949 the Netherlands attempted, without success, to regain control of the island; in 1950 it became part of the Republic of Indonesia. The economic history of that imperial relationship between the chambermaid and her European employers (a French hotel) is written right into the landscape: the poet sees the wealth of Java, rice and sugar, laid out in Flemish order, as though the Netherlands had permanently appropriated Java's plenty. (Within a year of the poem's publication, Indonesia was actually in the untenable position of having to import rice just for domestic consumption.)

But the imperial imagination, as Rich and Bishop suggested, is a fragile and dubious thing. A note to the poem quotes Webster's on a Dutch wife: "A rest for the limbs, used in beds in tropical countries, esp. in the Dutch East Indies. It consists of an open frame of rattan or cane, or often a long round bolster stuffed with strips of paper." The penultimate couplet is crucial: the Dutch wife provides a rest only for the limbs, none for the spirit. The poet in his form (these proud couplets) and the Dutch in their economic empire both think they embrace immortality. But Cassity has to reach back to seventeenth-century usage to get that forced rhyme; the obvious suppressed rhyme is "die." What the poet-speaker suppresses, Cassity knows: the chambermaid's silence hardly conceals the revenge of history. The Netherlands lost their colony forever in 1950, but the price of atonement has not yet been paid. Ten years after this poem appeared, part of the bill was presented: South Moluccans, representing another island in the former Dutch East Indies, firebombed the Hague Peace Palace—so much for inherent night being undone. In 1975 another group of South Moluccans took more than fifty hostages on a train and in the Indonesian consulate in Amsterdam. Two years later South Moluccan terrorists held fifty-four train passengers and a hundred Dutch schoolchildren and their teachers as hostages. The Dutch military eventually intervened, killing six terrorists and two hostages. When the public prosecutor asked the court to give ten-year sentences to the captured terrorists, 30,000 South Moluccan exiles rioted in Assen. The irony of these events was that, although the terrorists wanted independence for their islands, the Dutch government was no longer in a position to negotiate this issue, for South Molucca had been part of Indonesia since 1950. None of these events could have surprised Cassity (or those who knew his poem), since he saw the storm coming. Most tourist-poets concerned themselves with the cultural formation of the empire; Cassity asked about the consequences of empire.

American poets are usually aware, painfully so, of being the unacknowledged representatives of national culture, or vulgarity, wealth, and power, and implicated in the expansion of empire. Abroad, America equals money, a simple and binding relationship. When Stanley Kunitz's pocket was picked on a Roman tram, he felt oddly debased, humiliated:

> More even than my purse,
> And that's no laughing matter, it is my pride
> That has been hurt: a fine Italian hand,
> With its mimosa touch, has made me feel
> Blind-skinned, indelicate, a fool Americano
> Touring a culture like a grand museum,
> People and statues interchangeable shows,
> Perception blunted as one's syntax fails.

"The Thief" (1956)[48]

Entitled to outrage, he feels guilty instead; his coarseness has been exposed and its center has been touched—the cash. Even after living more than fifteen years in Brazil, Bishop felt the same onus. "Going to the Bakery" ends with an encounter between Bishop and a black man begging a token of sympathy for a recent wound. Suspecting that her alms will go only for liquor, she can do little but play her role:

> I give him seven cents in *my*
> terrific money, say "Good night"
> from force of habit. Oh, poor habit!
> Not one word more apt or bright?[49]

Americans are the world's consumers. "Buy, buy, what shall I buy?" she asks, only half-ironically. Forgiveness, perhaps, for incomprehension: "He speaks in perfect gibberish," trying to explain what has happened to him. When Bishop's readers saw this poem in the *New Yorker* in March 1968, they would have known, from the newspapers, that Rio too was on the slide of that year's catastrophes. The preceding year had seen 30 percent inflation, and in March there were violent demonstrations there. Three days before the poem appeared, New Yorkers read that the American consulate in São Paulo had been bombed. The familiar properties were in place for the South American scenario that would come as no surprise to New Yorkers. A week after the poem appeared, one demonstration in Rio left a student dead. By the end of the year, the turmoil had led to the arrest of former President Kubitschek, the suspension of constitutional guarantees, the dissolution of congress, and a declaration of martial law. Less than a year later, the military was back in control. Writing as these events were just beginning to slip into their relentless cycle, Bishop felt helpless, tainted, and estranged, an American with no more to offer than seven luckless pennies and a banality.

Affluence and a favorable exchange rate (in 1968 those seven pennies would buy a pound of sugar) give a tourist a sense of power; everyone has felt that and, however guilty or embarrassed at times, gratitude too for immunity from the small confusions and uncertainties that dog a tourist. But when a nation counts on that immunity and power (or, worse still, when one's hosts presume that such power is real) its humanity is endangered. Richard Wilbur has a poem on this theme, a fable about the birds for sale in Paris.

> Marché aux Oiseaux (1949)
>
> Hundreds of birds are singing in the square.
> Their minor voices fountaining in air
> And constant as a fountain, lightly loud,
> Do not drown out the burden of the crowd.

Far from his gold Sudan, the travailleur
Lends to the noise an intermittent chirr
Which to his hearers seems more joy than rage.
He batters softly at his wooden cage.

Here are the silver-bill, the orange-cheek,
The perroquet, the dainty coral-beak
Stacked in their cages; and around them move
The buyers in their termless hunt for love.

Here are the old, the ill, the imperial child;
The lonely people, desperate and mild;
The ugly; past these faces one can read
The tyranny of one outrageous need.

We love the small, said Burke. And if the small
Be not yet small enough, why then by Hell
We'll cramp it till it knows but how to feed,
And we'll provide the water and the seed.[50]

Those picturesque birds have been brought from exotic places to the capital, where they can be bought and sold by those who want to feel loved as well as powerful. This, Wilbur suggests, is the psychology of imperialism, but its basis in human nature generally is firm: affection is extended easily to the weak because it is self-serving; kindness to those who might be squashed suggests restraint and generosity. So powerful is the need to be regarded as beneficent that the mighty will reduce the victims of their magnanimity to helplessness. And, as the second quatrain suggests, the imperialist is out to deceive himself as well as others: protests must be heard as songs of joy. At the basis of imperialism (and of tourism too) is a tempting deception that mocks most human interchange.

American poets are commonly thought of as adversaries to political expansion, as advocates of disarmament. But the evidence is abundant that poets, like other observers, were captivated by the proliferation of American interests after World War II. More important, some of these poets, with the interests of the capital in mind (least of all is this an expatriated literature), have written distinguished poems that set out a sensitive, far-seeing critique of American expansion. Seeing the attractions of expansion, and feeling these attractions powerfully as poets, Bishop, Cassity, and others nonetheless took a critical perspective on expansion. Enthusiastic, implicated, and still critical in a measured way: these are the poets who have written best about the

American effort to take over where France, England, and Germany left off.

I have stressed the cultural purpose served by tourist poems, rather than what might be spoken of as the intentions of the poets, in order to show that these poems address a major experience shared by many middle-class Americans of the 1950s and later. I do not mean to suggest that these writers were State Department agents fulfilling a plan for cultural hegemony; rather few of these poets traveled for the State Department. Nor was there explicit discussion among poets of the offices of tourist poetry. The poets wrote about a subject that was held in focus by some conventions of treatment and elaboration; this was also a subject their own experience brought close to them, and they knew it to be close to the experience of their middle-class readers. This subject held one other attraction for poets then: it enabled them to write poems about social life.

A tourist-poet often writes about people, foreign people, with a fresh eye, and that is a powerful attraction for any poet. Poems about people raise some special problems for postwar American poets. The burden of literary tradition was especially heavy in this area. There were two conventional ways of writing about the social activities of Americans after World War II: one was the type-poem in which a character was drawn of a representative type, not of an individual (Wilbur's "He Was" [1950] and Merwin's "The Master" [1956] are examples).[51] The second method was to write with irony turned against a vulgar or crass American character (the bounder in Merrill's "Charles on Fire" [1960] is the best example).[52] But poems written about middle-class American social behavior from a sympathetic viewpoint were more unusual.[53] Immediate literary precedents, the weight of avant-garde scorn for the bourgeoisie, made it difficult to write poems of observation, curiosity, and sympathy or respect about Americans who have a claim to social normality; certain literary attitudes, such as the fear of sentiment, or of naiveté, were strongly exclusive, especially in the 1950s. Tourist poems offered poets a quick way around conventional attitudes. Although it might be difficult to write admiringly of the social activity of Americans in the 1950s—poets being too ironic and sophisticated to show sympathy so close to home—it was relatively easy to write warmly of foreigners.

Many of these poets tended to admire the same human aspects that would set clicking the shutters of any busload of foreigners. Paul Blackburn writing about the instinctive tenderness of a class-conscious sailor in the Adriatic ("The First Mate" [1955]) or the spirited gesture of a gypsy ("Whee!" [1956])—these are pleasant but unremarkable contributions to the genre.[54] What is noteworthy, though, is some rather pointed agreement among poets as to the particular European traits worthy of American admiration. Merwin wrote about the bond between European farmers and the land they till:

> You feel they would never
> Say the place belonged to them: a reticence
> Like love's delicacy or its quiet assurance.
>
> *"In the Heart of Europe" (1956)*[55]

How very un-American, which is exactly the point. These farmers represent an acknowledged core of European values: respect for the tacit, the calm, the refined, and the confident. On the contrary, Americans are typically quick to say proudly that the land they occupy is their own. They prefer relationships to be explicitly defined, partly because their history inspires no particular assurance about the future. In "St. John's, Hampstead," Gullans admires the "style of calm and dignified restraint" expressed in British funerary monuments. Those who repose there were public men who held a "common hope."[56] A sense of shared fate, of being a member of a group, was regarded by these poets as particularly European and, for obvious reasons, quite distinct from the American ethos. Writing about the small ways that Europeans instinctively know that their lives are tied to a collective civic life provided a means of urging moderation on those Americans of the 1950s who thought that the world was theirs. Merwin's poem begins: "Farmers hereabouts, for generations now / Have owned their own places"; any midwestern American would hear compatriots being addressed with that idiom. From its first lines, the poem draws an implicit contrast between European and American ways, though no invidious comparison is actually spelled out. The second line of Gullans' poem—"Of this smooth Georgian pomp none was ashamed"—makes clear too that he writes with an awareness of how embarrassing American pomp can be. Blackburn asks quite directly:

> When will we learn
> so naturally to
> quit, when what we have to do
> is done?
>
> *"Affinities II" (1956–577)*[57]

Even poems that purport to describe fondly the distinctly European ways of these travelers' hosts are in fact turned to American utility: the tourist poem allowed American poets to write, often obliquely, as social observers, yes, but also as critics of the extreme individualism of their own nation.

Sometimes too the barb was turned back against the pretensions of cultivated tourists.

> Oh, tourist,
> is this how this country is going to answer you
>
> and your immodest demands for a different world,
> and a better life, and complete comprehension
> of both at last, and immediately,
> after eighteen days of suspension?
>
> Bishop, "Arrival at Santos"[58]

Even poet-tourists, Bishop suggests (addressing herself), may imagine that they get (and still worse, are entitled to) more from their travels than in fact they do. Cultivation? Neither Bishop nor Merrill are so sure about that. Compared to the Caspar Goodwoods who know their limits, sophisticated travelers are not uniformly charming. These are the opening stanzas of Merrill's "Words for Maria":

> Unjeweled in black as ever comedienne
> Of mourning if not silent star of chic,
> You drift, September nightwind at your back,
> The half block from your flat to the Bon Goût,
> Collapse, order a black
> Espresso and my ouzo in that Greek
> Reserved for waiters, crane to see who's who
> Without removing your dark glasses, then,
> Too audibly: "Eh, Jimmy, qui sont ces deux strange men?"
>
> Curiosity long since killed the cat
> Inside you. Sweet good nature, lack of guile,
> These are your self-admitted foibles, no?
> My countrymen, the pair in question, get
> Up, glance our way, and go,
> And we agree it will not be worthwhile
> To think of funny nicknames for them yet,
> Such as Le Turc, The Missing Diplomat,
> Justine, The Nun, The Nut— . . .[59]

These poems by Bishop and Merrill set seasoned travelers next to perhaps simpler Americans: Bishop and Miss Breen from Glens Falls, New York; Merrill and "ces deux strange men." Moreover, both poems invoke those camp idioms ("So that's the flag. I never saw it before. / I somehow never thought of there *being* a flag") that most call into question the worth of sophistication. The critique of tourism suggested by these two poems is rather different from Emerson's: the issue here is not whether one skates on surfaces or dives for meaning. Bishop and Merrill set the terms instead for a social critique of tourism and sophistication. Maria and Bishop ("Please, boy, do be more careful with that boat hook!") are impolite. Miss Breen has "Beautiful bright blue eyes and a kind expression"; the two Americans in Athens move on discreetly, perhaps to another café. Melville seems to have been not entirely correct: a great deal of travel may not in fact have a liberalizing effect on the spirit. The sophistication that extended travel brings may not have much to do with genuine *bon gout*. And where then do the tourist-poets end?

At the beginning of this chapter I mentioned that tourist poems were only one of three conventional types of poems popular during the 1950s; European artists and animals provided the subjects for the other two. The common motive behind these three genres, if they can be called that, is a desire to speak for another: these poems are about places that are distant, about artists who are dead, and about animals that are mute. All three sorts of poems take pride in the ability to represent some subject that needs representation; they all demonstrate the power of poetry. This is a self-conscious kind of art, though for good, unusual, and (one might say) subtly patriotic reasons. The adequacy of American high culture was in serious question after World War II, exactly because the nation's economic and military institutions were moving into many of the places left unattended by the European powers. For poets to feel upon them the questioning eyes of fellow citizens, as well as of Europeans, was natural, and to concentrate their energies on those types of poems that display taste, sophistication, intelligence, and inventiveness was, after all, responsible. The still greater responsibility of writing critically as well as patriotically, these poets have managed admirably. I have not tried to suggest that only a new imperial power will produce tourist poetry; British poets too were writing tourist poems by the score during the 1950s.[60] A number of different impulses (some strictly literary—the desire to write descriptive or social verse; some economic and circumstantial—

the favorable exchange rate and low cost of airfare, the availability of travel fellowships) coincided to produce the tourist poetry I have described. My point is only that these poems performed a special service for the nation in the fifteen years or so following the war. That the responsiveness of poets to the needs of the national culture should issue in poems on the order of Hollander's "Lazienka," Bishop's "Questions of Travel," and, best of all, Merrill's "Thousand and Second Night" is proof enough that even the timeliest of what I have called, after Karl Shapiro, culture poetry has shown, in the last thirty-five years, extraordinary literary distinction.

4 · James Merrill: "Revealing by Obscuring"

The conventions popular in the 1950s were well known at the time, and that much easier to drop in favor of others when the time came to do so. James Merrill excelled within the conventions of the 1950s. "The Thousand and Second Night" is the very best, because the richest, tourist poem of the last thirty-five years. Yet when the 1950s conventions became unfashionable, Merrill only seemed an even more important poet: he appeared to excel too at the new conventions of the 1960s, though about these conventions he was rather cagey.

The term "confessional poetry" has earned widespread skepticism; as a generic term, it is misleading.[1] Yet it would be hard to trace the development of recent American poetry without reference to the influence of Allen Ginsberg's *Howl* (1956), Robert Lowell's *Life Studies* (1959), W. D. Snodgrass' *Heart's Needle* (1960), and the poems collected in Sylvia Plath's *Ariel* (1966). Whatever claims may be made on behalf of confessional poetry, it is plain that these books all contributed to the reinstatement of two closely related literary conventions: the notion that poems originate in their subject matter and the corollary that poets mean, at least literally, what they say. These are of course not "facts" about literature (nor even about these four books) but rhetorical rules whereby poems are understood, if not often written. My point here is only the obvious one that during the 1960s these conventions, which have their roots in common-sense notions about poetry, were more accessible than they had been in decades. Which is to say not only that many sixties poems invoke these conventions, but that many others deliberately flout them. My interest in this chapter is James Merrill's ironic wrenching of these rules. For a number of his most important poems originate in calculated reticence. Whereas confessional poets characteristically hold a sharp focus on subject matter, Merrill often writes around interpretable silences. Even more, the obliqueness I am describing conforms to the attitudes and proprieties invoked by Merrill's characteristic style.

Merrill himself has insisted that confessional poetry is as conventional as any other, that it has no special claims on truth telling.[2] Confessions, however, have a special place in his writing—from Francis Tanning's confession of wealth and sexual inexperience to Xenia in *The Seraglio* (1957),[3] to Merrill's seductive invocation of his muse, Psyche, in *From the Cupola* (1966)—

> Tell me about him, then. Not a believer,
> I'll hold my tongue while you, my dear, dictate.   (ND 38)

—right up to the coy opening lines of *The Book of Ephraim* (1976): "my subject matter / Gave me pause—so intimate, so novel" (DC 47).[4] Full disclosure, however, is the last thing one has reason to expect of Merrill. He has admitted that one part of the subject of *From the Cupola* is "an unknowable situation, something I'm going to keep quiet about." Yet he invites his readers "to guess at, to triangulate . . . [that] story, the untold one" (CW 146). Loaded silences are a rhetorical trope for Merrill. In "Part of the Vigil" he imagines himself, tiny, plumbing the inner passages of his lover's heart: "What if my effigy were down there? What, / Dear god, if it were not! / If it were nowhere in your heart! / Here I turned back. Of the rest I do not speak" (FS 24). And near the end of "Words for Maria" he feigns interest in his friend's buried life:

> About what went before
> Or lies beneath, how little one can glean.
> Girlhood, marriage, the war . . .
> I'd like once (not now, here comes Giulio)
> Really to hear—I mean—I didn't mean—
> You paint a smiling mouth to answer me:
> "Since when does L'Enfant care for archaeology?"   (FS 13)

Merrill's joke is that contrived obstacle to his hearing Maria's secrets—"here comes Giulio." Maria knows as well as Merrill's readers that what L'Enfant most enjoys is her *painted* face. These little tricks, rhetorical caresses of ignorance, have a serious tacit point to register. Speculating on the transience of glory, Merrill says: "—Might reputations be deflated there? / I wondered here, but Ephraim changed the subject / As it was in his tactful power to do" (DC 98). Quiet evasions like Ephraim's, like Merrill's, testify to a delicate system of human meaning whose categories, felt by people of understanding, might be compromised by express formulation. Reticence, for Merrill, is painstakingly deliberate and exact in its meaning: thus, in *The Summer People,* Andrew, Margaret, and Nora "dealt with Jack from then on / By never mentioning him" (FS 68). There is a class of people for whom silence is a badge of discretion and a measure of controlled power, the power to ignore.

There are more strictly literary ways to explain Merrill's inclination to bury certain subjects. Merrill himself has spoken of "buried meanings" as a kind of hedge against trivia: "Without something like them, one ends up writing light verse about love affairs."[5] But perhaps more important is his early declared allegiance to the commonplace that music and meaning rob from each other in poetry. These lines come from "The Drowning Poet" (1947):

> To drown was the perfection of technique,
> The word containing its own sense, like Time;
> And turning to the sea he entered it
> As one might speak of poems in a poem
> Or at the crisis in the sonata quote
> Five-finger exercises: a compliment
> To all accomplishment.   (FP 17)

The poet dedicated to his craft scorns referential meaning: He prefers poems that refer only to other poems (better yet, to translations of poems) and thereby honor the boundaries between art and life. By this understanding, allusions do not, in Eliotic fashion, deepen the resonance of themes; they gesture disdain for the bourgeois or common-sense expectation of moral wisdom from poetry. Thus the arch-poet, Apollo, "Inflicted so much music on the lyre / That no one could have told you what he sang" (1958; CT 52). Music properly overpowers sense. According to this Shelleyan revision of the French Symbolists, the poet aims "at something not unlike / Meaning relieved of sense, / To plant a flag there on that needle peak / Whose diamond grates in the revolving silence" (1964; ND 24).

Yet Merrill is self-critical always, and he has nicely revealed the blindness of a poetic that takes for granted the sanctified reserve of art. Here are some lines from "Mirror" (1958), a poem reworking the traditional art-as-mirror topos (the mirror is addressing the window):

You embrace a whole world without once caring
To set it in order. That takes thought. Out there
Something is being picked. The red-and-white bandannas
Go to my heart. A fine young man
Rides by on horseback. Now the door shuts. Hester
Confides in me her first unhappiness.
This much, you see, would never have been fitted
Together, but for me.   (ll. 13–20; CT 36)

Constructed order characterizes the special province of art, but the fullness and depth of this art's order are in question. For the mirror arranges surfaces on a plane, as some poets constellate images in verse. (Merrill, in a playful moment of self-parody, has referred to his own version of this poetic as " 'word-painting' " [DC 48].) The three indicative sentences stretched over lines 16–18 all but iron the human drama out of the narrative: the language makes little distinction between the closing of a door and a young woman's feeling when her first romance has ended. The mirror cannot connect events: the three sentences, without conjunctions, line up like beads on a string. The mirror prides itself on the thoughtfulness of its order (l. 14), but Merrill uses his buried-subject trope to show where an art of dazzling surfaces cannot penetrate: "Out there / Something is being picked." One must guess at what is being picked, but the mirror, blindly, supplies clues. The persimmon mentioned later in the poem (l. 30) is raised chiefly in the south, and the bandannas dear to the heart of the mirror may well be worn by slaves picking cotton. What the mirror cannot penetrate is the depth of human motive in both politics and love: *why* is something being picked? *Why* is that fine young man riding away? These are questions about the human presence beyond appearances, and the mirror cannot respond to them. For the mirror, as for a poetic of artfully disposed imagery, slaves are "red-and-white bandannas," and a failed romance is a man on horseback and a shut door. On occasion, however, Merrill has obliquely honored the humaneness of this sort of poetic: part of what it suppresses is destruction. There are moments in Merrill's verse (as in the opening five lines of "A Timepiece" [CT 8], or in this clause from "After the Fire": "Remembering also the gift of thumb-sized garnet / Bruises he clasped round Aleko's throat" [BE 6]) when his painterly style quietly indicates that below the dazzling surface lies the alternative to civilized manners: violence. But in "Mirror" Merrill suggests that the passing of this poetic in time is as natural and inevitable as erosion.[6]

.   .   .

In 1964 Merrill published "The Thousand and Second Night," a wonderful poem literally about a buried subject. James, the speaker of the
poem, likens himself to Hagia Sophia.

> The building, desperate for youth, has smeared
> All over its original fine bones
>
> Acres of ochre plaster. A diagram
> Indicates how deep in the mudpack
> The real facade is. I want *my* face back.   (ND 5)

C. B. Cox once noted that the subject of the poem is the anxiety of
middle age,[7] but beneath that subject lies another. Merrill himself has
said: "I don't know what the main subject is—the poem is flirtatious
in that sense."[8] In the third section, "Carnivals," Merrill leans rather
heavily on his trope of evasion—

> We had made our peace
> With—everything.   (ND 9)
>
> Here's the dwarf back with cronies . . . oh I *say!*
> Forget about it.   (ND 11)
>
> I spent the night rekindling with expert
> Fingers—but that phase needn't be discussed . . .   (ND 11)
>
> And now the long adventure
>
> Let that wait.
> I'm tired, it's late at night.   (ND 13)

—and for good reason: this middle section bears most directly on the
true subject of the poem. The opening quatrains refer to a change
James has undergone: his friends accuse him of having become a
"vain / Flippant unfeeling monster" (ND 9). Although he resents
that formulation ("To hear them talk"), he does not dispute the basic
diagnosis: "they were right." He has changed, and his recent meeting
with M. (on whom he once had a crush) and his wife comes into the
narrative as implicit evidence of that change. Their "war" is over because James has lost feeling for all past pursuits of Eros:

> A thousand and one nights! They were grotesque.
> Stripping the blubber from my catch, I lit
> The oil-soaked wick, then could not see by it.
> Mornings, a black film lay upon the desk

>   . . . Where just a week ago I thought to delve
>   For images of those years in a Plain Cover.
>   Some light verse happened as I looked them over: (ND 10)

"The Thousand and Second Night" is a morning-after poem; James surveys his past in hungover disgust. For James, Psyche and Eros, thought and feeling, mind and body, cannot reach each other; the right half of his face is paralyzed by that split. The witty lines on Great-Uncle Alistair's pornographic postcards enter the poem under the auspices of that colon: they describe scenes from Alistair's suppressed sexual fantasies, but James makes them serve as "images of those years in a Plain Cover"; James regards his own rendezvous with Eros as grotesque and comically pointless, much like Alistair's silly postcards. Alistair's daughter Alix wants to banish these sordid mementos: " 'We'll burn them. Light the fire' " (ND 11)—but James knows better the consequences of fire for Psyche and Eros. The two prose passages that follow offer a rationale for reuniting Eros and Psyche. The paragraph by "Germaine Nahman" claims that "the libertine *was* 'in search of his soul' " (ND 12).[9] The extraordinary sexual ambitions of Great-Uncle Alistair and of James himself might be understood, by this analysis, not as base debauchery but as quests back toward that infantile state in which "The soul . . . could not be told from the body." The libertine (Alistair, James) sought all along to bring Eros and Psyche together again. And James's limp face is testimony that they never were entirely separated. "Natural calamities (tumor and apoplexy no less than flood and volcano) may at last be hailed as positive assurances, perverse if you like, of life in the old girl yet" (ND 12). Just as the earth kicks back against the abuses inflicted upon her, so the body complains of the excesses imposed upon her. And these complaints are proof that the body is more than just *physis,* that James's "precious sensibility" has not been entirely wrecked, though now it may take a good "pinch . . . to recall how warmly and deeply those two [Eros and Psyche] did, in fact, love one another" (ND 12).

The true, and buried, subject of the poem is the difficulty one has reconciling ideas about love with erotic experience itself. Promiscuity may well be more common, more often central to homosexual than to heterosexual experience, and of course it is frequently cited as a major cause of homosexual anxiety. There is a sense, then, in which the subject of the poem has a special bearing on homosexuality. Specifically, the phrase "images of those years in a Plain Cover" may suggest that what James refers to as erotic grotesquerie dates from a period when he had not worn his homosexuality openly, that James's "change" is related to Francis Tanning's change in *The Seraglio:* they will no longer keep their preferences under cover. Merrill's use of Great-Uncle Alistair's postcards, however, seems especially oblique, for Alistair's fantasies are plainly heterosexual and James has already indicated that his erotic inclinations have been homosexual (ND 9). Yet Merrill introduces those postcards in order to suggest that the split between Eros and Psyche should not be smugly dismissed or clinically "understood" as a consequence of that homosexual promiscuity which Merrill depicts as a series of whaling expeditions (ND 10). For in the end Merrill will make very traditional claims for his conclusions:

> . . . The heart prevails!
> Affirm it! Simple decency rides the blast!—
> Phrases that, quick to smell blood, lurk like sharks
> Within a style's transparent lights and darks.   (ND 12)

This section of the poem (the five sestets following the prose passages) was the most difficult for Merrill to write (CW 145), and for good reason. His thematic conclusion, here as elsewhere, is easily formulated in conventional, trite language, and he steps free of the inert burden of such phrases only by openly displaying, without disowning, the staleness of these truisms. This rhetorical maneuver Merrill learned in writing "An Urban Convalescence." In fact, he claimed that just this trope—

> The sickness of our time requires
> That these as well be blasted in their prime.
> You would think the simple fact of having lasted
> Threatened our cities like mysterious fires.
>
> There are certain phrases which to use in a poem
> Is like rubbing silver with quicksilver. Bright
> But facile, the glamour deadens overnight.
> For instance, how 'the sickness of our time'
>
> Enhances, then debases, what I feel.   (1960; WS 5)

—was the turning point which led to *Nights and Days*.[10] The debasement comes when Merrill sees that his analysis of experience travels the well-worn grooves of contemporary journalism. To recognize that one's ideas are as common, as vulgar, literally, as the thoughts of those who daily deal in pontifications is the challenge Merrill modestly accepts in the books following *Water Street*. For instance, in *From the Cupola* he offers Psyche the counsel of commonplaces:

> Weeping? You must not.
> All our pyrotechnic flights
> Miss the sleeper in the pitch-dark breast.
> He is love:
> He is everyone's blind spot.
> We see according to our lights.   (ND 46)

To posit these sentences as conclusions is Merrill's way of mildly suggesting that there is nothing new under the sun. And much the same point is made by setting the Eros-Psyche myth in Stonington and by bringing the Tithonus story forward through the centuries, as he does in *The Immortal Husband* (1955). Merrill is plainly skeptical of the poetic claims often made on behalf of one or another unusual subject matter. He is a poet for whom subject matter is properly subordinate to style. He has never claimed, as so many of his contemporaries have (Olson and Ammons are obvious examples), to have many ideas of his own: "In neither / The world's poem nor the poem's world have I / Learned to think for myself, much" (DC 129). Commonplaces, truisms, clichés may sound their notes flatly, but the sense of such formulations resonates through long experience:

> . . . take
> Any poor smalltown starstruck sense of "love
> That makes the world go round"—see how the phrase
> Stretches from Mystic to Mount Palomar
> Back to those nights before the good old days,
> Before the axle jumped its socket so
> That genes in shock flashed on/off head to toe
> Before mill turned to maelstrom, and IBM
> Wrenched from Pythagoras his diadem.   (DC 32)

The resonance is directly due to the age-old truth (as they say) of the proposition.

Novelty and variety certainly have a place in Merrill's poetic: they are criteria of surface excellence, sheen. Subject matter (though not theme) is also something to be "worked up":

> Hadn't—from books, from living—
> The profusion dawned on us, of "languages"
> Any one of which, to who could read it,
> Lit up the system it conceived?—bird-flight,
> Hallucinogen, chorale and horoscope:

Each its own world, hypnotic, many-sided
Facet of the universal gem.
Ephraim's revelations—we had them
For comfort, thrills and chills, "material."   (DC 75)

Merrill's theme in the *Book of Ephraim* is the coming and going of love or, as he puts it, "The incarnation and withdrawal of / A god" (DC 47). Ephraim's transmissions on the Ouija board are, properly speaking, his subject matter—but that hardly matters. Ephraim and the subject of ghosts (a subject that may not be there at all) are no more than a vehicle for the theme Merrill long ago took for his own. To manage that theme, he now wishes for (of all things) a plain style:

. . . the kind of unseasoned telling found
In legends, fairy tales, a tone licked clean
Over the centuries by mild old tongues,
Grandam to cub, serene, anonymous.   (DC 47)

Although his deepened commitment to narrative verse holds some of his mannerisms in check, he is still the last poet whose plainness can be trusted, and I will suggest why plainness is at odds with the larger ambitions or Merrill's style.

But before turning directly to matters of style, I wish to look briefly at "Lost in Translation" (1974), Merrill's most recent rationale for constructed secrets. In this extraordinary poem, Merrill tells how, as a young boy, he spirited away a single, palm-shaped piece of a jigsaw puzzle successfully completed with "Mademoiselle" in 1939. This single missing piece reminds him of his boyhood infatuation for his governess and, more important, of his parents' divorce in 1939 (his father remarried two weeks later: hence the boy's fond imagination that "old wives who know the worst / Outsweat that virile fiction of the New" [DC 8]). Merrill indirectly recollects feeling torn between his mother and father:

. . . Houri and Afreet
Both claim the Page. He wonders whom to serve,
And what his duties are, and where his feet . . .   (DC 8)

That missing piece is a token of Merrill's lost footing, for it reminds him of his surrogate parent Mademoiselle, who kept her then dubious German ancestry a secret, and through her of the global fracture of 1939 that made her reticence prudent. Through a literary recollection of another French-German nexus, Merrill recalls "Palme," the poem Valéry wrote in 1917, one year before the threat of a German advance took him away from Paris, five years before Rilke translated the poem.[11] The tree in "Palme" manages to keep its footing in sand and, like a secret, bear its fruit in silence ("Chaque atome de silence / Est la chance d'un fruit mûr!"); it stands securely between earth and sky ("L'attirance de la terre / Et le poids du firmament!"), or mother earth and father sky/time, as Merrill imagines them in "The Broken Home" (ND 27–28). Rilke knew, Merrill suggests, how much of Valéry's poem would be memorialized in the translation only by silent loss, absence: a phrase like "d'un fruit mûr" becomes "das Reifen genau." ("Verger" and "parfumer," incidentally, are absent from this particular Valéry poem.) And Merrill claims to know, from looking at the German text,

> What Pains, what monolithic Truths
> Shadow stanza to stanza's symmetrical
> Rhyme-rutted pavement. Know what ground plan left
> Sublime and barren, where the warm Romance
> Stone by stone faded, cooled; the fluted nouns
> Made taller, lonelier than life
> By leaf-carved capitals in the afterglow.   (DC 9–10)

His secret homage to Rilke's self-deprivation is a haggard ghost of that stanzaic scheme (ABABCCDEED) buried in his own poem (ll. 19–30). And Merrill's image of the prosody as a pavement reinforces the recollection of that passage in *From the Cupola* in which the palm-Aphrodite gradually undermines the paved sidewalk at its base, just as Psyche's fantasy of Eros obscures her grimy housecleaning chores on Long Island Sound.[12] For the take-home message—and Merrill does choose the most inspirational passage of the Valéry/Rilke poem for his epigraph—is that even the waste and failure of misunderstanding and misstatement (on one level, his parents' divorce) harbors sustenance (on that same level, material for poems, Mnemosyne).

> Lost, is it, buried? One more missing piece?
>
> But nothing's lost. Or else: all is translation
> And every bit of us is lost in it
> (Or found—I wander through the ruin of S
> Now and then, wondering at the peacefulness)

And in that loss a self-effacing tree,
Color of context, imperceptibly
Rustling with its angel, turns the waste
To shade and fiber, milk and memory.   (DC 10)

Finally, the palm represents the translator himself. There are at least
six translators in the poem: Rilke; Mademoiselle, who misstates her
own ancestry; her nephew, the UN interpreter, who translates the
misstatements known as diplomacy; Maggie Teyte, the English musical translator of French songs, who disguised her name (Tate) so that
the French would pronounce it properly; Stonington, that translation
of Greece on Long Island Sound; and Merrill, who brings near English
the Valéry/Rilke poem and near stage-Arabic his parents' relationship
(Houri and Afreet). They all suggest that effacement, the keeping of
secrets, in the translator's code is as important to communication as
disclosure is. Rilke's direct translation of Valéry's stanza and his effort
to make exactitude take the place of Valéry's sensuosity (*fruit
mûr/Reifen genau*) suggest that plainness itself can be yet another
version of obscurity, of shadowy self-effacement.

These patterns of thematic secrecy correspond profoundly, I think, to
certain of Merrill's stylistic manners. Periphrasis, talking around a
subject, is the most obvious one. "Maisie," the poem following "The
Thousand and Second Night" in *Nights and Days,* is an extended periphrasis: Merrill never mentions that the subject of the poem is a cat.
These arabesques around reticence—"the mirror of the tide's / retreat" for wet sand (CT 59); "Great drifts of damask" for napkins
(ND 9)—are part of the fun of Merrill's writing. Some of the wittiest
moments in his verse occur when he twirls words euphemistically
around what need not be said. For example, these lines from the postcards section of "The Thousand and Second Night"—

She strokes his handlebar who kneels
To do for her what a dwarf does for him.   (ND 10)

—twist around the contortions of double fellatio for three. For Merrill,
the language of poetry is implicitly prefaced by a contractual "In other
words." In fact, the more obvious the periphrasis, the purer and more
apparent the playful spirit behind it—which is a grandly liberating
principle.

Because Merrill wears his periphrastic motive on his sleeve, he can pursue words and phrases that are off limits to his contemporaries. From the beginning, his diction has been precious—"smilingly" (FP 14; CT 9), "swifterly" (FP 23), "amberly" (FP 43), "lucent" (FP 67)—in ways that would make Robert Lowell or Charles Olson blush. Similarly, from *First Poems* to his most recent, Merrill has maintained easy access to that stable of words which trail behind them the label Poetic. In his early poems, bodies are "winsome" (FP 42) and, for a rhyme, can even be made to "wend" (FP 71). In *The Country of a Thousand Years of Peace* there are Miltonic "lowing beasts secure" (CT 11), and in "The Thousand and Second Night" on billboards "Loom wingèd letters" (ND 4). In *The Fire Screen* "Piebald hindquarters of another guest" identify someone vomiting in a toilet (FS 34). In *Braving the Elements,* Merrill sees his mother as "bepearled" (BE 14), just as in *The Book of Ephraim* his mirror is said to be "bespattered" (DC 86). Even more firmly impressed on his diction than these archaic poeticisms is that odd category of adjectives beginning with "a-" which, like tableaux, freeze actions into qualities. A few of these words are inconspicuous, ordinary: asleep (BE 16), awake (WS 27), ajar (CT 63; BE 30), aloud (CT 36). Others are less so, but still familiar: askance (FP 36), aghast (CT 27; ND 16), askew (CT 54), aloft (CT 6), agape (DC 63). But most of these adjectives are strikingly rare or novel: aspin (CT 6), atremble (CT 9), atilt (CT 11), aswirl (CT 47), atwirl (CT 33), ableach (CT 33), adrowse (CT 47), aflicker (WS 22; FS 43), aswim (ND 30), acrackle (ND 52), abubble (FS 24), ashiver (FS 33), aglitter (FS 47), aflush (DC 48), awince (DC 77). The list, little in itself, shows Merrill's willingness to indulge his own painterly mannerisms. He would be the last poet to use such words and phrases naively; he knows that the components of his diction—precious, archaic, poetic, and mannered—have been so firmly displaced from usage that their appearance nudges his poems outside the spoken language. But that may be greater gain than loss: Merrill's poems proudly occupy a special corner of the language where the possibilities of play are unlimited by mundane considerations of democratic usage. Likewise, syntax, which ordinarily preserves for narration or ratiocination the distinct categories of agent, action, and object, in poems like "Olive Grove" and "Thistledown" becomes a game of suspense; questions of who did what to whom are submerged in the fluencies of syntax, as in a solvent.[13]

Merrill demands all the special prerogatives of poetic language: diction, syntax, and, perhaps most strikingly, metaphor. He is a master of the obviously "clever" figure. Figurative language, for him, is ornamental and playful. The burden of striking figures is that they are so obviously "poetic" that they seem to display the powers of the poet more boldly than they do the facets of the subject. But this is a light burden for Merrill: he would never attempt to conceal his artfulness. His figures are almost tricks because they rest on certain set moves. For instance, one move that often generates a figural showstopper is to liken language to objects:

> ... On which (to the pilgrim who forgets
> His Arabic) a wild script of gold whips ...   (ND 4)

or the same move in the opposite direction:

> A mapmaker (attendant since Jaipur)
> Says that from San Francisco our path traces
> The Arabic for GREAT WONDER ...   (DC 83)

The most common move behind these witty figures (and of course it is not just Merrill's) is a mild personification: objects or animals are likened to people. Often these are just quick, deft touches, as with the "dove with Parkinson's disease" (DC 28) or the "snapshots old / Enough to vote" (DC 85). In other instances, though, these figures are sustained for a line or two, as if Merrill were in no hurry to be getting anywhere. Here are two lines describing a ski lift:

> Prey swooped up, the iron love seat shudders
> Onward into its acrophilic trance.   (BE 53)

And a few more toying with an etymological possibility:

> Moonglow starts from scratches as my oval
> Cheval-glass tilting earthward by itself
> —The rider nodding and the reins gone slack—
> Converges with lamplight ten winters back.   (DC 94)

Economy be damned: Merrill takes time to have fun. This is a freedom sanctioned, he knows from reading Auden, by no lesser precedent than *Don Juan,* with its "air of irrelevance, of running on at the risk of never becoming terribly significant" (CW 151); and Merrill has lately acknowledged his debt to Byron's master, Pope (DC 56, 92, 105, 116). For Merrill, energy, invention, and ornamentation—not signification—are what make poetry.

These stylistic manners are mostly idiosyncratic, the marks by which Merrill allows his language to be identified. There is, however, a greater ambition behind his verse, manifest mainly in diction and tone. He is unusual among his contemporaries, and more generally rare among American poets, in his effort to imply by his style a set of attitudes and values claimed by a whole class of American society. This is a difficult claim to substantiate, not because many other poets make the same effort (they do not: the effort itself is widely suspect) but because American class boundaries are elusive; to identify the style of an American class is doubly difficult. I will begin, therefore, by identifying the attitudes and values invoked by Merrill's writing and end by suggesting the class loyalties of those attitudes.

Some of these values have already been described: periphrasis, euphemism, mannerism—these tropes testify to Merrill's esteem for extravagance. He is a poet who, rather than unify style and content in post-Romantic fashion, prefers to set style at odds with content. His style often throttles content. And style, for Merrill, is a way of playing, not working—the force behind style is energy serving no particular end but itself. The characteristic tone of his verse is ironic, but only lightly so. In *The Book of Ephraim* he identifies

> the tone
> We trusted most, a smiling Hellenistic
> Lightness from beyond the grave.   (DC 59)

Neither naively jubilant nor bitterly sardonic, the tone he aspires to is one of undeluded good cheer. Here are the first two lines from his elegy for his friend Hans Lodeizen:

> Here they all come to die,
> Fluent therein as in a fourth tongue.   (CT 2)

Any magazine editor might have altered the second line to conform to the canons of 1960s poetic diction (the poem was actually published in the winter 1951–52 issue of *Origin,* which was militantly opposed to the reigning editorial policies of the 1950s): "Fluent in death as in a fourth tongue." The meter and sense would be preserved and that awkward legalism ("therein") avoided, but the line would be too heavy by a tone, too naively self-absorbed by a ton.

The proper word for Merrill's tone is *arch.* That tone is first heard, in Merrill's oeuvre, in the opening line of "Medusa":

> The head, of course, had fallen to disrepair
> If not to disrepute.   (FP 10)

This tone is often nicely tuned to syntax. Merrill effectively tosses off ironic parenthetical clauses so that the irony seems casual, incidental, a result more of his temperament than of any norm or principle of judgment implied by the irony. The tone of the lines from "Medusa" is established not in the main clause but in the "of course" and "if not" clauses. Rhetorically, this is a variety of understatement, for the qualifying irony of the lesser clauses throws an entirely new perspective on the main clause. Here are two more examples of this archness:

> Tell me, tongue of fire,
> That you and I are as real
> At least as the people upstairs.   (ND 27)

> From judgment, it would seem, he has refrained.   (BE 70)

The tone of the first passage, from "The Broken Home," is set by two words so placed as to seem parenthetical: "at least." The irony of the passage can be measured not just by the apocalyptic periphrasis for a candle flame, "tongue of fire," but by the difference between "at least as real" (which would be the ordinary syntax) and "as real / at least." Merrill's version of the phrase makes the ironic stab at his neighbors an afterthought—easy, for him. Similarly, the single line from "The Victor Dog" sets its tone in the throwaway clause, "it would seem." And the conditional mood turns the volume lower, as if the claims of the statement were being posited hesitantly and politely. Yet politeness, in this context, has little to do with concern for others: this archness can become, in the words of Merrill's friends, "vain / Flippant unfeeling" (ND 9).

Merrill is his own critic in this regard:

> My friend with time to kill
> Asked me the price of cars in Paradise.
>
> By which he meant my country, for in his
> The stranger is a god in masquerade.
> Failing to act that part, I am afraid
> I was not human either—ah, who is?
>
> He is, or was; had brothers and a wife;
> Chauffeured a truck; last Friday broke his neck
> Against a tree. We have no way to check
> These headlong emigrations out of life.
>
> Try, I suppose, we must, as even Valéry said,
> And said more grandly than I ever shall. . . .   (ND 8)

These lines from "The Thousand and Second Night" move as far toward self-criticism as Merrill has ever cared to go. He criticizes his own willingness to allow archness to become more than mischievous. On occasion Merrill can be snotty, often when he deals with people he considers, if only for the sake of a poem, his inferiors, either in terms of class or of sensibility. Take, for instance, this quatrain from "Days of 1971":

> Can-can from last night's *Orphée aux Enfers*
> Since daybreak you've been whistling till I wince.
> Well, you were a handsome devil once.
> Take the wheel. You're still a fair chauffeur.   (BE 65)

What Merrill tries to censure in the lines quoted from "The Thousand and Second Night" is this sort of glib condescension.[14] But, finally, the point of the passage is that he can only try. The first sign of his effort comes in the lines "I am afraid / I was not human either—ah, who is?" No sooner is he self-critical than his all-embracing skepticism lets him off the hook ("ah, who is?").

Merrill has developed this strategy into a trope for casually universalizing chagrin:

> She has brought a cake "for tomorrow"
> As if tomorrows were still memorable.   (BE 4)

> Tonight in the Magician's tent
> Next door a woman will be sawed in two,
> But right now she's asleep, as who is not, as who . . .   (DC 25)

>   I'll never know.
> Who ever does?   (DC 34)

> For it, poor soul, he did so, he was lost.
> Ah, so were we!   (DC 99)

World-weariness, the tone of the *perdu,* is an attitude Merrill dons like a theatrical mask; it is purely conventional, void of genuine emotional significance—pure style without content. In these two stanzas from "The Summer People" Andrew and Margaret toy with the conventionality of their own cries of despair:

> "Oh God, this life's so pointless,
> So wearing," Margaret said.

"You're telling me," Andrew agreed.
"High time we both were dead."

"It *is*. I have pills—let's take them!"
He looked at her with wit.
"Just try. You know we'd never
Hear the end of it."   (FS 68–69)

Clever to the end, they know that weariness, like various small courtesies, is demanded of them; it is a code attitude no more to be taken literally than the love such people express for four-hand piano, bridge, gossip, croquet, and entertaining (FS 58–59). Thus when James (to return to the passage from "The Thousand and Second Night") says "He is, or was," he is calling into question the propriety of this programmatic skepticism. The next two and a half lines describe the death of an ordinary worker, and these lines quietly accuse James of a failure of feeling, flip callousness. But Merrill goes only so far in implicit self-accusation: at this point the suspect archness resumes control of the passage and continues with the poem—"We have no way to check / These headlong emigrations out of life." Archness is Merrill's ground note: he cannot silence it, though he can acknowledge and regret, from time to time, its impoliteness or, worse, insensitivity.

Though archness is an apt term for describing Merrill's characteristic tone, it does not indicate the greater aspiration of his style. For that, another term will serve better: camp. In 1929 Ezra Pound described logopoeia:

> It employs words not only for their direct meaning, but it takes count in a special way of habits of usage, of the context we *expect* to find with the word, its usual concomitants, of its known acceptances, and of ironical play . . . It is the latest come, and perhaps most tricky and undependable mode.[15]

Merrill, more than any of his American contemporaries, successfully invokes by his tone and diction patterns of usage that add up to a coherent sensibility, one whose class allegiance or aspiration is explicit. Here are some lines from "Words for Maria":

I'm calling *you* henceforth The Lunatic.
Today at 4 a.m. in a snack bar
You were discovered eating, if you please,

> Fried squid; alone. Aleko stood aghast.
> Sappho has been to your new flat, she *says*.
> Tony, who staggered there with the Empire
> Mirror you wanted from his shop, tells how
> You had him prop it in a chair and leave
> That instant. Really now!   (FS 12)

The campiness of these lines is established largely by insistence: certain words are italicized to insist on one emphasis rather than some other, and the word "alone" is isolated by punctuation to suggest that it is full of meaning that need not, in some company, be elaborated upon. The tone suggests that there is a secret, something not being said, which would explain both the extravagance of Aleko's response and Merrill's implication that Sappho may not be telling the truth. Merrill's success with this tone is measured partly by his ability to make this voice *heard*. Still he can attribute it to anyone, even "the man in the moon": "The point's to live, love, / Not shake your fist at the feast" (FS 30).

The camp tone is less a dialect Merrill can use for some types of characters than a norm—social as well as stylistic—erected by his verse. With this tone goes a set of attitudes and values that is boldest in its political aspect.

> Where are the chimneys, the traffic? Instead come strange
> Horizons of ink, and livid treetops massing raggedly
> Beyond the sill like poor whites in a study
> Of conditions we must one day seriously try to change. (FS 37)

> THE AIR
> ABOVE LOS ALAMOS IS LIKE A BREATH
> SUCKED IN HORROR   TOD MORT MUERTE DEATH
> —Meaning the nearby nuclear research
> Our instinct first is to deplore, and second
> To think no more of.   (DC 77)

Politics, with few exceptions, is a subject Merrill deliberately, and wittily, disdains:

> . . . I rarely buy a newspaper, or vote.
> To do so, I have learned, is to invite
> The tread of a stone guest within my house.   (ND 29)

From the camp viewpoint, politics is stylelessly overladen with content; it can be ignored because the camp sensibility is premised, as Susan Sontag has noted, on detachment.[16] Merrill—and not just in his campier moments—claims an aristocratic aloofness from political activity.[17] Yet the anachronism "aristocratic" can be taken only metaphorically, even in Merrill's case: it indicates aspiration or desire rather than actual loyalty. The camp sensibility aspires to a stable, sanctioned position from which detachment can be easily afforded, or from which engagement is impractical. Sontag points out that the camp sensibility wants as well to take up one of the supposed burdens of the aristocracy: "Since no authentic aristocrats exist today to sponsor special tastes, who is the bearer of this taste? Answer: an improvised self-elected class, mainly homosexuals, who constitute themselves as aristocrats of taste."[18] This is not to say that Merrill's style is restrictively homosexual: often he uses phrases that are commonly upper-class without necessarily being camp: "ghastly scenes" (CT 28), "to launch one" (ND 25), "I dare say" (ND 54), "I'm pained" (ND 9), "mayn't I" (ND 53); and the diction of the "The Summer People" shows that Merrill makes no hard and fast distinction between upper-class and camp manners. The line Merrill is likely to insist upon is between upper- and lower-class diction: he typically distances himself from the language commonly understood as colloquial. For example, in "The Locusts" he makes a parenthetical joke of his second-hand rendering of a ruralism: "Come spring (he says) / The grubs will hatch" (CT 78). And in "Days of 1971" he resorts to a vulgar expression in a sentence that goes on to climb to high culture:

> One self-righteous truck
> Knocked the shit out of a eucalyptus
> Whose whitewashed trunk lay twitching brokenly—
> Nijinsky in *Petrouchka*—on the quai. (BE 68)

Street fighting to ballet—such is the distance Merrill puts between himself and what many of his contemporaries regard as colloquial usage.[19] Merrill has no truck with the Whitmanesque, or Wordsworthian, dream of speaking to or for "the people." Regardless of where his poems appear, of how many copies his books sell, or of which prizes are awarded him (so far he has received the three most prestigious American awards for poetry: the Bollingen, the National Book Award, and the Pulitzer), Merrill is a coterie poet by rhetorical choice: his diction and tone locate his poetry in a world where the reigning sensibility is camp. From Merrill's point of view, to have it any other way is frankly disgusting:

> Must I grow broad- and dirty-minded
> Serving a community, a nation
> By now past anybody's power to shock?   (DC 12)

Merrill seems to ask to be assessed as a minor poet, for camp has pronounced limits. By making a virtue of exaggeration, it cannot achieve justness, and a sane assessment of our most difficult experiences is part of what is asked of the greatest poetry.

Pound once said that the most intense form of criticism is new composition, and Merrill's verse is critical in just this sense.[20] He has been rightly praised for making his own way during a time when gusts of literary fashion tossed about many of his contemporaries. Poems such as "The Thousand and Second Night" and "Lost in Translation" seem from one point of view to have confessions to make; yet the conventions of confessional poetry are invoked only to be artfully eluded. Merrill's ironic pirouettes around these conventions are more than incidental. His unique position among recent American poets can be located by the social ambitions of his poetry. During the 1960s, while some of his contemporaries, under the influence of Merwin, were pursuing styles that apparently disowned social relations, and others, like Lowell, were attempting to democratize, with free verse, low colloquialisms and brand names, the densely metaphorical styles they learned in the 1950s, Merrill held on to his meters and chose his phrases with a sense of class.

So distinct a sense of class is implied by his style that he, at least as much as any of his contemporaries, has altered the politics of style in American poetry—which is to say that he has expanded the stylistic horizon of American poetry. Other American poets have succeeded in implying by their styles the attractions of a particular class or political view: during the thirties there was something of a vogue in leftist literary journals for dialect poetry, and a good deal of recent black poetry is written in dialect. But, for ideological as well as artistic reasons, Merrill would rightly resist that company; the proper analogy is to British poets, and chiefly to Auden. Merrill's distinction is his skeptical view of that American *idée fixe,* the democratic or classless style. Nor can this issue be strictly confined to poetic style. Alvin Gouldner has shown that contemporary intellectuals share a "culture of critical discourse," the rules of which require (1) that assertions be justified, (2) that justification not be through citation of authority, and (3) that the voluntary consent of those addressed be elicited by rational arguments.[21] A commitment to this sort of language holds intellectuals together ideologically. Merrill, with his insistence always on the tacit rather than the explicit, sets his writing directly against these norms. His opposition is not just to recent stylistic conventions established by poets like Lowell and Merwin, but rather to that sector of contemporary society so proudly set up to explain things. The *New York Review of Books* may praise Merrill, and even publish interviews with him, but this can only serve as evidence of its lack of genuine engagement with poetry. Merrill can never, as Lowell surely could, offer solace to intellectuals generally.

When Eliot defined the difference between major and minor poets, knowledge of the whole of a major poet's work, he said, makes one understand single poems better. The gathering of a volume of collected poems is one way that poets routinely ask to be measured; a less common route is the writing of a work that casts new light back on earlier work. Lawrence Lipking has spoken of one stage of poetic careers as the making of harmonia, works that draw to fulfillment the diverse tendencies of earlier books and poems.[22] Merrill has now completed a long poem, *The Changing Light at Sandover,* that came as a stunning surprise even to his longtime admirers, so weird a perspective does it throw on his earlier poems. And Merrill himself is aware of this: the Ouija sequence is salted with references to his earlier books (*First Poems, The Seraglio, The Country of a Thousand Years of Peace*) and poems ("The Thousand and Second Night," *From the Cupola,* "The Broken Home," "Matinees," "The Summer People," "Lost in Translation"), as if to press home the point that his career was all the time leading to this one epic poem. This is not to say that Merrill is eager exactly to weigh in with the great poets of harmonia; he is more than a little diffident about writing this kind of modern epic, "a low-budget / Remake—imagine—of the Paradiso" (DC 89). He seems to know that he is more likely to be remembered as the author of a handful of shorter poems. Yet Merrill's talent will never look the same as it did before the long poem appeared—that too he knows—which may be why in 1982 his publisher issued simultaneously a collected poems and a one-volume edition of the Ouija trilogy. The career itself is now being offered up for evaluation.

One of the ambitions of the Ouija poem is to proceed with little regard for decorum. Notions of propriety in style are now commonly thought of as more the property of scholars than of common readers, yet the apparent improprieties of this poem are forceful indeed. The question is whether one can treat matters of life and death, immortality, theology, and the fate of humanity with the light touch I have spoken of as camp. One can expect seriousness over the long haul (longer than *Paradise Lost, Paradise Regained,* and *Samson Agonistes* combined, in this case) without demanding solemnity from poetry. Stephen Spender, for instance, criticized the poem for "a kind of postponed responsibility, a passing of the buck from the unconscious mind of JM and DJ in this world to a possibly conscious mind of history in the next."[23] Merrill himself has been admirably straightforward about this matter: "The reader who can't swallow [the pill] has my full sympathy. I've choked on it again and again . . . But the point remained, to be always of two minds."[24] Some critics have swallowed the pill, taken Merrill's seriousness as axiomatic, and proceeded with the job of interpretation; one panel at the 1981 Modern Language Association convention was entitled "The Sacred Books of James Merrill."

If the Ouija poem is interpreted and assessed as visionary poetry, other problems, beyond the open question of belief, arise too. The quality of the vision itself, JM observes, is dyed rather "vivid / By the popular imagination" (M 103). Peter Stitt has referred to the poem's summary of western thought as "an intellectual sham."[25] A critic of visionary poetry might also observe that Merrill's vision is not rendered particularly compelling or memorable. The works of Ovid, Dante, Blake, or Pound, by comparison, make it clear how little of Merrill's effort is directed to the pictorial dimension of visionary poetry; the Ouija poem is addressed to the ears rather than the eyes. Calvin Bedient spoke of the *Book of Ephraim* as "more gossip than gospel," and there is a serious point in the phrase.[26] Much of the poem reports on activity or events at some distance from JM and DJ; the spirits tell more than they show, and so does JM. One weakness of the poem is that JM and DJ occasionally display dubious judgment when, for instance, they praise Auden's brilliance after some rather ordinary remark.[27] (Similarly, George Cotzias is often celebrated for extraordinary intelligence, though none of this is displayed in the poem.) That difference between what is heard and what can be observed is a continuing burden to the poem. Speaking of it as a visionary poem may well arouse damaging expectations, for this is a poem less of authority than of companionship.

The seriousness of the poem is not in its didacticism. Only camp followers or pedants, David Bromwich has remarked, would try to judge the poem by its argument.[28] Of all his contemporaries, Merrill is least likely to write a long, earnestly didactic poem; Olson, Lowell, Ammons, or Ashbery, yes, but not Merrill. The poem's cast of characters is telling on this score. Helen Vendler points out that the four major characters, JM, DJ, Maria Mitsotaki, and W. H. Auden, are bound together by their childlessness.[29] The first three were all good friends, but Merrill, as he himself has said, did not know Auden well, however much he admired him.[30] Setting him next to those Merrill knew well enough to love dearly is perhaps a sign of Merrill's literary intention, of his motive in the poem. For who would scoff most quickly at the idea of a long verse explanation of life and death? Reflecting in 1948 on Yeats's occultism in *A Vision,* Auden asked in terms that apply to Merrill: "How on earth, we wonder, could a man of Yeats's gifts take such nonsense seriously? I have a further bewilderment, which may be due to my English upbringing, one of snobbery. How *could* Yeats, with his great aesthetic appreciation of aristocracy, ancestral houses, ceremonious tradition, take up something so essentially lower-middle class— or should I say Southern Californian—so ineluctably associated with suburban villas and clearly unattractive faces?"[31] Merrill makes Auden recant his Anglicanism in the poem, but possibly Auden is a joker planted in the deck, arching the eyebrow of literary history. Auden certainly appreciated lightness, but not long explanations of the nature of things; instead he is a wise and quotable poet at just those points when he reduces the truth to something short, simple, unqualified, and tender. And this too has been Merrill's gift.

Imagine a world in which one's mother and father live on, life after life, with their failures reduced to foibles and circumstance. Imagine too that our friends do the same, and that we can go on talking with them long after they have been buried or burnt. Imagine, in other words, that distance and time separate no one. Dream as well that a poet's work does not obstruct his life with others, that the writing can be shared freely with loved ones. For in *Mirabell* JM says quite simply: "Art— / The tale that all but shapes itself—survives / By feeding on its personages' lives" (M 124). Later he admits that the ambition of artists corrupts emotions; the death of an artist's loved one can be an opportunity: "losses which we see / At once, no matter how reluctantly, / As gains. Gains to the work. Ill-gotten gains" (SP 94). And doesn't this poem turn just such losses—Maria Mitsotaki, George Cotzias, Robert Morse—to artistic gains? Not that Merrill has reason for a guilty conscience; the poem is written in devotion to these friends, and especially to one other, David Jackson. Imagining other worlds is to the point because the poem is imaginative in just this innocent, touching sense.

Devotion, Ephraim says, is "THE MAIN IMPETUS" (DC 103). The seriousness of the Ouija poem may well reside right there in that motive—devotion, in particular to his life with his lover. David Jackson—not Merrill—is referred to as "the psychic one" (M 13). The poem comes from "a composite / Voice" (M 172); unlike the others, this is their baby, so to speak. JM is a scribe, not for DJ exactly but for their shared imaginations—"it's all by someone else!" (M 167)—as *A Vision* is in part a celebration of the Yeatses' marriage. The question of belief, then, is an intimate one. Too much skepticism on JM's part would entail breaking faith with his lover and his personal life; too little would mean breaking faith with those readers who have come to learn his habits of mind. Yet this sounds like a calculation. The Ouija poem is just the poem Merrill should not have been able to write; it is a distillation of, as he puts it, "Popthink"—black holes, pyramids, magical electrons, and so on. Merrill is a love poet, perhaps the best of this era, not a culture poet. But apparently out of devotion to DJ and the life these two writers shared, Merrill seems to have tried to press against his own limits, taking up the muse of his contemporaries. Perhaps the buried subject of the Ouija poem is the sharing of a literary career and love's power to make one want to be someone else, Yeats or Dante, say, rather than Auden—or Merrill.

5 · Politics

The sixties were years when poets, along with students and professors, rediscovered politics—or so it is often said, with some reason.[1] In 1966 Robert Bly and David Ray founded Poets Against the War, and later they organized various public readings to benefit antiwar organizations. The only anthologies or critical studies of post–World War II political poetry concern Vietnam poetry.[2] And certainly the Vietnam war rolled thunderously into the writing of Bly, Robert Duncan, Adrienne Rich, Denise Levertov, and others in the mid-1960s. But a price is paid for an overemphasis on the 1960s, partly a poetic one: political poetry is now thought of too narrowly as protest poetry, as though a poet, when political, always protests—rather than, say, advocates, analyzes, or celebrates. The remainder of the cost for this myth of the 1960s can be computed in another currency. To think that, during the two decades preceding Lyndon Johnson's 1965 decision to send combat troops to Vietnam, no political issues concerned poets directly enough to make them write expressly political poems is to misunderstand social as well as literary history.

At least two other related political matters had a direct claim on poets well before the Vietnam war: the growth of an American economic empire and the increased influence of a group of Americans, occupational more than social, whose credentials were provided by institutions of higher education.[3] Both of these matters bear directly on the literary culture in a way that the Vietnam war never did. The connection between poetry and aspirations to empire has the sort of literary history that no poet can afford to ignore. And the institutions of higher education, in the United States, harbor not only the government's advisers and future administrators, and those who will determine the flow of information through the nation's various media, but also most of the audience for contemporary poetry.[4] Poetry readers are part of what is now spoken of derisively (on the right) as the New Class, those who labor not in primary production but in language and information.[5]

In the 1950s the concept of class, never powerful in American thought, was discounted in intellectual circles. Instead, consensus was spoken of as the noble successor to class conflict.[6] Edward Shils, in 1956, said that the "various social classes and groups are more aware of each other, empathize with each other more readily and respond more readily to each other's expectations than in any European society."[7] When social scientists employed the term "class," they often qualified it, as when Peter Viereck claimed that American classes are "fluid, unhereditary, and more psychological than economic," and Talcott Parsons spoke of American class continuity deriving not from the family but from occupational divisions.[8] Dissatisfaction with the sociopolitical term "class" had many causes. One was simply that America had never evolved a class structure comparable to that of European countries, and the recent experience of European conflict left Americans aware and appreciative of the differences between American and European society. Sociologists generally believe that class distinctions attenuate, regardless of national traditions, as industrial economies advance; the resolution of the war left the United States much further advanced in that way than its European allies.[9] But perhaps most important was the extraordinary prosperity Americans enjoyed after the war; it was tempting then to believe that the working class had moved up into the middle class. The Veterans' Administration, federal mortgage policy, and low interest rates all helped to expand credit to wage-earning consumers, and some of the conspicuous trappings of the middle class—suburban houses, new automobiles, home appliances—were more widely dispersed than ever before. (In 1956 over 57 percent of the outstanding home mortgage debt was financed at under 5 percent; in 1940 that figure stood at 20 percent.) The working class and the middle class began to look alike in the decade following the war, even though the distribution of income in fact changed hardly at all.[10]

There was one other appeal this notion of classlessness had during these years: it served the interest of intellectuals. With Roosevelt's first administration, academics entered government service in unprecedented numbers, and their influence was great. During the war, too, intellectuals in the officers' corps and the OSS had special duties. One of Kennedy's advisers remembered the wartime feeling of importance:

"there we were, captains and majors, telling the whole world what to do."[11] After the war, some intellectuals lost that spirit. Once Henry Wallace's presidential bid failed in 1948, it seemed to Charles Olson, for instance, that haberdashers had taken over the government, so he left Washington.[12] When Eisenhower was elected in 1952, over the intellectuals' candidate Adlai Stevenson, more intellectuals began to feel out of favor, but Eisenhower actually employed more academics than FDR had.[13] (American intellectuals have traditionally identified their interests with the Democratic Party, but beyond that Eisenhower did say that an intellectual is "a man who takes more words than is necessary to say more than he knows."[14]) In the 1950s American intellectuals had every reason to feel a part of the national culture. They had attached themselves to the upper-middle class that then seemed to be setting standards for the rest of the culture.

The decade should not be thought of as a dull time for intellectuals, for better than any other group they understood and responded to the extraordinary challenges being presented to America. It was they, after all, who were formulating not only particular governmental policies but also, in documents such as *Goals For Americans* and *Prospect for America,* the specific terms of the consensus.[15] The authority of these statements depended upon the ability of Americans to transcend class differences. Because intellectuals were more involved in governmental policy in the 1950s than they had ever been, and more influential ideologically than any other group, it was important to play down the relevance of class analysis, lest rival classes begin to feel bullied by their new de facto leaders. Intellectuals have not been popularly trusted, however highly they have been regarded, throughout American history.[16] The concept of classlessness helped to protect intellectuals in the 1950s from the traditional reproach and class resentment they had often experienced and never overcome.

The protection was imperfect, though. On February 9, 1950, Joseph McCarthy began his campaign against those "young men who were born with silver spoons in their mouths."[17] By the late spring of 1954, when the Army–McCarthy hearings were broadcast on television, the senator had lost credibility in his campaign against the "network of professors and teachers who are getting their orders from Moscow."[18] (Richard Nixon, of course, was the willing heir of McCarthy's anti-intellectualism: in the 1952 campaign he spoke of Stevenson as "Adlai the appeaser . . . who got a Ph.D. from Dean Acheson's College of Cowardly Communist Containment."[19]) McCarthy plainly thought of his efforts as a kind of class warfare.[20] Edward Shils has described McCarthyism as a late episode in the battle between intellectuals, on one side, and politicians and businessmen on the other, which began in the second quarter of the nineteenth century. Certainly intellectuals felt attacked as a social group, though Richard Hofstadter and others preferred to speak of "status politics" rather than class politics.[21] Peter Viereck said that "McCarthyism is the revenge of the noses that for twenty years of fancy parties were pressed against the outside of the window pane."[22] David Riesman and Nathan Glazer called McCarthy a political arriviste, and they employed the standard intellectual weapons of class rivalry against him and his constituents—condescension and intellectual pride.[23] But the most commonly invoked defense in this class battle was psychological: Riesman, Glazer, Bell, Viereck, and Parsons, like many other intellectuals, often analyzed McCarthyism psychologically, as if this antagonism had to be explained partially in terms of pathology rather than as an instance of only slightly disguised and relatively bloodless class conflict.[24]

McCarthy lost the battle, and the influence of intellectuals grew more decisive in the decade following the Army–McCarthy hearings. In the early 1960s Daniel Bell spoke of the university as "the primary institution of the new society."[25] The Kennedy administration was one highwater mark for intellectual influence, and in 1963 Lyndon Johnson brought even more academics to Washington, especially social scientists. In Johnson's War on Poverty, many sociologists for the first time in their careers became involved in administrative and policy decisions. Intellectuals had the attention of politicians: there were more academics in American government service then than ever before, or since. And the political efficacy of intellectuals had increased at just the time when their numbers were also soaring. Within only ten years, from 1950 to 1960, the number of college teachers had nearly doubled (to just under 200,000), and the indirect influence of this occupational group increased as the number of college students did. During the entire postwar period the number of colleges (now about 3000), faculty, and students grew tremendously. In 1940 some 1.5 million students were registered in colleges. By 1968, when Lyndon Johnson withdrew from the presidential campaign, that number had increased fourfold. Now there are about 10 million college students and 600,000 faculty. By 1979 about 30 percent of the adult population had some college training, and half of these people held college degrees. The political influence of this rapidly expanding sector of the population increased throughout the cold war years—especially after the Soviet success with Sputnik in 1957—and with few complaints from anyone after McCarthy's demise.[26]

In the late 1960s this sector appeared to both the government and, more important, to most of the national television audience, to have special interests that were at odds with the objectives of the majority. Garry Wills has argued that Vietnam was America's "first professors' war."[27] The foreign policy that led to and sustained that war was formulated by advisers to the government in accord with the liberal ideology popular among academics. And yet the main support for the antiwar movement plainly lay in the academic community too. The testimony of intellectuals who changed their minds (Dr. Spock, Daniel Ellsberg) was particularly moving to students and understandably infuriating to Lyndon Johnson. The more firmly that liberal intellectuals became associated with the antiwar movement, the easier it became for the Republican Party, with its roots in the upper-middle class, to tap the dissatisfaction of the lower-middle and working classes. Nixon's 1968 victory showed that support among intellectuals had become a major liability for the Democratic Party. The emerging Republican consensus was expressly antiacademic, and the conflict between working classes and intellectuals has been no secret since the mid-1960s.

With the expansion of the Republican Party's appeal among the working classes came a reinvigorated attack on liberal intellectuals. The Marxist model for class analysis locates continuity in the family, and this seemed an accurate explanation of social standing in European society, where one is born into a class. In American society, continuity has instead been sought in the occupational structure: plumbers are working class, theater managers are lower-middle, insurance brokers are middle, doctors and professors are upper-middle, and so on out of sight.[28] In the last three decades, however, the occupational structure has changed: the service sector has increased greatly, only partly because of the growth of government. Intellectuals with the interests of the Republican Party close to heart see in this sector the formation of a New Class with ideological coherence and special interests of its own. The ideological center of this class is said to be avowedly liberal and enamoured of idealistic politics: "The New Class sees itself . . . as a 'conscience constituency' motivated only by ideas and ideals, whereas others are driven only by baser impulses and issues 'of the stomach.' "[29] The ideological adversaries of the new class claim that these idealistic political advocates have certain advantages over most citizens in terms of exercising political influence. One advantage is that the new class exercises virtual control over the flow of information in America. Jeanne Kirkpatrick, for example, has said, "What wealth is to the capitalist, what organization is to the old-style political boss, what manpower is to the trade unionists, words are to the new class"—for its members are teachers, journalists, publicists, social workers, administrators.[30] The political objective of this class is thought to be reform, achieved through government regulation, chiefly of industry. Those who own large interests in industry, the upper class, feel their prerogatives eroding under the combined pressure of proliferating regulation and the increasing power of managers who are part of the new class.[31] What makes this tension significant in terms of electoral politics is the success of the upper class in forming an alliance, represented by Reagan's victory, with the lower-middle class. The primary class conflict in America now, because of the success of that alliance, is between a lower-middle class that has assumed responsibility for bourgeois values and a segment of the upper-middle class that regards itself as liberal.[32] The latter, most of which is seen as the new class (doctors with their own practice are not part of the new class, but employed doctors are), is being squeezed out.[33]

The primary qualification for membership in the new class is neither income nor family background, but education. More consistently than money, geography, religion, or family, a college degree indicates a high proclivity for liberal values and political opinions. During most of the last thirty-five years, while the number of Americans who give and receive college educations has increased several times over, this social sector has not been discussed politically. Now that the intelligentsia has lost political authority, the importance of higher education in terms of ideological and class formation is discussed more openly than before, and the intelligentsia is once again under attack from the right. Over the last three decades, intellectuals have had an extraordinary history: they acquired great influence and political prestige and then lost influence after dissenting on the issue of foreign policy in the mid-1960s. As a subject for poets, the recent history of intellectuals is rich, complex, and central to the national culture. Moreover, most of the audience for poetry comes from this class, which makes the analysis and representation of the subject all the more compelling.

From the end of World War II until the early 1960s, American poets had little to say about the differences between the intelligentsia and the working classes. American intellectuals, among whose growing numbers were nearly all readers of poetry, certainly felt some tension. (George Oppen fled to Mexico in 1950 rather than face a HUAC subpoena; he was silent until he returned in 1959.) And the politician whose name is commonly invoked to refer to the problems of the era gained fame by aggravating that tension. When poets questioned McCarthyism, the terms were not usually political in an explicit sense.

Richard Wilbur wrote "Speech for the Repeal of the McCarran Act" in 1951—and published it in the tiny avant-garde magazine *Origin,* not in the *New Yorker* where many of his other poems routinely appeared. The McCarran Act of September 1950 required Communist organizations and their members to register with the attorney general, even though membership was not illegal. (If an organization was later declared illegal, as seemed entirely possible at the time, its members would then be subject to prosecution by virtue of their self-incriminating registration.) Wilbur opposed the law on the grounds that it endangered the social fabric by raising the cost of candor and thus encouraging perjury.

> Let thought be free. I speak
> Of the spirit's weaving, the neural
> Web, the self-true mind, the trusty reflex.[34]

The poem is circumspect and tactful. Nothing is made of the fact that lawyers and politicians knew the bill to be ill conceived and impractical; it was more a political banner than a legal measure. Wilbur speaks from what was then a broad ideological base: not the protection of the civil liberties of the left, but the defense of intellectual freedom. Opposition to the bill was a liberal cause. Truman vetoed it, but Congress easily overrode the veto. Hubert Humphrey (after once voting for the bill) delivered so fulsome an oration against its passage that he was thought to be attempting a filibuster—that effort of course failed.[35] And the one poet to address the issue took a very high road in a very small magazine. Poets seldom spoke of the one corner of the class structure that concerned them most directly.

One notable exception is Charles Gullans' "Return Voyage, 1955," a poem about a homecoming poet-tourist's regard for his countrymen:

> With slow, fat bodies and their sleek, fast cars,
> I could dislike them, now, repatriate,
> I could despair. It is not hard to hate,
> Nor is it hard to play the patriot:
> Fools and their folly fill the public hour,
> Glib in their loyalty and their despair.
> · · · · ·
> Extremity, the national disease,
> Is mine no less than theirs. The question, then,
> Is who are they and what are they to me,
> "The earth's new giant breed, the American,"
> My separate and our joint identity.[36]

The 1950s was no time for poets to repatriate. Americans knew, especially if they had traveled, that they were then expected, in Gullans' words, to "dominate an age." Poets dream (Vergil and Whitman did) of speaking for such a nation. The criticism Gullans directs at his countrymen is measured, not categorical: "imperfect policy . . . passionate confusion of the scope / Of moral empire with imperial power." Part of the measure is his own complicity, and this is crucial. He claims no immunity from the national disease and offers no cure. But neither is there desperation in the poem because he believes, as academic liberals had every reason to believe, that "our world yields to the form of hope, / The shape of thought." In 1955 American intellectuals were happy to be supplying those shaping thoughts, and their hope for progress seemed well founded; in December 1954 the Senate censured McCarthy. The class antagonism he had expressed against intellectuals had been terrifying but not decisive in any general way. The professors stayed in Washington, many of them even in the State Department.

Although poets did not write about the class antagonism of workers and intellectuals, they did write—and sometimes very well—about the upper classes and their privileges. These gloating lines from Robert Bly's "Poem against the Rich" (1962) mark one end of a continuum of prevalent attitudes toward wealth:

> Each day I live, each day the sea of light
> Rises, I seem to see
> The tear inside the stone
> As if my eyes were gazing beneath the earth.
> The rich man in his red hat
> Cannot hear
> The weeping in the pueblos of the lily,
> Or the dark tears in the shacks of the corn.[37]

Bly is sensitive to what the rich miss altogether—this apparently strikes him as a simple matter. Qualifications are unnecessary, perhaps impossible, within the surrealist method he was employing. Until the early 1960s this categorical treatment of the wealthy classes was uncharacteristic. More commonly, after World War II, poets wrote with an awareness of a connection between the poems and the ads in the *New Yorker*. Here is Richard Wilbur's "The Regatta" (1947):

> A rowdy wind pushed out the sky,
> Now swoops the lake and booms in sails;
> Sunlight can plummet, when it fails,
> Brighten on boats which pitch and fly.

Out on the dock-end, Mrs. Vane,
Seated with friends, lifts lenses to
Delighted eyes, and sweeps the view
Of "galleons" on the "raging main."

A heeling boat invades the glass
To turn a buoy; figures duck
The crossing sail—"There's Midge and Buck!
I know his scarf!"—the sailors pass.

The hotel guests make joking bets,
And Mrs. Vane has turned, inquired
If Mr. Vane is feeling "tired."
He means to answer, but forgets.

She offers him binoculars:
A swift, light thing is slipping on
The bitter waters, always gone
Before the wave can make it hers;

So simply it evades, evades,
So weightless and immune may go,
The free thing does not need to know
How deep the waters are with shades.

It's but a trick; and still one feels
Franchised a little—God knows I
Would be the last alive to cry
To Whatzisname, "I love thy wheels!"

Freedom's a pattern. I am cold.
I don't know what I'm doing here.
And Mrs. Vane says, "Home now, dear."
He rises, does as he is told;
Hugging her arm, he climbs the pier.
Behind him breaks the triumph cheer.[38]

Wilbur's poem seems modeled on the famous poem by William
Carlos Williams, "The Yachts" (1935). Williams comes to realize that,
however impressive the spectacle, a regatta ought to be understood as
an emblem of the class struggle in which the poor are doomed to suffer; he finally sees the meaning of the yacht race as horrifying.[39] Wilbur, on the other hand, speaks not of the power of the wealthy, but of
their vacancy. Mrs. Vane, Midge, Buck—the names pin the characters
to postwar social types. Their feelings—her "Delighted eyes," the possibility that Mr. Vane "is feeling 'tired' "—and perceptions—"I know

his scarf!"—are as vapid as Victorian poetic diction. The wealthy spectators, like the boats, are weightless and ignorant of depths, and yet a poet knows too that his work is as bound by conventional turns as these people are. Wilbur makes no unforeseen move. The stretching out of the last quatrain into a sestet is "but a trick." (What's a couplet to a versifier?) All that is unsettling is the Shakespearean chill of complicity in the last stanza, and this alone gives the poem more gravity than *vers de société.* Perhaps freedom is a pattern, but who is Mr. Vane? At the end, Mrs. Vane seems to lead away Wilbur himself, somewhat confused: "I don't know what I'm doing here."

Instead of examining the strains and contradictions in the relation between workers and intellectuals, poets tended to write about the very poor and the well-off, which often meant servants and their employers. This focus near the extremes of the class structure effectively raises the question of class in almost abstract purity: if class is not the determinant factor in the relation between servants and employers, where differences seem plain and powerful, then the importance of class in any social relationship is rather open to doubt. Wilbur's "A Summer Morning" (1960) registers the familiar irony about servants taking more direct pleasure in their circumstances than their employers do: as he puts it, they possess "what the owners can but own."[40] That is one way, an old one, of discounting the exploitation of one class by another. But another strategy has stronger appeal to liberals, who want both servants and a clear conscience: according to this view, the paradox about servitude is that it works both ways, binding both parties by natural obligation. This is the opening strophe of Elizabeth Bishop's "Manuelzinho," which first appeared in the *New Yorker* in 1955:

> Half squatter, half tenant (no rent)—
> a sort of inheritance; white,
> in your thirties now, and supposed
> to supply me with vegetables,
> but you don't; or you won't; or you can't
> get the idea through your brain—
> the world's worst gardener since Cain.
> Tilted above me, your gardens
> ravish my eyes. You edge
> the beds of silver cabbages
> with red carnations, and lettuces
> mix with alyssum. And then
> umbrella ants arrive,

or it rains for a solid week
and the whole thing's ruined again
and I buy you more pounds of seeds,
imported, guaranteed,
and eventually you bring me
a mystic three-legged carrot,
or a pumpkin "bigger than the baby."[41]

One reason Bishop can write so brilliantly about the class relations between a landed foreigner in Brazil, where the poem is set, and a Brazilian tenant-farmer is that she is insistently candid about the most illiberal sentiments. She knows how to make her liberal readers squirm and snicker guiltily. Just those two words, "imported, guaranteed," do the trick: behind them is the notion that nothing of domestic origin is reliable, which is dangerously close to the speaker's attitude (a parenthesis notes that "A friend of the writer is speaking"—yes, but not one condemned by the author). But perhaps the second and third lines are still more explicit: since Manuelzinho is white and in his thirties— that is, not Indian, not black, and no longer a child—there is really no excuse for his behavior. Although the poem is well fueled by any number of outrageous remarks, audacity alone would be nothing. Tone, on the other hand, is everything. Speaking that first sentence aloud, one can hardly help but turn the head to the side, speak through a smiling, clenched mouth, and widen the eyes: the exasperation is right there in the parallel constructions, the parentheses, the line breaks, the rhyme. Just as plainly, with the next sentence, the tone changes almost to plaintiveness, largely because of one word, "ravish," which, at the head of the line, gets emphasized and drawn out. The diction is simple, and the syntax too; in this strophe there is not one of the flashy figures she is known for. One cannot miss the human voice here.

Nothing could be more important to the view of class relations expressed in the poem than that the speaker's voice be thoroughly convincing and individual. Regardless of her relative wealth, and of her chauvinistic prejudices, the speaker feels genuine affection for this bizarre gardener: "In the kitchen we dream together / how the meek shall inherit the earth— / or several acres of mine." The prerogatives of class are, first of all, unenforceable. She gets curiosities instead of vegetables because her particular gardener is an eccentric. In fact, perhaps Manuelzinho should be said to enjoy the prerogatives of class, since he is the one who effectively claims "a sort of inheritance"—just what a class structure is meant to institutionalize. But even if wealth could assure class privileges, a sense of irony ("or several acres of mine") and a human imagination—

> Twined in wisps of fog,
> I see you all up there
> along with Formoso, the donkey,
> who brays like a pump gone dry,
> then suddenly stops.
> —All just standing, staring
> off into fog and space.
> Or coming down at night,
> in silence, except for hoofs,
> in dim moonlight, the horse
> or Formoso stumbling after.
> Between us float a few
> big, soft, pale-blue,
> sluggish fireflies,
> the jellyfish of the air . . .

—make it impossible or at least base to think simply in class terms, though nothing is more human than occasional base moments. The poem draws toward a close with the recollection of one of Manuel-zinho's strange hats, a bright green one:

> Unkindly,
> I called you Klorophyll Kid.
> My visitors thought it was funny.
> I apologize here and now.
>
> You helpless, foolish man,
> I love you all I can,
> I think. Or do I?
> I take off my hat, unpainted
> and figurative, to you.
> Again I promise to try.

Her unkind remark, to visitors, was easy and ugly, she knows. She is the victim of her own class prejudices, and rather than deny them ("Or do I?") she counts on her conscience and good will to make the future with her tenant farmer tolerable. Finally, what ought to be a simple social relationship (if Marxists are on the right track), between employer and servant, is presented as even more complicated than this clever, ironic speaker understands ("helpless, foolish man" indeed!). Manuelzinho and his employer are presented as individuals who, despite the economics of their relationship, cannot be properly comprehended as only representatives of social classes. A generous spirit and a good conscience—what could be more liberal?—are the only reliable guides to the dark maze of obligation and affection these people live in. The prerogatives of class are finally trivial, and the idea of a class structure, quaintly naive.

The notion of class is potentially divisive. Poets, and intellectuals generally, had no reason to encourage divisiveness in the 1950s, partly because they were enjoying the benefits of a cultural consensus, partly because in these years haunted by fear of nuclear holocaust divisiveness seemed too dangerous. Gullans said that extremity was the national disease. Extremism coupled with great power is terrifying. Thinking of McCarthy, HUAC, loyalty oaths, and atomic war, he said: "I fear their judgment, and I fear their fear / To face the deep compulsions of the hour." From 1945 until August 1949 America enjoyed atomic hegemony; restraint then seemed a moral obligation. After the Soviets exploded their first atomic weapon, restraint was a matter more of prudence than morality. "This is now a different world," said Arthur Vandenberg, chairman of the Senate Foreign Relations Committee.[42] What Gullans and other poets worried about was whether Americans could quickly learn a moderation that was conspicuous nowhere in the culture.

Gullans, Wilbur, and Rich all wrote about this subject with notable restraint. Wilbur spoke of the need for "Grace" (1947), for the pause Nijinsky could make in midair and the deliberation of Hamlet:

> Even fraction-of-a-second action is not wrecked
> By a graceful still reserve. To be unchecked
> Is needful then: choose, challenge, jump, poise, run. . . .
> Nevertheless, the praiseful, graceful soldier
> Shouldn't be fired by his gun.[43]

This is a language of moderate argumentation with all the tools of discursive rhetoric in place (the concessions, the qualifications, the adversatives).

> Not that missiles will be cast;
> None as yet dare lift an arm . . .

> Let us only bear in mind
> How these treasures handed down
> From a calmer age passed on
> Are in the keeping of our kind.
> We stand between the dead glass-blowers
> And murmurings of missile-throwers.
>
> Adrienne Rich, *"The Uncle Speaks in the Drawing Room"* (1951)[44]

"Even," "is needful," "Nevertheless," "Not that," "None as yet,"
"Let us only"—after 1965 or so, poets pretty well stopped using this
reasonable language, but in an age of consensus these nods toward
shared beliefs were appropriate—especially when the subject was a
matter of state. By 1965 these words and the rhetorical contract they
rest upon would be gone from American political poetry—at great
cost, I think—for at least a decade.

At the very end of Eisenhower's presidency and the beginning of
Kennedy's, a good deal of national attention focused on armaments.
Kennedy's first defense budget was epoch-making. (When Eisenhower left office in January 1961, he predicted a $1.5 billion surplus
for fiscal 1962. Seven months later, Kennedy announced a planned
$5.3 billion deficit, due mainly to his proposals for increased national
security and the space program. The deficit turned out to be $6.3 bil-
lion.) The Geneva agreements against nuclear testing expired in
1961, and testing resumed. At the beginning of September, Kennedy
announced that the Soviets had exploded the first atom bomb since
1958. A few days later they exploded another, and by the end of the
month the total was up to fifteen. Robert Lowell then wrote:

> Back and forth, back and forth
> goes the tock, tock, tock
> of the orange, bland, ambassadorial
> face of the moon
> on the grandfather clock.
>
> All autumn, the chafe and jar
> of nuclear war;
> we have talked our extinction to death.
> I swim like a minnow
> behind my studio window.
>
> *"Fall 1961"*[45]

Like any number of Americans, Lowell was feeling that time was tediously running out on the chance for negotiating an end to the arms

race. The fire looked inevitable. Patience, restraint, faith in discourse—some of the qualities characteristic of 1950s poetry—were
starting to sound strained. Poets seemed small fry at the time, and the
big fish, the statesmen, were not preparing for peace. The Soviet representative to the Vienna conference walked out in protest of the
American attempt to install Dr. Sigvard Eklund of Sweden as director-
general of the International Atomic Energy Agency—that was just two
weeks before the first Soviet test, in fact. The Soviets claimed that
American belligerency in Berlin—in August Soviet and American
tanks faced each other in the divided capital—made the resumption of
testing necessary. Yet the poets were still not ready to give up the rhetorical obligations, and advantages, of consensus. Just a few months
before Lowell wrote his poem, Gullans listened to the crash of waves
and the report of gunfire from a training camp:

> The heavy guns that shudder through the day,
> Miles up the coast, are not so far away.
> Nations rearm with steel and with cold nerve.
> I sit here doing nothing. I observe:
> The beach, fine rubble, detritus of war
> Between the assaulting water and the shore;
> Guns that as pointlessly assault the air,
> Precisely mimicking what they prepare,
> Terror of battles that erode mankind.
>
> *"Gunnery Practice, Seaside, Oregon, August 16, 1961"*[46]

One of the signs of consensus is an unwillingness to raise political
questions in a partisan way. Kennedy had campaigned on the notion
of a missile gap; rearmament was obviously a partisan issue. Yet poets
tended not to treat the subject of mounting nuclear terror as strictly
political. Gullans speaks of military gunfire as pointless. In Kennedy's
judgment, though, there was great point to the American attempt to
strengthen itself militarily in 1961: one point was the broadening of
the Democratic political base that would support his liberal policies;
another was the strengthening of American political authority in relation to the Soviet Union. However, these were strictly political considerations—and hence ignored. Military destruction is likened instead
to the motiveless erosion caused by waves beating on the Oregon
coast. A poet observes both processes from a great distance, uninvolved and unable to do anything beyond showing how senseless destruction is. Of course even a poet can hope that mindless behavior
will stop when understanding improves. Gullans suggests, only

faintly, that understanding, certainly not political confrontation, may prevent greater military casualties in the future.

Intellectual liberalism was broadly appealing in the early 1960s, as Kennedy's professors came to Washington. Even for those who were not seduced by the promises of Camelot, political questions tended often to be understood in intellectual rather than political terms. The best American poem on nuclear holocaust that I know—and this was the chief political subject for poets of the late 1950s and early 1960s—is one of Mark Strand's earliest pieces, "When the Vacation Is Over for Good" (1962):

> It will be strange
> Knowing at last it couldn't go on forever,
> The certain voice telling us over and over
> That nothing would change.
>
> And remembering too,
> Because by then it will all be done with, the way
> Things were, and how we had wasted time as though
> There was nothing to do,
>
> When, in a flash
> The weather turned, and the lofty air became
> Unbearably heavy, the wind strikingly dumb
> And our cities like ash,
>
> And knowing also,
> What we never suspected, that it was something like summer
> At its most august except that the nights were warmer
> And the clouds seemed to glow,
>
> And even then,
> Because we will not have changed much, wondering what
> Will become of things, and who will be left to do it
> All over again,
>
> And somehow trying,
> But still unable, to know just what it was
> That went so completely wrong, or why it is
> We are dying.[47]

Strand is not at all a political poet, and yet this subject seems perfect for his characteristic style. His poems often show some stunning passivity in the face of a horror; the fatalism in his work leaves horror and ordinary social life more or less indistinguishable. The diction is unremarkable; the clauses are strung together rather listlessly by copulas, until the possibility of syntactic force in this "sentence" is eliminated by strings of dangling participles. Except for a flash in the third strophe, not much happens in the poem; knowing, telling, remembering are verbals beginning a series that ends with dying. The style shows extraordinary equanimity in the face of a nuclear blast. There is nothing plainly stylish about the poem, as though almost anyone could speak it. Like most of the poets of this time, Strand insists on complicity with his audience—"*we* are dying"—though what binds poet and audience together in 1962 is a common fate, rather than a commitment to shared values or conventions of rational discourse. The only ostentatious aspect of the poem, to a poet's eye, would be the figure in the fourth strophe. Comparing the radiated air to the buzzing richness of full summer is nice, and gives the poem a clever title that makes another point too: "we" are like schoolchildren who have a lesson to learn. The poem ends with us, while dying, trying unsuccessfully "to know just what it was / That went so completely wrong," as though nuclear war were something to figure out. Strand's treatment of this political subject is not political: the poem ends, as Gullans' "Gunnery Practice" does, with the suggestion that intellectual effort is called for. Nuclear war was the perfect political subject for an age of consensus. Everyone ought to be terrified of the prospect; the normal political divisions of the population along class, party, or ideological lines seem irrelevant in the face of nuclear threat, though in fact that threat was heightened by a Democratic, liberal president who openly avowed the interests of intellectuals, as his predecessor had not.

By 1965 the belief in consensus was feeble. The civil-rights movement had shown that the nation was in for a period of serious social strife. The assassination of Diem, Kennedy, and Malcolm X, the policedogs and firehoses in the south, and the Watts riots of the summer of 1965 all brought bloody violence before the eyes of most Americans. Moreover, that year the Marines landed for combat in Vietnam, and intellectuals were beginning to question the wisdom of intervention. With the erosion of consensus, too, went the reticence of poets about the tension between intellectuals and the working classes. Poets had good reason to think of themselves as part of the intelligentsia; somehow the intellectuals were commonly thought to have removed themselves, at least in terms of taste, from middle-class vulgarity. Their newly jaundiced eyes, as though from some separate place, could be turned on the classes occupying the recently proliferated suburbs. In 1965 it seemed that the lower-middle and middle classes, not the intellectuals or the wealthy, were in control of America, and most poets disapproved of the situation. The traditional notion of American "classlessness" took a new shape in the mid-1960s: what was once an alleged sign of American consensus then became emblematic of monolithic dullness and ignorance.

Hardly anyone had a kind word for the suburbs, or indeed for the changes brought by the increased political power of the working and managerial classes, but the terms of criticism varied substantially. Turner Cassity's "Epigoni Go French Line" (1966) revolves around the more generous pole of opinion on the subject:

> Egalitarian and full of plastics,
> S.S. *France,* efficient, safe, and banal,
> Mirrors double in the English Channel.
> One reflection has her own statistics;
> One has patently an extra funnel.
>
> She, that other, follows where the real
> Distorts her; just below the water, just,
> But only just, describable—her past
> Already idiom, her loss detail.
> Imperfectly, the structured meaning lost
>
> And connotation gone, hers, nonetheless,
> Prevail. Time is the steward of decor.
> In auctioned fittings that no longer are,
> Persists the image that forever is:
> Ease, class on class, and in the distance, war.
>
> Meanwhile, if enamel, glazes, metal
> Bear the mark of Cain, here, being human,
> It lends them what the *France* can never summon.
> Simply, well aware it may be fatal,
> Luxury is drive toward the uncommon.[48]

Cassity suggests that class privileges (specifically, here, whether one has a cabin, a berth, or stays at home) are finally purchased with blood; the world of segregated classes, in a sense, reached a conclusion with World War II. Who can lament the passing of that world? No one very loudly, but a poet can gripe a bit. The phantom prewar ship, the *France*'s reflection, has a human edge, the spirit that always wants a bit more. That was a flashier world, with Wallis Simpson and stain-less steel pianos, but somehow it led only to world war. The poem closes with a dutiful acceptance of the modern liner qualified only by nostalgia:

> The Channel clouds; the ships merge utterly;
> Our faith now is in the *France,* for good or ill.
> But when the bored forsake the guarding rail,
> The life preserver, spotlit, still reads *Normandie.*

The campy sheen of a 1930s movie is a moment of indulgence—merely that. The *Ile de France* did in fact lose one funnel, when it was rebuilt in the late 1940s after its use as a troopship early in World War II, its internment by the British, and its postwar service carrying French soldiers to Vietnam. Then came calm decades of ferrying tour-ists back and forth across the Atlantic. The *Normandie,* also operated by the French Line, was meant to outdo the *Queen Mary* in luxury and to replace a more utilitarian liner, the *France,* that had been a U.S. troopship during World War I. But the *Normandie* (whose third fun-nel was a dummy) could not, when the time came, surrender its lux-ury: a workman's lamp accidentally ignited a pile of mattresses for 12,000 kilroys, and the water that doused the fire sank the ship at New York in 1942. *La Normandie* (1883–1901), reduced from four to two masts in middle age, the *France* (1912–1934), the *Ile de France* (1927–   ), the *Normandie* (1935–1941)—the lines of succession crisscross a bit. The ghost of the extravagant youngster, the *Norman-die* (which Cassity, as a child, once visited), is borne as a memory, an amputated funnel, on one of the last and most reduced liners to make the crossing.[49] Campiness, nostalgia—these are styles of remem-brance, finally serious. We pay for peace and efficiency with a small hunger for quaintness, and the bargain is sound.

In the mid-1960s the middle-class suburbs and the working classes were submitted to strenuous criticism by poets. The common com-plaint was not just that these classes lacked taste, though that point was made, but also that these citizens were not *listening* and that in-telligence had disappeared from the body politic. What had happened was that the consensus of intellectuals, workers, and much of the middle classes, treasured through the 1950s and early 1960s, broke down over the issues of desegregation, foreign policy, and university administration. Many poets, rather predictably, turned against the in-tellectuals' former silent partner.

Whereas poets had previously resisted a class analysis of the tension

between intellectuals and nonintellectuals, they tended now to focus
on the suburbs in terms of the most narrow determinant of American
class standing: income. In the mid-1960s, not without reason, the suburbs were seldom mentioned in poems without some reference to affluence. These early lines by Robert Bly are about driving through
Scarsdale, an executive's suburb:

> . . . I think of the many comfortable homes stretching for miles,
> Two and three stories, solid, with polished floors,
> With white curtains in the upstairs bedrooms,
> And small perfume flagons of black glass on the window sills,
> And warm bathrooms with guest towels, and electric lights—
> What a magnificent place for a child to grow up!
> And yet the children end in the river of price-fixing,
> Or in the snowy field of the insane asylum.
> The sleet falls—so many cars moving toward New York—
> Last night we argued about the Marines invading Guatemala in
>   1947,
> The United Fruit Company had one water spigot for 200
>   families,
> And the ideals of America, our freedom to criticize,
> The slave systems of Rome and Greece, and no one agreed.
>
> *"Sleet Storm on the Merritt Parkway" (1962)*[50]

The political poetry of the 1960s is strikingly class-oriented. The last
words of Bly's poem suggest how painful the breakdown of consensus
seemed to the intellectuals who were accustomed to having their appropriate members formulate policy, and respectful executives ad-
minister those policies. In the fall of the same year, 1967, Denise
Levertov wrote virtually the same poem: her "Tenebrae" draws to a
close with the lament that these station-wagoned, freezer-stuffing suburbanites are "not listening, not listening."[51] And they used to listen
so well. Many intellectuals felt that the suburbanites were willfully ig-
noring the greed and malice behind American foreign policy. Bly was
insistent on seeing this problem in strictly political and economic
terms: American foreign policy was revealed in 1947 to be merely an
extension of American international business interests. The inhu-
manity of those business concerns ought not to be debatable, but neither is slavery debatable. All the talk about such political and
ideological matters seemed sadly hollow—on both sides of the debate.
The Marines did not invade Guatemala in 1947, though the suggestion that they did sounds plausible enough. Everyone's words, Bly's

too, float above the level on which troops land, families go hungry or soft. The suburbanites can agree only upon the conventions of consumption—guest towels and little perfume bottles. Intellectual activity has frozen into a conflict of different points of view. George Oppen argued that the middle classes are essentially "shoppers, / Choosers, judges"; consequently,

> They develop
> Argument in order to speak, they become
> unreal, unreal, life loses
> solidity, loses extent, baseball's their game
> because baseball is not a game
> but an argument and difference of opinion
> makes the horse races. They are ghosts that endanger
>
> One's soul.[52]

The complicity expressed by most 1950s poets was gone by 1965. No more reasonable "we"; only Strand's (and Merwin's) dying "we" survived the 1960s. Poets of the later 1960s seemed suddenly to speak from outside the walls.

Bly's early effort to hold a political, economic focus on class tension was not widely shared, and even he gave it up soon for another. Instead, the class hostility once understood as political and economic in origin was soon regarded by many poets as psychologically motivated, and then soon the whole matter of class antagonism was oddly resolved. James Wright's "Autumn begins in Martins Ferry, Ohio" (1962):

> In the Shreve High football stadium,
> I think of Polacks nursing long beers in Tiltonsville,
> And gray faces of Negroes in the blast furnace at Benwood,
> And the ruptured night watchman of Wheeling Steel,
> Dreaming of heroes.
>
> All the proud fathers are ashamed to go home.
> Their women cluck like starved pullets,
> Dying for love.
>
> Therefore,
> Their sons grow suicidally beautiful
> At the beginning of October,
> And gallop terribly against each other's bodies.[53]

"Therefore" must carry a lot of weight: an apparent nonsequitur is meant to express a less apparent logic. These workingmen are too proud to go home and deny love to their wives: the cycle of repression and violence begins there. Unable to satisfy themselves or their women, they concoct a suburban cult of masculine aggression—at least as spectators. Violence, the poem suggests, is being bred not altogether deliberately in the lower-middle class suburbs. (These are the same suburbanites, from around Wheeling, West Virginia, who heard McCarthy launch his anticommunist drive in 1950.) It is only a short step from this notion about the source of American violence to the grander claim that the war in Vietnam can be traced right back to the cultural priorities of American suburbs—despite the historical involvement of liberal intellectuals, not the suburban middle classes, in formulating the foreign policy of the Kennedy and Johnson administrations.

> At the edges of southeast Asia this afternoon
> The quarterbacks and the lines are beginning to fall,
> A spring snow,
>
> And terrified young men
> Quick on their feet
> Lob one another's skulls across
> Wings of strange birds that are burning
> Themselves alive.

> Wright, "A Mad Fight Song for William S. Carpenter, 1966"[54]

Once the terms were shifted from politics to psychology, it was easy to reestablish the connection of complicity—for everyone knows how repression leads to violence even in the best of us. This is a human fact; inherently, it has nothing to do with one or another class, or even with one particular country. Wright grew up in Martins Ferry, Ohio. "A Mad Fight Song" for the West Pointer who ordered his own troops napalmed begins with Wright's own memory of playing football.[55] The poet's alienation from the suburbs is irrelevant here; steelworkers, watchmen, poets have all been touched by this warping of the psyche. Whether Wright came from the suburbs is not so important: Carpenter and those Martins Ferry ballplayers are all sad and attractive in their self-destructiveness. The divisions between one class and another amount to very little in a poetry that leaps across cultures and oceans from strophe to strophe, leaving only an occasional outrageous conjunction to mark the space crossed.

> It's because the milk trains coming into New Jersey hit the
> right switches every day that the best Vietnamese men are
> cut in two by American bullets that follow each other like
> freight cars
> . . . . .
> It's because taxpayers move to the suburbs that we transfer
> populations.

Bly, *"The Teeth-Mother Naked at Last"* (1970)[56]

The conjunctions of logical relationship, which ten years earlier
were used by Wilbur, Rich, and others to maintain an amicable relationship between poet and reader, no longer serve discursive ends. Bly
and, to a lesser degree, Wright speak oracularly about politics and society, as if vision rather than understanding were needed. The techniques of this visionary political poetry do not permit the exercise of
analytical intelligence. Close discrimination is hardly possible in a poetry of rapid juxtapositions; concessions, qualifications, and subordi-
nations are ruled out on technical grounds. In place of the rational
virtues, Bly and others offer vision, quick but penetrating, and at
times vision seems especially called for. As a young man, Pound argued that art is "necessary only when life is apparently without design; that is, when the conclusion or results of given causes are so far
removed or so hidden, that art alone can show their relation."[57] Bly
writes as though his art were necessary to expose hidden relations.

This proud attitude is implicit in the surrealist technique of juxtaposition—and how oddly consoling it is in this context. For if unnoticed relations were to be illuminated, the connection between
Vietnam and American intellectuals ought to have been high on the
list. Since many nonliterary American intellectuals bear responsibility
for advocating an interventionist, antiguerrilla foreign policy, they and
the poets who address their community should be wary of too proud a
denunciation of the war once its consequences had become apparent.
(This is not to say that Bly's audience included government advisers,
but rather that many of the intellectuals and students among his readers were involved through institutions of higher education with the
mainly nonliterary intellectuals who urged an interventionist policy in
Southeast Asia and elsewhere.) Bly of course never supported intervention, but intellectuals as a group enthusiastically supported the
one American president who most explicitly avowed such a policy—
John Kennedy; furthermore, it was the Democratic liberals who regarded the university as central to American society.[58] How much
harder, and more dignified, it would have been for Bly in 1970 to re-

mind his audience of the ugly consequences of their obvious (not hidden) former enthusiasms. How helpful it might have been then to make academics face the prospect of a society in which the university was peripheral or, worse still, of an economy without the support of an interventionist, antiguerrilla foreign policy. In the 1980s the first of these prospects has had to be faced (though without, to put it simply, any guidance from poets). The second has remained unconsidered (but still remote), with the consequence that literary intellectuals still commonly criticize the global reach of American political and economic interests without admitting the price that would have to be paid, even by intellectuals, for a less extended economy.

In the later 1960s, as the Vietnam war became the one overarching political subject, American poets tended to produce many variations of a single poem. Poet after poet stepped to the rostrum to speak of a culture with a death wish. Political or social distinctions between different classes or parties amounted to little in these poems; America wanted to die, and that meant everyone. The development of this genre can be traced back to one moment in the recent past, though its roots extend back through Pound, Whitman, and Blake to the biblical prophets.

> Inauguration Day: January 1953
>
> The snow had buried Stuyvesant.
> The subways drummed the vaults. I heard
> the El's green girders charge on Third,
> Manhattan's truss of adamant,
> that groaned in ermine, slummed on want. . . .
> Cyclonic zero of the word,
> God of our armies, who interred
> Cold Harbor's blue immortals, Grant!
> Horseman, your sword is in the groove!
>
> Ice, ice. Our wheels no longer move.
> Look, the fixed stars, all just alike
> as lack-land atoms, split apart,
> and the Republic summons Ike,
> the mausoleum in her heart.[59]

In the 1952 election, New York went solidly for Aldai Stevenson, the candidate favored by intellectuals. Robert Lowell was deeply disappointed at Stevenson's stunning loss to Eisenhower;[60] intellectuals felt shut out of office. This poem gives a powerful sense of how it was then to stand in the cold: frosty, yes, but for a poet invigorating too; with alienation came fresh access to biting, severe statement such as a poet has to be grateful for, though perhaps only in the short run. The political stakes of the 1952 election looked especially high to intellectuals; as Lowell represents them, they were cosmic. General Grant ended his bloody wilderness campaign with the battle of Cold Harbor, the worst slaughter of the war—that is the historical reference Lowell thought appropriate to Eisenhower's election. Even for New Yorkers, though, speaking of Eisenhower as an outland candidate was stretching things some: two years earlier, he had been president of Columbia. Yet Stevenson was plainly the northeastern, urban favorite, and he lost miserably. The forces behind Eisenhower's victory, as Lowell saw them, included a tradition of warrior-presidents such as Grant but, more important, the deathly spirit of America, the mausoleum in the heart of the nation. So sweeping is Lowell's vision here that even the stars are meant to figure in this historical moment, and in an odd way. Those fixed stars are being cracked open, like atoms, to mark a world-historical moment. Lowell manages, quite surprisingly, to associate Eisenhower with nuclear fission, even though the only person ever to order the military use of nuclear weapons was the outgoing Democratic president. (Of course, Eisenhower was involved in the decision to devastate Dresden, in protest of which Lowell refused induction and served a six-month prison sentence.) Lowell's effort to magnify the political loss suffered by Democrats, especially the urban, intellectual Democrats, was so strenuous that Civil War history, astronomy, and an odd manipulation of recent military history were all made to lend resonance to the moment. Given this bird's-eye view of the culture, a single political division becomes the axis for dividing the cosmos. In 1953, when to most observers the nation was settling in for a snooze, the culture seemed in extremis to Lowell; so he reverted conspicuously to the extremist style of his war book, *Lord Weary's Castle*. It would be another fifteen years before the culture would seem similarly doomed to many of his contemporaries.[61]

Nearly all the salient properties of the 1960s period piece, the cultural critique poem, are there in "Inauguration Day." The most important of these is perspective: poem after poem at this time strained after a large view. Usually the signs of strain are plainest in the conclusions, where poets show that their real point is grand. Robert Hass's "Bookbuying in the Tenderloin" (1967) ends:

> The sky glowers. My God, it is a test,
> this riding out the dying of the West.[62]

More typical, though, is an insistently national conclusion: an episode narrated in the poem is made to point a moral about the cultural death of the nation.

> I lie down between tombstones
> At the bottom of the cliff
> America is over and done with.
> America,
> Plunged into the dark furrows
> Of the sea again.
>
> Wright, *"Stages on a Journey Westward"* (1963) [63]

Nearing the end of the most ambitious of these period poems, "The Teeth Mother Naked at Last," Bly intones: "Now the whole nation starts to whirl, / the end of the Republic breaks off."[64] Like Whitman, these poets want to speak for the country, even at the risk of rhetorical rotundity. In the later 1960s, a national consensus was a fast-yellowing memory, but these poets show how haunting and seductive a memory it was. For a poet, the thrill is not in saying that the culture is dying, but rather in being in a historical moment when one might plausibly write: "Now the whole nation starts . . ."

In order to regain a collective voice, one very different from that of the 1950s, some options had to be forgone. To put the matter plainly, poets after the national voice of the mid-1960s, like politicians, gave up splitting for lumping. One of the stock devices of the cultural critique poem was reference to American history, for historical consciousness and national identity reinforce each other; nowhere is the tendency to make distinctions more forcefully repressed. The historical incidents that these poems cite form a kind of family group: Puritans killing turkeys, New England slaveships, Hamilton's plan for a central bank, the battle of Cripple Creek, Indians and buffaloes, pioneers and Conestoga wagons, Spanish missionaries, the assassination of President McKinley, the 1930s breadlines.[65] Abrupt junctures, beginnings and ends, these are the historical moments that count most for poets. Periods of gradual change, of compromise, of concentration, are apparently uninteresting, because they involve taking seriously differences that can be measured only with patience and discrimination.

The worst consequence of these cultural critique poems is that they encourage a lack of proportion in political thought. Here is a very good poem in this genre by Robert Hass that raises the relevant issue, "Politics of a Pornographer" (1972):

> Like America, his art consists
> in the absence of scale. He is no less

mad, but his Oedipus
meets, always, at the crossroads
his mother and trembles in the sun.
The dust is mallow
and the light is mallow-brown.
In his mind there are only
a summer meadow, breasts,
the mossy tuft, his cock,
and twining legs.
There is no walled city come to.
The sphinx proposes nothing.
There is no plague.[66]

The pornographer's art is pure or, as it might have been called a decade earlier, extreme. Circumstance counts for nothing at all: his
mother is always there. Without contest, without Laius, desire comes
to Oedipus in the road. Character and cleverness are without use because the sphinx has no special authority. There is only sun and geni-
tals, fast fulfillment without trial. All is overripe. The political poetry of
the later 1960s often seems hot and swollen too. The confrontation of
rival political postures in these cultural-critique poems seldom led to a
genuine qualification: the adversary was regarded as so alien and
wrong that nothing could be learned by scrutinizing him.

In many of the poems of this period, political leaders and candidates
were judged severely in moral terms, as if a political judgment were
somehow inadequate in force to the circumstances. The implicit view
of politics was above all impatient, like the customer loudly insisting
that he has not had his money's worth. The most frequent moral
charge leveled against politicians was the old and always pertinent
one: Lyndon Johnson did not tell the truth about his Vietnam policy in
the presidential campaign of 1964. He presented himself as the dove
to Goldwater's hawk. Just after the election, his advisers told him that
he would have to escalate the war or withdraw entirely.[67] Fidelity to
the policy of his predecessors compelled Johnson to escalate and
thereby violate his own campaign statements. Poets, and many other
commentators, often focused on his inconsistency, not on the systematic force of a foreign policy drafted largely by intellectuals in the
service of both political parties. Instead, Johnson was commonly
dismissed as immoral, and many poets, it must be admitted, lent their
art to the common view. Robert Duncan spoke of military and political leaders as "liars and masters of the Lie."[68] Bly made the same
claim in a wittier way when, referring to the American death wish,
he said:

> This is the thrill that leads the President on to lie . . .
> He lies about the number of fish taken every year in the Arctic,
>   he has private information about which city *is* the capital of
>   Wyoming, he lies about the birthplace of Attila the Hun.[69]

In the late 1960s there was adequate evidence to establish that the government was an unreliable source of information: this was an easy charge to make stick. Bly and Duncan could indict the Democratic administration for falsehood and hypocrisy, and no one would be surprised or moved in any way.[70] Even to speak of the military as conspirators thinking to use Johnson "as they thought to use Hitler / without losing control of their business of war" would not wrinkle many brows in 1965.[71] These poets were wheeling out big guns for fixed targets:

> Men like Rusk are not men:
> They are bombs waiting to be loaded in a darkened hangar.
>
> > *Bly, "Asian Peace Offers Rejected without Publication" (1967)*

> . . . and the very glint of Satan's eyes from the pit of hell of
>   America's unacknowledged, unrepented crimes that I saw in
>   Goldwater's eyes
> now shines from the eyes of the President
>   in the swollen head of the nation.
>
> > *Duncan, "Up Rising" (1965)*[72]

Later came moments of greater leniency, as when Anthony Hecht in 1978 wrote of the "engaging roguishness" of the young bomber pilots who flew so high above their targets that they could not appreciate the suffering they were causing.[73] But the moral critique of American political leaders logically ended in the claim that they were devils.

Moralism in American politics did not begin in the mid-1960s, and certainly not with poets either. Senator Eugene McCarthy is reported to have said of Johnson in a private meeting of doveish Democratic senators: "We've got a wild man in the White House, and we are going to have to treat him as such."[74] As I have suggested, demonology was an appropriate response, in a fashion, to the broken promises of the 1964 campaign. More generally, a moralistic perspective suits a nation that has come to think of politics almost exclusively in terms of personalities and electoral campaigns. Every four years, two people are judged, opinions are formed (as Oppen said), and then most Americans turn back toward the parts of their lives that engage them during the offyears. By focusing on the betrayals of the Democratic leadership, charging individuals with immorality, some poets helped to persuade their audience that the Vietnam war was a matter of leadership, that, come the 1968 election, another leader might be found who would not be immoral. If candidates would speak the truth, Americans might vote on whether to intervene in the political affairs of Korea, Vietnam, Dominican Republic, Cambodia, or Laos.

That an interventionist foreign policy is necessary, as many political counselors have argued during the last thirty-five years, in order to preserve the relative wealth of American citizens and the health of the American economy; that, even if it were politically possible in the mid-1960s to reverse the policy of intervention, the economic price for this change would be staggering to all Americans—these issues have little to do with electoral campaigns, and the poetics of the mid-1960s virtually assured that they would have to be raised by political scientists and historians, not by poets. Poets typically drew striking juxtapositions and searched for powerful images—the "velvety hairs" of the death wish, "like a clothes brush in the intestines."[75] A generation of American modernist predecessors, especially Pound, made a poetic of juxtaposition and image seem unavoidable. Those poets who had tried to restore the conjunctions and syntax of premodernist poetry were part of a period of political and cultural consensus that had passed quickly in the early 1960s; that effort had simply failed to sustain a collective voice. The impatience one hears in mid-1960s poetry follows directly from the failed consensus. In the early 1960s, poets seemed to lose their grip on an audience of American intellectuals who were influential in the political arena. The extremism of the mid-1960s poets now looks like a desperate attempt to regain lost authority.

Certainly in the mid-1960s poets seemed to gain authority, in the sense that their audience increased astonishingly.[76] That new audience was achieved indirectly through federal aid to education, but partly too by a choice of sides. A number of poets dealt with the differences between antiwar demonstrators and the Democratic Party as if an election were at stake: they glorified the young demonstrators.

> The beautiful young men and women!
> Standing against the war their courage
> has made a green place in my heart.
> In the dark and utter destitution of winter
> the face of the girl is a fresh moon
> radiant with the Truth she loves,

the Annunciation, the promise
faith keeps in life.

Duncan, *"Earth's Winter Song"* (1968)

I see Dennis Riordan and de Courcy Squire,
gentle David Worstell, intransigent Chuck Matthei
blowing angel horns at the imagined corners.
Jennie Orvino singing
beatitudes in the cold wind
        outside a Milwaukee courthouse.
I want their world—in which they already live,
they're not waiting for demolition and reconstruction.
        'Begin here.'
Of course I choose
revolution.

Levertov, *"Part I (October '68–May '69)"*[77]

These lines (a shame to quote them, really) are the nadir of political poetry of the later 1960s. Students were angelic, politicians were demonic, and worst of all poets, like voyeurs, trafficked freely in between. This is what choosing sides can come to for poets: a sentimental simplification of history.

My assessment of recent political poetry begins with a single question: if one read only poems, how refined an understanding could one have of American political life after World War II? Refinement is the issue here. From the poetry alone, one would certainly know something of the key events of the period, but *Time* magazine is more informative on that score. Wordsworth made the point that "the human mind is capable of being excited without the application of gross and violent stimulants . . . To endeavour to produce or enlarge this capability is one of the best services in which, at any period, a Writer can be engaged; but this service, excellent at all times, is especially so at the present day."[78] However narrow it is to praise poems only for subtlety, the registration and maintenance of fine distinctions are especially to be appreciated in political poetry, perhaps more generally too in culture poetry. From recent poets, one gets a special view of the last thirty-five years—a class perspective, I think. The poets follow the issues that touch the intelligentsia most directly, as well they might. Many poems acknowledge no distinction between the interests of intellectuals and those of the nation at large. As a consequence, when intellectuals began to feel disenfranchised in the mid-1960s, all humane, literate values, some poets suggested, were being trampled down. As I argued at the outset, the recent history of intellectuals has a special importance not only to this newly burgeoned class but to the entire nation. One test of a poet's political integrity, of a willingness to be critical even when criticism is unpopular, is whether the audience of the poet is scrutinized as earnestly as other classes are. By this measure, it must be admitted, the literary record is unimpressive.

6 · *Robert Lowell's* History

Robert Lowell was more elaborately belaureled than any other poet of his time. After the publication of *Lord Weary's Castle* (1946), his second book, he won the Pulitzer Prize. The following year he received a Guggenheim Fellowship and was appointed Poetry Consultant to the Librarian of Congress, at the age of thirty. (Lowell's early master, William Carlos Williams, was denied that position six years later, when he was seventy years o'd.[1]) In 1951 Lowell's third book, *The Mills of the Kavanaughs,* won the Harriet Monroe Prize, awarded by *Poetry* magazine. For *Life Studies* (1959), his next book of poems, he received the National Book Award and shared the Guinness Award with W. H. Auden and Edith Sitwell. Two years later his book of translations, *Imitations,* won another Harriet Monroe Prize and took half of the Bollingen Translation Prize. In 1964 he received a Ford Grant for Drama and the Obie Award for two of his plays, *My Kinsman, Major Molineux* and *Benito Cereno.* In 1966 he was given the Sarah Josepha Hale Award in recognition of a distinguished contribution to New England literature. Three years later Yale awarded him an honorary Doctor of Letters. For a lifetime of achievement in poetry, he was given the Copernicus Award in 1974. In 1977 his last book of poems, *Day by Day,* took the National Book Critics' Circle Award and earned Lowell the National Medal for Literature from the American Academy of Arts and Letters. All of this was well deserved. The only surprise is that when Lowell published three books, *History, For Lizzie and Harriet,* and *The Dolphin,* simultaneously in 1973, the book he thought gave shape and structure to his career, *History,* received only a chilly greeting from critics and readers; *The Dolphin* got the Pulitzer.[2]

Lowell was never a modest poet. Norman Mailer spoke of Lowell's "literary logrollermanship"—and who but Mailer would know better a writer's need "to keep the defense lines in good working order"?[3] In 1974 John Hollander said that Lowell "seems obsessed with his place in histories / Of intelligence."[4] Lowell makes his friend Jarrell ask, from beyond the grave, "What kept you so long, / racing the cooling grindstone of your ambition?"[5] (That ambition would leave him panting dully, especially in a book of 368 pseudo-sonnets, was a real fear.) Those who knew Lowell have recalled his eye for the competition; he was often eager to learn what was thought of one or another poet.[6] More important, he wrote ambitiously, always trying for the memorable line within his reach.

> History has to live with what was here,
> . . . . .
> drenched with the silver salvage of the mornfrost.   (p. 24)

Those are the opening and closing lines of the first poem in Lowell's most ambitious book, *History*—what comes within these framing lines is beside the point, for the moment. These lines show a great drive to write, foot to the floor, with power, and they mark the range of that power too. Who, besides Lowell, dared to write such "wisdom lines," as though the stonecutters were waiting?

> we lack staying power, though we will to live.   (p. 26)
>
> the price of slavery is ceaseless vigilance.   (p. 50)
>
> What little health we have is stolen fruit.   (p. 171)
>
> fame, a bouquet in the niche of forgetfulness.   (p. 52)
>
> a gentleman is an aristocrat on bail.   (p. 101)

And who too was as adept, clever, and evocative at description?

> lost in the dark night of the brilliant talkers,
> humor and honor from the everlasting dross!   (p. 140)
>
> blank with the cobbled ennui of feudal Florence.   (p. 179)
>
> the sickroom's crimeless mortuary calm,   (p. 114)
>
> They come this path, old friends, old buffs of death.   (p. 135)
>
> I go to bed Lord Byron, and wake up bald.   (p. 166)
>
> we too were students, and betrayed our hand.   (p. 152)

Lowell believed in his translation of Gongora: "Words / give marble meaning and a voice to bronze" (p. 68). For the poet's traditional role of giving memorable expression to understanding, Lowell was more willing than any of his contemporaries to risk the critic's charge of sentimentality, naiveté. This old and simple ambition should be recognized as the primary reason Lowell never wandered far from metrical verse. He had to write blank verse, because this is the medium of memorable verse in English, but he did not have to write sonnets. Those fourteen-line stanzas are in fact a bit much, as though he were poet enough to stand up to even the most famous author of memorable lines. Stanzas did not come naturally to Lowell. He knew he was a poet of "loaded and overloaded lines" (p. 118), and this is why Valéry's challenge was so unsettling:

> "All our French poets can turn an inspired line;
> who has written six passable in sequence?"
> said Valéry. That was a happy day for Satan. . . .   (p. 193)

Yes, satanic to suggest that stichic poets come cheap! But this is just the problem of *History:* too often lines or quatrains, rather than poems, stand out in memory. A poet of mighty lines ought naturally to have trouble weaving lines together into strophes or stanzas. Lowell surely did. Most of the lines I have quoted conclude poems, for what can come after an inscription, but recollection, a name and dates?

The English sonnet throws all the weight on the conclusion. But English or Italian, the sonnet form has one distinctive characteristic: the volta, or turn. At each turn, some measure of closure brings the poem to a momentary pause; too severe a closure breaks the poem apart, leaving a quatrain, sestet, or octave sitting by itself. The simplest way to avoid this difficulty is to repeat, more or less, one statement in the different structural units of the poem; or (a bit more complicated) to set one statement in an adversative relation to a preceding statement. Those, of course, are only the most conventional ways of coping with the sonnet structure; they come easiest. The ghost of the sonnet structure was powerful enough to urge Lowell now and then to a severe closure after six or eight lines. He sometimes broke his poems in two exactly because of his hunger for mighty lines. "Mother and Father 2" begins with eight lines about his reading habits as a young man, but with the ninth line—"I think of all the ill I do and will"—the subject changes with a generalization about his whole life (p. 114). Something similar happens in "Walks," when in the tenth line Lowell says, "Conservatives only want to have the earth." The first nine lines concern the simple lives of the tribes preceding King David; the last five enigmatically reflect on the connection between hierarchical societies and political liberty. The poems in *History* are seldom obscure for more than six lines, though a number of poems do not survive the turn intact; one powerful line is enough to nudge Lowell's attention in a new direction. This apparently most fixed of English forms turned, in Lowell's hands, into an instrument for improvisation.

In a book of 368 pseudo-sonnets, there is room for error, so long as the successes are great. Which they are. If the ghost of the sonnet sometimes leads Lowell to premature closure, it also has a hand in his best poems too. "Che Guevara" begins with five lines on Che's death, followed by a quatrain on the New York cityscape. Lines 10–12 set up a relationship between the illegal aliens from Latin America and the illicit love affair Lowell was engaged in. The closing lines pull together all the various strands of the poem: the hunted, Che, illegal aliens, illicit lovers, Charles I, are hunters too; when they are caught and cut off, like a branch of a tree, the larger process—justice, the health or pacification of the state or of a marriage—is well served. Behind many of the most successful of the *History* poems is a negotiation between the complicated stanzaic format of the sonnet and a poet who tends to cash in his poems for a lasting line.

All of the mighty lines I have quoted come from the book that shows Lowell's ambition best. Vergil, Dante, Pope—these are the poets whose careers in themselves were crafted, one move after another.[7] In his fiftieth year, Lowell began the volume that later became *History;* he drew *Notebook 1967–68* to a close with a sequence entitled "Half a Century Gone" and a last poem, "Obit," as if his life and work were turning a last corner.[8] Nowhere else does he speak so directly of his own weakness as a poet ("somehow never wrote something to go back to"), and here too he quotes the best critic of his first book (p. 195), and the later, dimmer lights as well (p. 204). He can afford to quote the critics here, I think, because this is the book where his greatness is plainest. Of course there is reach, even cheek, everywhere in this proudly titled book, not least in the form. Lowell positioned his book directly between two poetic poles of the English language: William Carlos Williams, who often referred to the sonnet as the very deadest of poetic forms, and Shakespeare, whose sonnets have served as a mine of poetic diction for more than one generation of poets (so obviously are they bona fide poems) and as the beginning of poetic taste, the first poems, for generations of readers. Lowell wanted the book to work for both sorts of readers, and he meant the poems to stand up to the comparison, perhaps here and there even to come out on top.

For there is one thing in *History* that neither Shakespeare nor Williams achieves: encyclopedic grandeur. The book begins almost with the Christian world's beginning. Abel, not Adam, is Lowell's first man, partly because Lowell would see historical man as more a victim than a beginner, but surely too because Abel is the abecedarian beginning of the story: the beginning of the alphabet, of manslaughter, of Christian narrative, and of Lowell's book. The end of *History* is "ciphers." Between Abel and ciphers is Lowell's summa: the book contains poems spanning his entire career and its much touted development. "In the Cage" is explicitly labeled: "(First Written in 1944)"; it appeared in *Lord Weary's Castle*. Lowell was direct about his desire to pull all his work together. His readers do not need to know that the Rome sequence in *History* comes to a close with a poem, "Rome in the Sixteenth Century," that was born from a single line of another poem, "Dea Roma," scribbled in the notebooks for *Land of Unlikeness,* nor that "Charles V by Titian" was a mature attempt at a poem, "Charles V, After Muhlberg [suggested by Titian]," which Lowell copied into a still earlier notebook and dated 30 August 1935, when he was eighteen years old. These are mere details of provenance and can only help to justify the feeling Lowell's readers must have in reading this summa: that in the late 1960s and early 1970s Lowell had easy access to the style, long before renounced, that had made him instantly famous when *Lord Weary's Castle* appeared right after the war. And this is only another way of saying that Lowell deliberately made it known that, in his fiftieth year, he was writing with his full powers.

This poetic ambition, the effort at the magnum opus, is a poet's version, Lowell knew, of the imperial aspirations of the politically powerful. Those political dreams are seen under the sign of Abel. The ethical perspective of the book comes out in the first of Lowell's mighty lines:

> History has to live with what was here,
> clutching and close to fumbling all we had—
> it is so dull and gruesome how we die,
> unlike writing, life never finishes.   (p. 24)

All things must pass, and few come to fullness; this is an old but powerful lesson—one that the first word (his title) turns against the imperial ambition of this book. In Lowell's poems, the empire—Rome's, America's, his own—is being constantly eroded by transience and error:

> O Rome!
> from all your senates, palms, dominions, bronze
> and beauty, what was firm has fled. Whatever
> was fugitive maintains its permanence.   (p. 51)

It is not just that we die, though that is bad enough, but that our highest efforts go wrong from goofs. Life will never take a polish because somehow the wrong things, the fugitive details, the shallow Tiber, survive into prominence. The difficulty is there in the word that turns into the next quatrain, "finishes"—polishes, mainly, but also ends, and that secondary sense leads on to Abel, whose life was brought to an end. That the term should generate this pun, an accidental but overpowering significance, is just the point. For the historian who holds by this skeptical commonplace, there can be no talk of progress or decline; transience and error are constants. Nor can visions of apocalypse be taken seriously. Lowell begins his treatment of the 1968 elections by debunking his own dreams of the one move that would change things entirely, the leap from the window ledge; instead, along with Gramsci in a Roman prison, he affirms the even roll of time. "I saw the world is the same as it has been" (p. 173). And after the Republicans had dusted off that old contender Nixon, Lowell acknowledges the limits of the future: "What can be is only what will be" (p. 176). What will be is mediocrity. The task for most of us is simply accommodation, "to live with what was here."

For a poet, this viewpoint presents problems. The most obvious threat of this commonplace is stale language, to which Lowell did indeed succumb, as in the badly flawed octave of "Rome in the Sixteenth Century," where he speaks of "the hand of time." A list of such warts could be easily produced, and Donald Hall has done that.[9] A still more encompassing pall is generated by a thematic commonplace: Lowell is constantly tempted and often lured into a predictable, easy grimness. A number of poems come to no very surprising end with a funerary image of one sort of another. And the great are too often merely debunked or sullied:

> Did the fish leaping
> have leisure to see their waters had collapsed,
> that even Jefferson's philanthropy
> offered a great award for their extinction?
> Landthirst, whiskeythirst. We flip extinct matches
> at your rhinoceros hide . . . inflammable earth.   (p. 85)

This kind of journalistic exercise leads directly to a pouty bitterness, as here; or, worse, to hysteria before the icon of Lincoln:

> You may have loved underdogs and even mankind,
> this one thing made you different from your equals . . .
> you, our one genius in politics . . . who followed
> the bull to the altar . . . death in unity.
> *J'accuse, j'accuse, j'accuse, j'accuse, j'accuse!*
> Say it in American. Who shot the deserters?   (p. 88)

Those of the great or powerful who bear up to this poet's scrutiny are few, since the most noble, intelligent accomplishment is renunciation, not conquest, and the price of renunciation is so high that history provides mainly grounds for easy bitterness; a sense of measure is sometimes lost. The sestet of "The Death of Alexander" is clearest about this theme:

> No one was like him. Terrible were his crimes—
> but if you wish to blackguard the Great King,
> think how mean, obscure and dull you are,
> your labors lowly and your merits less—
> we know this, of all the kings of old,
> he alone had the greatness of heart to repent.   (p. 40)

Lowell's syntax here is strenuous, his language fully flexed, though the immediate subject bears the strain with difficulty. Lowell's poem might be thought to suggest that Alexander, at the end of his life, repented of his terrible crimes, and this of course was not quite the case. During his last campaign, Plutarch says, he relented on his plans to conquer India, only because his troops refused to cross the Ganges. Plutarch does not tell of any final repentence, but he does present a character who often repents of particular deeds, and this is Lowell's point. The most striking turnabout concerns the destruction of Thebes and the selling of the Thebans into slavery; Plutarch says that years later Alexander was distressed at his own harshness in this matter and made some amends. Likewise, Alexander repented of permitting Xerxes' palace to be set aflame and quickly had the fire extinguished. He was remorseful over the stringent terms of surrender he offered to Darius, when Darius' captive wife died in childbirth. Plutarch also tells of Alexander's despondent remorse after impulsively, drunkenly slaying Cleitus. And late in his reign, when it seemed that one of his officers, Antigenes, who had attempted to defraud the king and been banished from the court as a consequence, would kill himself rather than live in humiliation, Alexander rescinded the punishment.[10] Aside from these incidental second thoughts, Alexander made no repentence. Lowell is slightly misleading on this subject, though not at all inaccurate (accuracy must count for a lot in a poem like *History*); he seems to be caught up in a narrow stream of strong feeling. So few of the great have renounced power that the few who may possibly be seen as somehow renouncing it (Alexander, Charles V) are subjected to extreme defense, to weakly justified celebration.

The problems raised by Lowell's skepticism are serious, and they often enough overpower his writing, but the poetic payoff too was great. What this doubting view of human aspiration offered was a way of witnessing political struggle without being confined either to the loyalties of one party to a struggle or to a dull neutrality.

The March 2

Where two or three were flung together, or fifty,
mostly white-haired, or bald, or women . . . sadly
unfit to follow their dream, I sat in the sunset
shade of our Bastille, the Pentagon,
nursing leg- and arch-cramps, my cowardly,
foolhardy heart; and heard, alas, more speeches,
though the words took heart now to show how weak
we were, and right. An MP sergeant kept
repeating, "March slowly through them. Don't even brush
anyone sitting down." They tiptoed through us
in single file, and then their second wave
trampled us flat and back. Health to those who held,
health to the green steel head . . . to your kind hands
that helped me stagger to my feet, and flee.   (p. 149)

This is one of the poems that was hardly altered at all from one edition of the *Notebook* to the next, and for good reason; it came easily and he had it right from the start.[11] As early as 1952, Lowell was trying to write this way. He then told Allen Tate: "Nothing's harder than getting the unpretentious variety of letters or conversation into a poem. I've been turning out a lot lately, none of it good yet. It's either pedestrian, pompous or queer. But what I'm groping after really seems worth mastering."[12] The variety of diction and tone in this particular poem results not just from a freedom from any one stiff loyalty but more from an even-handedness that, given the circumstances, ought to be authoritative. The first line sets the casualness of his comrades (he once wrote "heaped," but "flung" better insists on the accidental formation of the group) against the biblical measure of the truly devout, those who gather together in God's name; the irony is gentle and only self-deflating. If this confederation does not quite measure up to its most dignified tradition, neither is the base language of television advertising—"to follow their dream"—quite right either; this group meets in that vast area in between. The tone here is arch, but nowhere flip; the difference between Lowell's archness and Merrill's is crucial. However light Lowell can seem, he is never far from earnestness: "our Bastille, the Pentagon . . . my cowardly, / foolhardy heart." Those appositions locate the seriousness. He admits, with amused sophistication, to fearful quaking but also claims, all the more forcefully for the line break, courage beyond prudence; insofar as the Pentagon is the Bastille to be stormed, one must be foolhardy—or, better, ironic—just to stay with the fight. The end of the first sentence, closing the octave, is above all else convincingly good-humored: "how weak / we were, and right." To speak of a political poem of 1967 as good-humored, urbane, and yet serious is high, rare praise.

Lowell's seriousness might possibly be questioned in the octave, but surely not in the sestet, where the poem turns and turns again, in the plainest of idioms. The trampling second wave of troops comes without warning or explanation, all the more surprising after the mincing first contingent—and also without reason. There is no suggestion of malice or of motive at all; the stunning charge is only part of the unexplained circumstances, perhaps even a goof.[13] Lowell renders no reproach, only an urbane but plain toast to "those who held" but also to a soldier who, out of simple human kindness that knows nothing of political encampments, broke ranks and helped him regain his footing.[14] The last turn, not altogether a surprise, is that having toasted those who held, he flees, recovering the sophisticated composure of the octave, where his cowardice was admitted in advance. The poem ends with comprehensive resolution, Lowell having given up nothing: not his irony about the composition of the demonstrators, his doubt about the possibility of success, his admission of his own weakness, or above all else his claim to a sensibility that, however urbane, includes admiration for simple virtues directly expressed—"your kind hands." The poem is richly sensitive, intelligent, and wholly conscionable, as rather few political poems, especially of 1967, are.

Lowell's skepticism often meant that he would write most approvingly of political figures when they moved out of the political arena. One way to make peace with the transience and confusion of the historical process is to renounce power; marriage is another way. In "Ulysses" he describes marriage as a "dark harbor of suctions and the second chance" (p. 159). Having failed to return home with his men, Odysseus has a second chance of attaining satisfaction: by living harmoniously, domestically, with Penelope. Political men are doomed to fail, only more or less miserably, and the poet who takes up their cause must write elegiacally about their defeat. But the one harbor Lowell treats altogether respectfully is domesticity. And having this area of human life to write about affirmatively greatly expands the range of *History* and deepens the pathos of many poems. Lowell once said that he wished those critics who speak of his being a violent poet would see that instead he is heartbreaking.[15] He was thoroughly right.

Sunrise

There is always enough daylight in hell to blind;
the flower of what was left grew sweeter for them,
two done people conversing with bamboo fans
as if to brush the firefall from the air—
Admiral Onishi, still a cult to his juniors,
the father of the Kamikazes . . . he became a fish-hawk
flying our armadas down like game;
his young pilots loved him to annihilation.
He chats in his garden, the sky is zigzag fire.
One butchery is left, his wife keeps nagging him to do it.
Husband and wife taste cup after cup of Scotch;
how garrulously they patter about their grandchildren—
when his knife goes home, it goes home wrong. . . .
For eighteen hours you died with your hand in hers.   (p. 132)

To write movingly about friends is one thing, a poet is more or less expected to do that; but to write movingly about national enemies, to find affection where none is expected, was a challenge Lowell loved to respond to. He found it easy to answer to circumstances that seem a bit off: that they should chat through their last bombing raid; that she should nag him to get on with the suicide, as she might have nagged him to look after the car; that they should drink scotch rather than saki; that the man responsible for relentless strategic attacks on American ships should kill himself incompetently. The fine thing was to be able to write that last line, as plain, direct, and characteristically sad as a line he wrote long before about a friend: "Ford, / you were a kind man and you died in want."[16]

Of all the poets who have tried their hand at political poetry in the last thirty-five years, Lowell is the most accomplished and surely the most ambitious. One measure of the quality of his effort is the coherence of the poetry around several expressly political beliefs; another is the cogency of the beliefs themselves. *History* embodies nothing so systematic or impersonal as an ideology, but the judgments and sympathies in the poems reveal a set of political ideas that bear on each other— which is perhaps only to say that this is a more intelligent than opinionated book.

Lowell's politics were focused on the appeal of imperial and revolutionary cultures: opulence and excitement. Rome, even as late as the fourth century, offered enough of "The Good Life"—

> . . . trees flower and leaves pearl with mist,
> fan out above them on the wineglass elms,
> life's frills and the meat of life: wife, children, houses;   (p. 50)

—to make the officers left in Rome after Constantine withdrew (330 A.D.) "anxious to please," at the expense of "vomiting purple in the vapid baths." Lowell made no bones about his own complicity in those experiences fostered by empires and revolutions—namely, quick changes.

> Marcus Cato 234–149 B.C.
>
> My live telephone swings crippled to solitude
> two feet from my ear; as so often and so often,
> I hold your dialogue away to breathe—
> still this is love, Old Cato forgoing his wife,
> then jumping her in thunderstorms like *Juppiter Tonans;*
> his forthrightness gave him long days of solitude,
> then deafness changed his gifts for rule to genius.
> Cato knew from the Greeks that empire is hurry,
> and dominion never goes to the phlegmatic—
> it was hard to be Demosthenes in his stone-deaf Senate:
> "Carthage must die," he roared . . . and Carthage died.
> He knew a blindman looking for gold
> in a heap of dust must take the dust with the gold,
> Rome, if built at all, must be built in a day.   (p. 43)

The poem begins with self-incrimination—for a common, domestic betrayal. His own willful deafness to his wife he compares to the deafness of demagoguery: Cato becomes a political genius when late in life he ceases listening to others, and of course the Roman senate was deaf as well. The imperialists hear not, and neither do they see, but they get the gold. What is all but stated is the painful truth that a poet trying to incorporate history from Eden to the Hudson must take a lot of dust for a little gold, and probably also betray the living ones he loves with insensitivity—a "petty decadence," he wrote in a draft of the opening line.[17]

As an alternative to imperial opulence and self-indulgence, history offers austerity, which Lowell regards as consistently loathsome. (In fact, as the case of Cato suggests, austerity too can be self-indulgent.) The barbarians from the north were provincials with nothing more urging them on than "the wind / . . . and a gently swelling birthrate" (p. 53). Lowell's criticism of America is not that it is imperialistic, like Rome, but that it is merely predatory where Rome was grand: "our bombers are clean-edged as Viking craft, / to pin the Third World to its burning house" (p. 53). The grandeur of Rome was sensual, monumental, not ideological; Mediterranean, not Nordic. The austerity of the ideologue, Saint-Just and Cato the Elder are the type, is odiously inhumane (p. 76). In an early draft of the poem he was then calling "Saint-Just, Saint of the Guillotine, 1767–1793," Lowell wrote: "It's deplorable that these men so young—still / unfinished, dead before the age 25 / should so violently force themselves on their / world."[18] Lowell's complaint about austerity is not just that its severity is cruel but also that civilization, taste, is corrupted by it.

Waterloo

A thundercloud hung on the mantel of our summer
cottage by the owners, Miss Barnard and Mrs Curtis
a sad picture, ⅔'s life-scale, removed now, and no doubt
scrapped as too raw and empire for our taste:
Waterloo, Waterloo! You could choose sides then:
the engraving made the blue French uniforms black,
the British Redcoats gray; those running were French—
an aide-de-camp, Napoleon's perhaps,
wore a cascade of overstated braid,
there sabered, dying, his standard wrenched from weak hands;
his killer, a helmeted, fog-gray dragoon—
six centuries, this field of their encounter,

kill-round of French sex against the English *no* . . .
La Gloire fading to *sauve qui peut* and *merde*.   (p. 78)

Cascade of braid, weakening hands, wicked dragoon—all of this was
perfect, in its camp way, and sadly missed. Imperial grandeur is
stagey, even crude, and indefensible in strictly moral terms (the land-
ladies are right about that), but the last line claims that protestant
moralism is ignoble and vulgar too in its effect on the French imagination. An empire is a conception of collective identity and of sublimity
and gradation. Without it the picture is gray.

Lowell will take the power and the glory every time (how else
should a poet choose?) even at the cost of championing Napoleon:
"Dare we say, he had no moral center?" (p. 77). Or, worse still, Stalin.

> Winds on the stems make them creak like manmade things;
> a hedge of vines and bushes—three or four
> kinds, grape-leaf, elephant-ear and alder,
> an arabesque, imperfect and alive,
> a hundred hues of green, the darkest shades
> fall short of black, the whitest leaf-back short of white.
> The state, if we could see behind the wall,
> is woven of perishable vegetation.
> Stalin? What shot him clawing up the tree of power—
> millions plowed under with the crops they grew,
> his intimates dying like the spider-bridegroom?
> The large stomach could only chew success. What raised him
> was an unusual lust to break the icon,
> joke cruelly, seriously, and be himself.   (p. 143)

This is an outrageous poem. Stalin, Lowell suggests, must not be
judged too harshly, for he too is part of the process. Like a leaf, he be-
haved according to his nature, looking only for success, and that is a
biological need. (In this poem, Lowell urges the English *no* to face up
to the shades of gray in the natural process.) Lowell does not push his
point quite as hard as he might have, or as he once did: the penultimate line, in the first three editions, spoke of "the usual lust"; and
unpublished typescripts refer to "our common lust to break the icon,"
and "Everyman's lust to smash clichés and icon."[19] As the poem went
through successive revisions, Lowell prudently drew back a bit from
the claim that Stalin was just doing what comes naturally to us all,
being an individual; the *History* version says that his daimon was unusual, but in no way unnatural. And that approximation to nature is

all that is needed, of course, to call into question the pertinence of moral judgment, for how can one judge a natural phenomenon? Lowell's avatars of power often seem to be nearly beyond judgment.

Lowell was always inclined to go a long way in sympathy with the powerful, at least in his poems (in the polemical pages of *Commentary* he was more careful to align himself with the insistent anti-Stalinism of New York intellectual circles by saying that "No cause is pure enough to support these faces" of Stalin and Mao on posters upheld by students marching in Rome.[20]) The leaders he found most despicable were not the tyrants or the conquerors—a redeeming word or two could be found for Attila, Timur, or Hitler; but for the wholly predictable "Leader of the Left" he had only bitter contempt (p. 150). Leaders ought, first, to be individuals; if they are humane as well, that is extra. Lowell, like most liberals, put a lot of stock in the ability of particular individuals to alter the course of history. In the winter of 1967, the editors of *Partisan Review* asked various intellectuals, "Does it matter who is in the White House? Or is there something in our system which would force any President to act as Johnson is acting?" To ideological leftists, the effects of American policy are determined by systematic priorities, not by individual executives. But to Lowell's mind, as to those of most liberals, "nothing could matter more than who is in the White House."

> It's not like the arts. Two very foolish novelists with opposed beliefs or temperaments would write equally foolish novels, but two equally foolish presidents would have widely differing effects on our lives, the difference between life and death. Yet a great president somehow honors his country, even if what he effects is debatable. I suppose Lincoln was our most noble and likable president. The country is somehow finer for having had him, yet much that he accomplished was terrifying and might have been avoided by the run-of-the-mill Douglas. I wish Stevenson had been elected. Maybe he would have done nothing (I don't believe this) but at least he would have registered what he was doing. I can't imagine him not losing a night's sleep over Hiroshima, even if he did drop the bomb. I think he might not have.[21]

A highly placed individual not only makes consequential decisions, determined partly by character, but he or she also serves as a measure (like *La Gloire*) of the state of the nation, its level of refinement. This is a poet's politics—Pound would have understood exactly. Lowell's

forlorn glance back fifteen years to the defeat of Adlai Stevenson by
Eisenhower shows how much this poet was of the intellectual, liberal,
Democratic Party. On the night when Stevenson lost in 1952, Lowell
wrote to Tate: "We're feeling blue about the election. Ike is a sort of
symbol to me of America's unintelligent side—all fitness, muscles,
smiles and banality. And Stevenson was so terribly better than one had
a right to expect. We too feel too hurt to laugh."[22]

The leader to whom Lowell was most attached in the late 1960s was
Eugene McCarthy. He followed McCarthy along part of the campaign
trail and spoke publicly on his behalf. After the California primary
went to Robert Kennedy, and Kennedy was shot down, Lowell realized
that McCarthy's chances of receiving the Democratic nomination
were nil, and he wrote a sentimental poem about his candidate:

> I love you so. . . . Gone? Who will swear you wouldn't
> have done good to the country, that fulfillment wouldn't
> have done good to you—the father, as Freud says:
> you? We've so little faith that anyone
> ever makes anything better . . . the same and less—
> ambition only makes the ambitious great.   (p. 175)

Lowell's is a melioristic argument based on the liberal notion of
progress, and a belief that simple qualities of character, such as ambition, change the world—this was a hard argument to render persua-
sive in 1968. Less than a month before writing the poem "For Eugene
McCarthy," he told a group of Yale seniors that "we need a government of order and liberty, a merciful and intelligent government."[23]
Mercy and human kindness were qualities Lowell thought worthy of
political consideration, and about this, as about the transience of life
and the error of all efforts, he could write well.

> Hell
>
> "Nth Circle of Dante—and in the dirt-roofed cave,
> each family had marked off its yard of space;
> no light except for coal fires laid in buckets,
> no draft of air except the reek, no water,
> no hole to hide the excrement. I walked,
> afraid of stumbling on the helpless bodies,
> afraid of going in circles. I lost the Fascist
> or German deserters I was hunting . . . screaming
> *vecchi,* women, children, coughing and cursing.

> Then hit my foot on someone and reached out
> to keep from falling or hurting anyone;
> and what I touched was not the filthy floor:
> a woman's hand returning my worried grasp,
> her finger tracing my lifeline on my palm." (p. 130)

This poem moves nicely toward its emblematic conclusion (Lowell rather liked to close poems with tableaux, and this is where the poem is most his own); its point is perfectly clear. Human mortality is the thing that can keep us from hitting absolute bottom. (J. Glenn Gray, Lowell's source for this poem, makes quite a different point about the experience: "I hastily withdrew my hand, but not before I felt a responsive clasp from hers, unmistakably amorous." Gray writes about the intimate connection between love and war, Aphrodite and Ares, not about mortality.[24]) Whether one is pursuing, fleeing, or wandering, the lifeline runs across all palms, waiting to be touched. How pointless to pursue ideological antagonists (or are they rather national adversaries? German deserters might well not be ideological Nazis) when all causes will have to be deserted in the end, when hell takes in people of all sorts, all coughing, cursing, and suffering their dark fate. Only pity will do.

McCarthy, he told the Yale students, was the candidate of mercy and intelligence. Nixon's victory brought out the other side of Lowell's feeling, the side, it has to be said, that makes the pathos compelling:

> *We must rouse our broken forces and save the country:*
> I even said this in public. The beaten player
> opens his wounds and hungers for the blood-feud
> hidden like contraband and loved like whisky. (p. 178)

There is that sharpness in Lowell that has no mercy to give, only vengeance to seek, "to find with joy this bitter ink is sweet."[25] The craving to lance—others, yes, but more movingly himself—this is what makes his very traditional expressions of mercy or pity, as in "Hell," powerful. Home he remembers as the place where "hurting others was as necessary as breathing, / hurting myself more necessary than breathing" (p. 125). But that need to feel the pain of sacrifice was not only private: "The liberal . . . / bites his own lip to warm his icy tooth" (p. 75), knowing that sacrifice is a sign of good faith, conscience.

In the late sixties, violence was commonly thought of politically—in terms more of effect than of justification. Lowell wrote of it politically but also personally, even when he seemed impersonal. Several poems in *History* denounce the cycle of "violence cracking on violence" (p. 145). One of these rhetorical efforts, "Can a Plucked Bird Live?" is especially poor: Lowell speaks of "raised hands" as the "guns that will not kill the possessor," as though imagining a classroom.[26] A better poem derives from a quite different conception of the matter; the initial adversative (unusual in Lowell) relegates the argument here to the status of a qualification only.

Sheep

But we must remember our tougher roots:
forerunners bent in hoops to the broiling soil,
until their backs were branded with the coin
of Alexander, God or Caesar—
as if they'd been stretched on burning chicken wire,
skin cooked red and hard as rusted tin
by the footlights of the sun—tillers of the desert!
Think of them, afraid of violence,
afraid of anything, timid as sheep
hidden in some casual, protective crevice,
held twelve dynasties to a burning-glass,
pressed to the levelled sandbreast of the Sphinx—
what were once identities simplified
to a single, indignant, collusive grin.

(p. 37)

This poem is ostensibly about the Jews who were held slaves by the Egyptians. Lowell depicts them as enduring a moronic existence because of their unwillingness to resort to political violence. The Egyptians and the Greeks left records of their existence, and their lives were full with the excitement of conquests and the sustenance of marriage, but these slaves left only the sand they tilled. Without violence there is no history. The memory of these "tougher roots" ought, the opening line suggests, fortify us with this lesson.

Parts of "Sheep" were originally in a poem, "1936," that later became "Anne Dick 1. 1936" and concerns Lowell's violent aggression toward his father. Specifically, the grin was worn by his parents in their aluminum coffins, and a marginal note reads: "Think of them afraid of violence, timid, as sheep."[27] The episode described in "Anne Dick 1" and referred to again in "Father" and "Mother and Father I" was plainly a source of guilt for Lowell. He was the aggressive adolescent, his father was the passive, then contemptible, old man. What he did not appreciate in 1936 was his father's restraint: "holding out the letter, / and demanding 'Did *you* write this?' / How could he show my mother's hand?"[28] Lowell came late to an appreciation of his father's generous restraint, acknowledged in "To Daddy," a disruptively lonely poem in *History* because it departs entirely from the sonnet form (even here there are three lines, for the three people in the family, of fourteen syllables each, out of deference to the form that is being violated). The fact that the political argument for violence, adumbrated in "Sheep," derives from a poem about his father's passivity suggests how tangled Lowell's thoughts were on this subject: at times, it seems, dignity can be maintained only through violence (this is the adolescent viewpoint in "Anne Dick 1," but it is suggested too in that word "indignant" at the close of "Sheep"); yet in the end restraint may sometimes show generosity and wisdom rather than sheepishness. Lowell never sorted out his thoughts on this subject, and the poems in *History* suffer as a consequence, for he sometimes writes about feelings for which he cannot take much responsibility.

The second and third poems on Israel are flirtatious in just this way. Lowell visited Israel in 1969 and writes of it as a traveler, but one who is a bit of a voyeur. He feels titillated by the aura of violence there, "I loved the country, her briskness, danger, / jolting between salvation and demolition"—though he admits, in a witty way, to thorough ambivalence about the justice of Israel's cause:

> I could have stayed there
> a month longer and even stood conscription,
> though almost a pacifist, and still unsure
> if Arabs are black . . . no Jew, and thirty years
> too old.   (p. 30)

The temptation to stay there "a month longer" indicates only how frivolous his remarks were at the time. (The beaming, presumptuous lines in "Israel 3"—"spend ten days there, or as I, three weeks, / you find the best and worst of countries" [p. 31]—are best forgotten altogether.) The first drafts of "Israel 2" give an indication of how Lowell came to be lured into such writing. The poem originally began: "I can't come out with the obvious true on any subject." And then a later draft: "These sidesteppings and obliquities unable / to take the obvious truth on any subject."[29] A still later one carried the subtitle, "Truth." The clever, light tone of lines 3–5 was not part of the early drafts, which had as lines 3 and 4: "almost a pacifist, by no means certain / the Arabs were wrong."[30] At one point, it seems, Lowell was explicit that his attraction to the violence of Israel was based on self-disgust at his lack of force and directness as a poet. That this is a poor reason for praising one party to an armed struggle, no one, least of all Lowell, needs to be reminded.

In the late sixties, many poets and other writers became camp followers. The most followed camp was full of students and poets like Denise Levertov and Robert Duncan, who wrote with greater sentiment than intelligence. Lowell felt the attractions of the student antiwar movement: "there's a new poetry in the air, it's youth's / patent, lust coolly led on by innocence" (p. 159). The students, like the Israelis, sometimes seemed to be having quite a time: "Joy! Indescribable apprehension. House-arrest / for women, children, foreigners and dogs" (p. 95)—that's the thrill of revolution. Yet, in the main, Lowell kept a healthy distance:

> The roaddust blinds us, tactics grow occult,
> the terror of spending the summer with a child,
> the revolution has happened in the mind,
> the fear of stopping—when the soul, even the soul
> of ruin, leaves a country, the country dies. . . .   (p. 155)

Too much traveling with the movement, Lowell knew, was corrupting of the spirit: the normal, domestic, parental orders ("spending the summer with a child") come to seem dull only to a jaded sensibility.

History was written by a poet who was in no hurry to escape from his own generation or class, and this is part of the book's integrity.

Romanoffs

Let's face it, English is a racist last ditch.
We plead guilty, the laws of history tell us
irrelevant things that happen never happened.
The Blacks and Reds survive, but who is White?
The word has fallen from the English tongue,
a class wiped out, their legacy, non-existence.
The new blade is too sharp, the old poisons.
Does arrogance give the ruler solitude
to study the desolation of his thought—
the starred cellar, where they shot and then dismembered
Tsar, Tsarina, the costly hemophilic children—
"Those *statesmen,*" said Lenin, "sent 16 million to death."
Such fairy stories beguiled our brainwashed youth—
we, the Romanoffs with much to lose.   (p. 99)

To understand history in terms of laws entails some blindness to all that does not conform to exclusive categories.[31] Those irrelevant things—mitigating circumstances, errors, good intentions, the lives of the superannuated classes—disappear from the Marxist field of vision, and even the distinctions they rest upon fade shyly from the language. What remains is the barren choice between Bolshevik and tsarist morality. Lowell's point is that the abdication of Nicholas II set a bad example. The younger members of the privileged classes, despite their own self-interest, are easily gulled into believing in the polarized categories of the Marxists. The exact strength of Lowell's conviction in this regard can best be measured, I think, by the weakness of the poem. Ironically, the poem is governed rather autocratically by a principle, or opinion. The argument is that principles and politics tend to simplify history, yet the poem too is simplified by a strenuous conviction. Lowell represents his adversaries as a debater would. "A racist last ditch," "fairy stories," "brainwashed"—from first to last, he proceeds intemperately. The poem displays no manner of judgment or attitude of restraint that might more fully represent the detailed richness of history. In a sense, this lack of restraint suggests the vigor if not the depth of Lowell's conviction; "Romanoffs" is a more willful than convincing poem.

Differences of class are regarded skeptically in *History*. A strictly economic definition of class is explicitly rejected in "Rome."

> Rome asked for the sun, as much as arms can handle—
> liquidation with principle, the proconsul's
> rapidity, coherence, and royal *we*. . . .
> Thus General Sulla once, again, forever;
> and Marius, the people's soldier, was Sulla
> doubled, and held the dirt of his low birth
> as licence from the gods to thin the rich—
> both pulled pistols when they heard foreign tongues,
> praised defoliation of the East. . . .
> Their faith was lowly, and their taxes high.
> The emperor was killed, his metier lived—
> Constantine died in office thanks to God.
> Whether we buy less or more has long
> since fallen to the archeologist's pick.   (p. 41)

Sulla (137–78 B.C.) rose to power over Rome largely by representing the patrician interests that Marius attacked. He was notorious for exterminating his friends along with his enemies cruelly and illegally.

Marius (156–86 B.C.) had no political program but gained a reputation as a friend of the people by condemning in public speeches the nobility for effeminacy. Not much better than his antagonist Sulla, Marius butchered his enemies when Sulla left Rome on an expedition; he died of a pleurisy, Plutarch suggests, that followed from profound despair at the prospect of Sulla's victorious return from the Mithridatic war.[32]

Two incidental points should be noticed about Lowell's use of these two Roman rulers. The first is that he must have chosen Sulla and Marius as instances of the weakness of a class analysis with a special appreciation for the complications involved. True enough, Sulla was the patrician of the two: his father was a Roman nobleman, and Marius' was a laborer from outside of Rome. Sulla, however, inherited nothing from his father and was commonly reproached for his lack of means. (He acquired wealth by courting a common but rich woman who—like Sulla's stepmother—left him her estate.) Plutarch in fact makes a special point of the dubeity of Sulla's class standing (*Sulla*, IV.1). (The complications Lowell must have had in mind could just as easily be ferreted out by word play, when he speaks of the dirt of Marius' low birth: *dirt, soil, sully, Sulla.*) The second point worth making here is that Lowell leaves chronology a bit murky in order to address his poem to modern prejudices. According to the usual modern pattern, the representative of the people follows the patrician; this is the way Lowell's poem seems to have it. In fact, though, Sulla began as lieutenant, then consul, and tribune, under Marius. Marius early came to resent Sulla's renown among the nobility, but despite his rankling at class distinctions he considered Sulla, a mere officer, beneath his rivalry. Sulla's reign followed that of Marius.

Notwithstanding these complications, Lowell is direct about his argument: whether a leader represents one class or another does not matter in an empire with a formulated ideology, the royal *we*. Under its own steam, an empire rolls over people, though the notion of class strife is often used to disguise this fact. What Sulla and Marius share, besides a propensity to cruelty, is suspicion of foreigners, disregard for colonized peoples. Marius scorned the use or study of Greek because it was the language of mere slaves. For firewood, Sulla destroyed the sacred groves, the academy, and the lyceum at Piraeus; at Epidaurus, Olympia, and Delphi he ransacked the sanctuaries for treasure. Lowell uses a Vietnam-era phrase, to bring his point round to its American target. The suggestion that Marius followed Sulla helps to direct attention toward the American claim that its own imperialism, based on an avowed belief in democracy, is more righteous than that of its totalitarian antagonists. Which class rules in whose name is not always clear and not so important, Lowell suggests; Constantine was a pagan ruler, but he legalized Christianity. Whether those who exercise power appreciate the integrity of members of other classes, citizens of other nations, or followers of other religions, this is the more important question in assessing rulers. In fact, however, cosmopolitanism is a class perogative in an American context, and in this sense Lowell is willing to invoke class distinctions. Or, more accurately, his urbane style presumes a fascination with foreign tongues that is traditionally displayed by the upper classes. The idioms of *History* make it clear that, however much he may have benefited from William Carlos Williams' writing, Lowell would strenuously oppose any form of exclusive ethnocentricism. He does invoke class distinctions, though less obviously than Merrill does, insofar as they can be defined in terms of taste rather than income. Merrill and Lowell would agree that canons of taste measure humaneness more accurately than egalitarianism can.

From 1966 to 1976, Lowell lived in New York, on the West Side (he gives his address in *History*). He once spoke of having had his great years as a writer there.[33] Then he moved to England, divorced Elizabeth Hardwick, and married Lady Caroline Blackwood. His decade in New York included the years of *History*. During the 1950s, we have seen, New York had strong claims to being a literary and intellectual center, but thereafter the draw of the city weakened steadily until now it is hard to conceive of a single center to American culture. It was exactly 1967 to 1973, the years Lowell was working on *History*, when the political consensus was most strongly shaken, mainly by the antiwar movement; it was a commonplace then that the center of political authority was displaced from the culture at large. Lowell's book, more than any other, attempts to hold a single center. He knew personally many of the writers and figures who were most associated with New York cultural life. "Do you only suffer for other famous people . . . ?" he is asked in "Publication Day" (p. 182). (An incidental example: his anonymous friend "Across Central Park" [p. 144] is Jacqueline Kennedy Onassis.[34]) This book is about his involvement both with the ideas, books, and historical figures customarily thought to embody the European and American intellectual traditions, and with the political and cultural figures of his generation. In 1967, when he was writing the first version of *History*, Lowell was asked what the split between the Johnson administration and American intellectuals was likely to mean. He answered cleverly: "I don't know what the split between the President and the intellectuals *means*."[35] Of course he knew the intent of the question, and he had six months in prison in 1943–44 to think about what it meant to dissent from a President's policies. He had publicly declined a presidential invitation to the White House in 1965 in protest of Johnson's Vietnam policy. But he also put his letter declining the invitation through at least five drafts and then gave it to the *New York Times*.[36] Lowell knew in 1965 and in 1967 that, however much intellectuals might dissent from the administration, they were very much involved with it, and Lowell would never have had it any other way. One small bit of memorabilia he hung on to from the 1968 McCarthy campaign: a Fairmont Hotel desk slip to Lowell conveying the message that Senator Robert Kennedy had tried to call five days before he was assassinated in Los Angeles.

Lowell's *History* is a thoroughly centrist book, though far from an uncritical one. One of its most scathing poems is "The New York Intellectual" who writes ponderously for Irving Howe's journal and in Lowell's eyes is a "sick provincial," thoroughly "out-of-it" (p. 151). The myopia of New Yorkers Lowell knew well, but he had not given up on them. *History*'s closest antecedent must be the *Cantos* (acknowledged by Lowell in "Cicero, the Sacrificial Killing"), where Pound also gives a digest of the piths and gists of the best writers and thinkers as he saw them—and that is just the point of divergence too. For Pound was no centrist: his notion of the best that had been thought, said, and done—Kung, Cavalcanti, John Adams, de Gourmont—was strikingly at odds with the consensus view—Mortimer Adler's, say.[37] In 1968, writing about the assassination of Martin Luther King, Lowell brought "Two Walls" to a close with a line Pound, to his credit, never could have written: "I lie here, heavily breathing, the soul of New York" (p. 169). That, incredibly enough, was Lowell's ambition for a time.

And his success was great, in an inauspicious moment. Lowell knew that the notion of an American center was dubious during those years, and he deals with the doubts well. In his own background the question of provinciality came up early, when he left Harvard to study with Allen Tate and then with John Crowe Ransom at Kenyon College, for Tate and Ransom were, during the 1930s, like Yvor Winters, provincials on principle. Lowell's best poem to Tate recalls a visit in March 1937,[38] when Europe was having its "last fling of impotence and anger":

> above your fire the blood-crossed flag of the States,
> a print of Stonewall Jackson, your shotgun half-cocked . . .

to shatter into the false windmills of the age.
The cornwhisky was whiter than the purest water;
you told dirty, stately setpieces in Cumberland patois;
you said your tenant with ten children had more art
than Merrill Moore. "Do they expect me to leave the South
to meet frivolous people like Tugwell and Mrs. Roosevelt?"
Ford, playing Russian Banker in the half-light, nagging,
"Don't show your cards, my dear Tate . . . it isn't done."

(p. 120)

Tate's cards do show. In March 1937, European statesmen and those close to power in America, such as Rexford Tugwell and Eleanor Roosevelt, faced problems of great consequence. England was then beginning a feverish armament program; the British admiralty in March announced alternative routes to India, in the event of war with Italy in the Mediterranean. At the beginning of the month, the French socialist premier, Leon Blum, had to initiate a breathing spell on social reforms because the treasury was empty; his government fell three months later. On March 18, Pope Pius issued an anticommunist encyclical, and three days later another one denouncing the Nazis. In Spain, the loyalists successfully repelled 40,000 well-armed insurgent forces in the siege of Madrid and then defeated the Italian-Spanish insurgent army at Guadalajara, bringing Franco's prestige to a low point. (In April Franco consolidated the rightists in one party, and Guernica was destroyed.) The Chinese government was unifying its forces in preparation for the war with Japan that broke out in July. At home, the major of New York, Fiorello La Guardia, denounced Hitler and the Nazi government in terms that aroused the fury of the German press and caused Secretary of State Hull to express his official regrets to the Nazi government. Tate's statesmanship, Lowell suggests, was then confined to prepared tales ("tall" ones, the 1969 and 1970 editions say) related in an adopted dialect. Tate, like his rifle, was half-cocked, Lowell thinks, looking back. An early manuscript draft of this poem refers to the .22 rifle as "a symbol for Allen's leftist cronies from New York."[39]

All of Tate's "moonshine" (which became "cornwhisky" only with the 1973 edition) is the defensiveness and, in this particular historical moment, frivolity of a sulking provincial. Tate lived in Greenwich Village from 1924 until 1928, when he left for Europe. Returning in 1930, he expected to do freelance work in New York but was disappointed by the city he found, especially by the leftist tone to the literary scene; after a month he left for Tennessee. Tate's brother gave him a farm near Clarksville, overlooking the Cumberland River. In the thirties Tate became involved in the literary-political movement known as agrarianism. And Lowell is struck by Tate's unwillingness to meet with the New Yorker Tugwell (professor of economics at Columbia, contributing editor to *New Republic*) who was then the undersecretary of agriculture. Tate seemed to be enjoying a pout at a time when the country was in a political, economic, and specifically agricultural crisis. While the major nations of the world were arming against each other, Tate was imaginatively armed against his countrymen. Lowell would not mean to suggest, though, that his mentor was an isolated crank: Tate represented a genuine constituency with a deep history and place in the national consciousness; in mid-April 1937, the U.S. House passed an antilynching bill, which seems as odd in any global chronology of 1937 as Tate does surrounded by the paraphernalia of the confederacy. Two weeks later Congress approved an act confirming the permanent neutrality of the United States. Provinciality was then, as now, a national shortcoming, an especially costly one for those who are left trying, with little support, to hold the center.

In a still more important poem on the same subject, "Munich 1938, John Crowe Ransom," Ransom fares no better than Tate did.

> Hitler, Mussolini, Daladier, Chamberlain,
> that historic confrontation of the great—
> voluble on one thing, they hated war—
> each lost there pushing the war ahead twelve months.
> Was it worse to choke on the puke of prudence,
> or blow up Europe for a point of honor? . . .
> John Crowe Ransom, Kenyon College, Gambier, Ohio,
> looking at primitive African art on loan:
> gleam-bottomed warriors of oiled brown wood,
> waving broom-straws in their hands for spears;
> far from the bearded, bronze ur-Nordic hoplites
> of Athens and Sparta, not distant from their gods.
> John said, "Well, they may not have been good neighbors,
> but they haven't troubled the rest of the world."   (p. 127)

Earlier printings of the poem carried the date 22 August 1968—the day after the Russians moved into Czechoslovakia. The hoplites, the African warriors, the Nazis, and then the Russians stand in one line. Daladier, Chamberlain, and Ransom are associated with a policy of appeasement resting on a provincial presupposition: that the historical process can be confined to one locale—the Sudetan, Africa, Gambier.

Lowell knew, as Ransom apparently did not, that for the imperialist there is no such thing as the rest of the world; aggression is finally global by its own logic. The responsibility of the statesman is finally not so different from that of the poet or man of letters: to see life whole. Lowell's poems criticizing his early teachers are not surprisingly about his own poetic ambition. The history of modern literature, in fact, revolves around a number of great provincials—Hardy, Yeats, Lawrence, Joyce—but how tempting still to think, along with Arnold (and Whitman), that there is one especially advantageous place to stand, at the cultural center, if one hopes to see the whole.

About the time that the first version of *History,* then called *Notebook 1967–68,* appeared, Lowell went on record as having "never been New Left, Old Left, or liberal. I wish to turn the clock back with every breath I draw, but I hope I have the courage to occasionally cry out against those who wrongly rule us."[40] At the time it seemed to some that he had committed his writing to the New Left cause, though now the preoccupations of *History* seem far closer to those of the liberal consensus of the 1950s. The poet who wishes to speak only from time to time as the moral conscience of the body politic bears no systematic opposition to the authority of his government; he rather objects to some of the exercises of that authority. Lowell's interest in individual leaders, his discounting of their particular ideologies and of their class, his effort to psychologize the positions of those who were plainly illiberal in their loyalties, his hope for some increment of progress and a modicum of compassion—these are the concerns of the avowed liberals of Lowell's generation. I make this point not to disparage Lowell's achievement, although the term "liberal" has indeed come to be used casually as a disparagement. Nor can this designation have an especially exact significance. On the contrary, from the end of World War II until the early 1960s, it was a usefully inclusive term for identifying the capacious center of American political opinion.

The years 1967–68, when Lowell was beginning work on *History,* were perhaps the height of the hunting season on liberals. After the Democrats chose that old liberal Hubert Humphrey in 1968, it was hard to hold the liberal ground with banners flying; for a while, the center of American politics was thoroughly debased in the eyes of many influential academic and literary intellectuals. That Lowell would then undertake his magnum opus in the liberal vein shows a kind of firm integrity that, to the literary historian who weighs the achievement of one poet against the mass of his or her contemporaries, looks especially impressive. How common it was in the late 1960s simply to assume that the center was uninhabitable.

Political positions have to be assessed in terms of their practicality, humaneness, consistency, inclusiveness, and justice, surely. American liberalism has been subjected to severe criticism on most of these grounds in the last fifteen years or so. This is not the place to defend liberalism from such attacks. But Lowell's work does demonstrate, to my judgment quite soundly, that postwar liberalism had sufficient range of vision and intelligence, and commanded enough emotional power, to enable a poet of unusual ability to write the sort of book that guarantees him the status of a major poet. It cannot be said that American liberalism has had no major imaginative embodiment in the last thirty-five years. It has indeed its *History,* which is one of the most successful book-length poems of this period (Dorn's *Slinger* is the other, I believe). And the imaginative command of an ideology must also be measured when an ideology is assessed by historians, especially by literary historians.

7 · Pop Culture

Between high and popular culture falls a shadow that has left much of the discussion of this subject by American intellectuals rather gloomy. The editors of *Partisan Review* saw that "many writers and intellectuals now [in 1952] feel closer to their country and its culture," and yet "the artist and intellectual who wants to be a part of American life is faced with a mass culture which makes him feel that he is still outside looking in."[1] *Partisan Review* had a special stake in this subject. Its editors were remarking a change in the cultural climate since the 1930s, when pages of that journal and of others on the left, had discussed the cultural promise of the working classes in America, should they ever attain rightful access to the appropriate institutions. In the early 1950s the signs of promise were not bright. American workers were prosperous as never before and had unprecedented access to education, museums, symphony orchestras, to European literature in translation, to inexpensive reprints of classic literature, yet this was the decade of *Pillow Talk*, the *Hit Parade*, and *Peyton Place*. "Why is Brooklyn," one writer asked, "so much richer and bigger, so much more literate and educated—and with more leisure—so much less productive culturally than was Florence?"[2] The readers of *Partisan Review* knew that intellectuals had to face the fact—not at all hard at the time—that the 1930s optimism of the left was ill founded. The more painful and equally pressing conclusion then seemed to be that the quality of mass culture revealed an embarrassing limitation of liberal democracy.

Part of what troubled many intellectuals then was the homogenization of the national culture, as Dwight Macdonald put it.[3] "Mass culture is not the culture of a class or group throughout history," one sociologist remarked, but "the culture of nearly everybody today, and of nearly nobody yesterday."[4] Political egalitarianism had been a widely shared objective among intellectuals, certainly since 1930, but cultural egalitarianism seemed a nightmare. Leslie Fiedler argued that in fact the proliferation of mass culture was part of a class war: the petty bourgeoisie was attempting to achieve cultural hegemony by driving out the high and low art "on either side of their average own."[5] According to Herbert Gans some years later, the question was "which culture and whose culture should dominate in society, and represent it as the societal or national culture in the competition between contemporary societies and in the historical record of cultures or civilizations."[6] There can be no doubt about who won the war. Kojak and Rockford, dubbed into zombies, can be seen on German television every week, and one's francs are prevailed upon by chanteurs doing Bob Dylan in the corridors of the Paris Metro. Popular culture is global, but Americans have some priority in the field; Southern California and Las Vegas seem to have captured the imagination of the world.

Even in 1952 the issue of the struggle was obvious. The only real uncertainty then, about which there was some range of opinion, concerned the proper attitude of writers and intellectuals toward the cultural hegemony of the lower-middle class.[7] Philip Rahv concluded dismally that "if under present conditions we cannot stop the ruthless expansion of mass-culture, the least we can do is to keep apart and refuse its favors."[8] A few years earlier Irving Howe, with greater wisdom, had said that "So long as we live in a class society, mass culture will remain indispensible even to those who have learned to scorn it . . . The price of public experience may be a kind of contamination, but in view of the alternative it is not too high a price to pay."[9] Delmore Schwartz confessed to "the pious hope of a possibility" that "universal education, in combination with the very mechanical agencies which make mass culture profitable, may create and sustain a genuine educated class partly by the mere increase in the number of intelligent readers."[10] For the popular culture itself, little appreciation or pleasure was expressed (or confessed); Schwartz's optimism rested on the possibility that popular culture could enable something else to thrive.[11]

Looking back after eighteen years, Irving Howe noted that with the end of the 1950s the debate about mass culture simply stopped. "For years hardly a word could be found in the advanced journals about what a little earlier had been called a crucial problem of the modern era."[12] Howe had no regret about the silence, though, because the later phases of the mass-culture critique, which began with Clement Greenberg's famous essay "From Avant-Garde to Kitsch" (1939) in

Partisan Review, seemed to him hypocritical and politically distracting anyway: "If you couldn't stir the proletariat to action, you could denounce Madison Avenue in comfort."[13] Gans has claimed that the debate subsided because intellectuals in the 1960s acquired greater income, power, and status; they had little reason to snap at the hands that fed them better than ever.[14] At just the moment when sociologists, historians, and literary critics quieted down, American poets, to their credit, began to work out a variety of attitudes toward popular culture that went far beyond the scope of the 1950s debate, however flawed some of the poems on this subject may be.

The point here is that poets have recently tried to accommodate their art to a culture dominated by a mass, or lower-middle class, imagination. Very far from condescending to this part of American culture, or even from building bridges to an adversary, the poems I will discuss explore those ways in which the poets' imaginations are indeed part of that mass culture from which the New York intellectuals of the 1950s felt so removed.

Incorporating popular cultural subjects into poetry directly involved questions of poetic style. Most poets, like O'Hara and Ashbery, sought stylistic techniques somehow modeled on their subjects. But others, such as Hecht, Hollander, and Cassity, used the concentrations and emphases of traditional poetic techniques as a source of measurement—sometimes critical, sometimes fond—of their subjects. And these, I think, are the richer poems, for they successfully and courageously hold pop culture up to the test of comparison with that culture represented by the masters of English poetry.

The date 17 July 1959 will serve to mark the moment when the issue was taken up in poetry. "The Day Lady Died," Frank O'Hara's well-known elegy for Billie Holiday, begins:

> It is 12:20 in New York a Friday
> three days after Bastille day, yes
> it is 1959 and I go get a shoeshine
> because I will get off the 4:19 in Easthampton
> at 7:15 and then go straight to dinner
> and I don't know the people who will feed me
>
> I walk up the muggy street beginning to sun
> and have a hamburger and a malted and buy
> an ugly NEW WORLD WRITING to see what the poets
> in Ghana are doing these days[15]

Hamburger indeed. The contours seem to have been shaved off the experience the poem reports. Poetry from New York or Ghana, Verlaine, Hesiod, Brendan Behan, or Genet (lines 14–18): the time, the place (trains named after "points in time," as they say), even the language matters little. The whole world and all of history is right there in Manhattan, on 17 July 1959, for the buying, piece by piece, of Strega, Gauloises, Picayunes (lines 21–25). Distance is reduced by the pulp press, which is dominated by the lower-middle class (the *New York Post,* not the *Times*); poetry, modernism, these international zones of experience have no special force here. All art is brought close not by tradition, as Eliot had said, but by mass production, cheapness.

All principles for arraying emphasis and registering discriminations have been flattened. The rhyme in the third line is only a chance thing, and the first of the poem's nineteen "and"s (in the same line) makes an arbitrary connection. And as syntax and prosody go, so does social order: O'Hara says that he will be the dinner guest of strangers that night and then recounts (ll. 14–21) his efforts to find suitable gifts for Patsy and Mike, who are made to seem his hosts.[16] This easy familiarity, O'Hara suggests—Patsy, Mike, Linda—should not be too easily sniffed at; the reference to the well-known translator of Homer invokes an ancient sanction for gift giving and the entertaining of strangers—and for paratactic syntax. The power of the poem is in its inadvertent, banal approach to an earnest genre: the subject of the elegy does not even emerge until the poem is nearly complete, as though the great theme (death) can now only be talked around:

> . . . a NEW YORK POST with her face on it
>
> and I am sweating a lot by now and thinking of
> leaning on the john door in the 5 SPOT
> while she whispered a song along the keyboard
> to Mal Waldron and everyone and I stopped breathing.
>
> (ll. 25–29)

Beside the example of Billie Holiday, well eroded by the time she worked with Mal Waldron (1957–1959), *Partisan Review* complaints about the difficulty of making art in a culture so leveled by mass culture as America was in 1959 sound disingenuous. For most of her career, her audiences were small and sometimes difficult of access. In 1947 the New York Police Department denied her a cabaret licence, as many other jazz musicians were similarly punished for drug offenses. (During her final illness, she was arrested in her New York hospital room for illegal possession of drugs.) She was a singer who knew well how difficult reaching a fit audience might be, but even in her decline, O'Hara says, she took one's breath away and this elegy is literally directed at the renovation of that cliché of mass-culture advertising, the "breath-taking performance." The poem ends with much more than the apparent universal swoon for a great torch singer. "Everyone," he says in the last line, suggesting that a poet might well take pleasure in 1959 from the fact that some art can directly reach us all, and that nearly all art, African, French, and Irish, can be had now for the asking. The Bastille had been stormed, and if it turned out to be emptier than expected only the expectations deserve criticism. New York, even the *New York Post,* was moving still.

One year after O'Hara's elegy appeared, John Hollander wrote "Movie-Going," cutting an urbane middle path among New Yorkers. O'Hara was frankly anti-intellectual and camp about films. In a poem somewhat like his Billie Holiday elegy, he comes across a headline indicating that Lana Turner had collapsed. O'Hara's short, slight poem leads up to the jokey last line: "oh Lana Turner we love you get up."[17] Movies are wonderfully immediate, lively, and vulgar for O'Hara—not serious, in the *Partisan Review* sense.[18] To Irving Howe, they seemed simply trivial: "In the theatre . . . one is seldom brought to those heights of consciousness that a genuine work of dramatic art can arouse . . . The movie house is a psychological cloakroom where one checks one's personality."[19] Hollander takes up his subject in strictly metropolitan terms: "Drive-ins are out, to start with," for they are suburban of course; but beyond that the question of being in or out is a matter of style, of what is acceptable to the urban sensibility.[20] Easy enough to clown delight with the tawdry excesses of theater decoration; that much is almost taken care of by the prosody alone. The poem is comprised of mock-epic iambic hexameter lines tacked together in couplets by offrhymes—always a bit overdone and deliberately off in style; the form expresses not a critical judgment but Hollander's good-natured approach to the subject. He goes further in justifying the movies, only a little facetiously, in terms of their intellectual and moral effects. The poem ought to have been published in *Partisan Review* (for which Hollander had been regularly reviewing poetry since 1955).

> And having frequently to cope
> With the abominable goodies, overflow
> Bulk and (finally) exploring hands of flushed
> Close neighbors gazing beadily out across glum

> Distances is, after all, to keep the gleam
> Alive of something rather serious, to keep
> Faith, perhaps, with the City.

Hollander writes about this subject with the New York intellectuals apparently over his shoulder, so carefully does he head off objections. The inconveniences of moviegoing, he suggests, are exactly those of city living: a glut of cheap satisfaction, the push of crowds, routine molestation, and a gloomy view of the future. The poem is not quite an allegory, certainly no epic or elegy, though the moves of all these literary kinds keep the poem agitated. Hollander works hard to hold the poem to two planes at once.

> Never ignore the stars, of course. But above all,
> Follow the asteroids as well: though dark, they're more
> Intense for never glittering; anyone can admire
> Sparklings against a night sky, but against a bright
> Background of prominence, to feel the Presences burnt
> Into no fiery fame should be a more common virtue.
> For, just as Vesta has no atmosphere, no verdure
> Burgeons on barren Ceres, bit-players never surge
> Into the rhythms of expansion and collapse, such
> As all the flaming bodies live and move among.
> But there, more steadfast than stars are, loved for their being,
> Not for their burning, move the great Characters: see
> Thin Donald Meek . . .

Then follows the requisite procession of demigods. The lesson—and the poem is cast as a series of lessons ("One must always be"; "the second feature . . . will teach you"; "helping us learn"; "Never ignore"; "Try to see"; "Finally, remember always")—has everything to do with the urban life. Settling, coping, persevering, noticing—these are the proudly modest metropolitan virtues, learned largely because of the corruptions of popular culture. Hollander turns on its head the common complaint that the popular arts work by what Wordsworth (referring to Gothic novels) termed "gross and violent stimulants" that eliminate the mind's ability to make subtle discriminations.[21] On the contrary, Hollander argues, because of the very grossness of popular culture, the glut of it, and one's repeated exposure to formulas (or even to the same movie), one's attention turns, as a connoisseur's does, to the surprises in small details, the "asteroids" in their "humbly noble orbits." Popular culture is greedy and demands immersion. Even the most innocent minds, however, Hollander shows, sustain this greediness only by finding distinctions, observing grades, where none seem called for. An art that teaches careful measure, even by coarse means, deserves some praise, if only a playfully overdone elegy.

The poem begins to draw to its close with a catalogue of West Side moviehouses, many of which have declined into supermarkets. "Honor them all," Hollander says,

> Remember how once their splendor blazed
> In sparkling necklaces across America's blasted
> Distances and deserts: think how, at night, the fastest
> Train might stop for water somewhere, waiting, faced
> Westward, in deepening dusk, till ruby illuminations
> Of something different from Everything Here, Now, shine
> Out from the local Bijou, truest gem, the most bright
> Because the most believed in, staving off the night
> Perhaps, for a while longer with its flickering light.

> These fade. All fade, Let us honor them with our own fading
> sight.

Hollander has his tongue in his cheek, but not so firmly that he cannot praise. The poem is designed to celebrate the institutions of popular culture, or rather to honor them in retrospect, respectful in part of their authority. Looking back, the old movies seem quaint, like steam locomotives at a water tank. Looking west from New York, one can speak of the landscape, altogether conventionally, as "America's blasted / Distances and deserts." Imagining further one could say that America's future lay with Mars: "parched, / Xanthine desolations, dead Cimmerian seas, the far / Distant past preserved in the blood-colored crusts; fire / And water both remembered only." The movies then seem a fragile tie, all the more valuable for being fragile, to a quaint past and apocalypse the only future. So great was the power of the New York critique of mass culture that Hollander was driven to this overly wrought framing of "the colors of our inner life." To speak well of the movies, one need not fret about nuclear apocalypse, desert landscapes, or even the dull hollowness of life itself, for these terms, however clinching they seem to a debate, reflect a stagey, blunt extremism that undermines the cause of moderation espoused so artfully, thoughtfully, and warmly throughout most of this fine poem.

The truth of the New York mass-culture critique has certainly not been lost on poets. Hollander and O'Hara both, in different ways,

seem to write almost deliberately against Howe and others. Poems
about popular films imply a special reason for writing about the institutions of pop culture, for the movies enjoy a breadth of audience and
force of influence that poets sometimes envy. However, poets of the
last twenty years have been challenged, as the critics were not, to
write sympathetically of popular culture without the illusions of the
1930s. The challenge to poets was genuine—the drafting of a meaningful peace between high culture and the American lower-middle
class—and their success in meeting it, I think, less so. Balancing admiration and criticism when speaking of institutions, like moviehouses, is an altogether familiar activity. One can easily enough
admire a potentiality or an objective and at the same time criticize a
product; failures can be attributed to what Kenneth Burke spoke of in
1937 as "the institutionalization of the imaginative."[22] Blame it on the
system.

Where the poets went well beyond the New York intellectual critique of mass culture was in writing about the people who thrive on
pop culture, not just about the institutions themselves. Writing about
people can be different, though the line between individuals and institutions sometimes wavers. The balancing act is more precarious
where people are involved because the ultimate judgment is taken to
heart. Although the difficulties in writing well about the imagination of
the lower-middle class have not been resolved, a number of very good
poems about the people to whom popular culture is addressed have
appeared in the last decade. Poems about people start with an edge
over those about institutions in the sense that human sympathy is almost conventional in poetry, except in satire.

Elizabeth Bishop's poem "Filling Station" (originally in the *New
Yorker*) gives a sense of how removed poets felt from the people in
1955—how removed and yet curious too. "Oh, but it is dirty!" she
begins, as though reacting to more than the filling station itself.

> Father wears a dirty,
> oil-soaked monkey suit
> that cuts him under the arms,
> and several quick and saucy
> and greasy sons assist him
> (it's a family filling station),
> all quite thoroughly dirty.[23]

She manages, altogether characteristically, to implicate herself in a
class perspective on these people—and this is mere explication, not

criticism, of the poem. They are workers simply, soaked in their labor as in oil. The father, in his monkey suit, appears vaguely bestial, and the sons, saucy and greasy, a little impertinent to her view. The question that cracks open the poem disturbs just this perspective: "Do they live in the station?" Are there any pesonal lives in this family filling station? Some comic books on a doily covering a taboret next to a begonia: these are the icons of their lives beyond labor—"extraneous," as she says.

> Somebody embroidered the doily.
> Somebody waters the plant,
> or oils it, maybe. Somebody
> arranges the rows of cans
> so that they softly say:
> ESSO—SO—SO—SO
> to high-strung automobiles.
> Somebody loves us all.

Probably neither the father nor the sons embroidered the doily or watered the plant. The missing person, of course, is the never named mother, who stands for a whole dimension of the working life that was not immediately apparent to Bishop. Care, attention, delicacy, and a desire for color keep the comic books in place. Yes, somebody—a mother—loves even the dirty ones. But Bishop herself writes as an observer, respectful in the end, but admittedly and contentedly distant.

The passing of time alone has done little to make this distance seem less great; poets continue to stand off from this subject. In 1979 Anthony Hecht published an extraordinary narrative poem, "The Short End," focused on an alcoholic housewife's last moments of consciousness. He writes about Shirley Carson as a novelist might, from above, seeing nearly all, and from inside, feeling the memories. The distance between Hecht and his character, which (by virtue of narrative conventions) expands or contracts at his will, does not limit his access to her imagination, his professed understanding of her. For him, she is a social type, lower-middle class; her husband Norman was once a salesman but

> These days he came home from the body shop
> He owned and operated, its wall thumb-tacked
> With centerfolded bodies from *Playboy*,
> Yielding, expectant, invitational,
> Came home oil-stained and late to find her drunk

> And the house rank with the staleness of dead butts.
> Staleness, that's what it was, he used to say
> To himself, trying to figure what went wrong . . .[24]

This predictable irony ("owned and operated") holds Shirley and Norman at an assured remove from Hecht's full sympathies, and those of his readers, and permits him the space he usually requires to display his mastery of the art of elaboration.[25]

But Hecht does take Shirley seriously and has a frank go at the problem worrying Norman, "what went wrong." The decor at the Carsons' gets the poem underway:

> "Greetings from Tijuana!" on a ground
> Of ripe banana rayon with a fat
> And couchant Mexican in mid-siesta,
> Wrapped in a many-colored Jacobin
> Serape, and more deeply rapt in sleep,
> Head propped against a phallic organ cactus
> Of shamrock green, all thrown against a throw
> Of purple on a Biedermeier couch . . .

Shamrocks, Biedermeier, Jacobins, and Mexicans together evoke a rootlessly international taste, familiar and plainly incoherent, as Hecht's no less international idiom is not. Like Bishop, Hecht wants to penetrate to the personal life behind the vulgarity, but in this poem the woman is no missing person. Shirley's story is taken back to her honeymoon in Atlantic City, where Norman was obliged to spend his days at a convention for traveling salesmen. Shirley passed the days surveying how little the boardwalk had to offer—bumpum cars, bowling alleys, and "Sophisticated Nightwear For My Lady." The central section of the poem recounts an evening encounter with some of Norman's coarse colleagues and their companions. One salesman, Maurice, "Whose nickname, it appeared, was Two Potato," took charge of the evening.

> Two Potato proclaimed himself
> Their host, and winked at them emphatically.
> There followed much raucous, suggestive toasting,
> Norman was designated "a stripling kid,"
> And ceremoniously nicknamed "Kit,"
> And people started calling Shirley "Shirl,"
> And "Curly-Shirl" and "Shirl-Girl." There were displays

Of mock-tenderness towards the young couple
And gags about the missionary position,
With weak, off-key, off-color, attempts at singing
"Rock of Ages," with hands clasped in prayer
And eyes raised ceilingward at "cleft for me,"
Eyes closed at "let me hide myself in thee,"
The whole number grotesquely harmonized
In the manner of a barbershop quartet.
By now she wanted desperately to leave
But couldn't figure out the way to do so
Without giving offense, seeming ungrateful;
And somehow, she suspected, they knew this.
Two Potato particularly seemed
Aggressive both in his solicitude
And in the smirking lewdness of his jokes
As he unblushingly eyed the bride for blushes
And gallantly declared her "a good sport,"
"A regular fella," and "the little woman."
She knew when the next round of drinks appeared
That she and Norman were mere hostages
Whom nobody would ransom. Billy Jim asked
If either of them knew a folk-song called
"The Old Gism Trail," and everybody laughed,
Laughed at the plain vulgarity itself
And at the Carsons' manifest discomfort
And at their pained, inept attempt at laughter.
The merriment was acid and complex.
Felix it was who kept proposing toasts
To "good ol' Shirl an' Kit," names which he slurred
Both in pronunciation and disparagement
With an expansive, wanton drunkenness
That in its license seemed soberly planned
To increase by graduated steps until
Without seeming aware of what he was doing
He'd raise a toast to "good ol' Curl an' Shit."
They managed to get away before that happened,
Though Shirley knew in her bones it was intended,
Had seen it coming from a mile away.
They left, but not before it was made clear
That they were the only married couple present,
That the other men had left their wives at home,
And that this was what conventions were all about.

> The Carsons were made to feel laughably foolish,
> Timid and prepubescent and repressed,
> And with a final flourish of raised glasses
> The "guests" were at last permitted to withdraw.

This episode, in a sense, does explain what went wrong for Shirley and Norman. Their brief exposure to the manners of traveling salesmen was indication enough of how little the Carsons' world held out for Shirley. The story is told with loathing and contempt for "the plain vulgarity itself" and the mean spirits of Maurice, Felix, and Billy Jim. Shirley and Norman are not yet of this world; she herself rises above it, as Hecht does, by seeing clearly and cleverly the predatory motives of her hosts. Hecht presents these motives, all too simply, as distinctly masculine. The three male characters are all quoted, but the women, Madge, Bubbles, and Astrid, are made to bear no direct responsibility for the evening. In fact, Shirley remembers the convention as disturbingly male:

> . . . men's voices
> Just slightly louder than was necessary
> For the table-mates they seemed to be addressing.
> It bore some message, all that baritone
> Brio of masculine snort and self-assertion.
> It belonged with cigars and bets and locker rooms.
> It had nothing to do with damask and chandeliers.
> It was a sign, she knew at once, of something.
> They wore her husband's same convention badge,
> So must be salesmen, here for a pep talk
> And booster from top-level management,
> Young, hopeful, energetic, just like him,
> But, in some way she found unnerving, louder.
> That was the earliest omen.

Somehow the crassness of this men's world overwhelmed her, until now she too calls Norman "Kit." (Her only spoken lines in the poem—" 'Cooler,' she'd say, 'yer gettin' really icy,' / She'd say, 'so whyantcha fix yerself a drink?' "—express her own acquired vulgarity.) Some late autumn afternoon long after the convention, Shirley and Kit stop on a highway near Wheeling, West Virginia (which Joe McCarthy and James Wright have rendered emblematic of Middle America), to take in "A LIVE ENTOMBMENT—CONTRIBUTIONS PLEASE." George Rose "has forsworn the vanities of this world" and allowed himself to be buried alive for thirty-eight days in a coffin contributed, of course, by "The Memento Morey Funeral Home." After seeing (through a glass shield) in George's blank blue eyes "A boredom so profound it might indeed / Pass for a certain otherworldliness," Shirley herself turns away from the crowd and her husband to consider the barren industrial landscape before her. A vision of her eleventh-grade Latin teacher comes to her and instructs her to renounce all, in preparation for the resurrection of this mock Christ:

> Consider deeply why as the first example
> Of the first conjugation—which is not
> As conjugal as some suppose—one learns
> The model verb forms of 'to love,' amare,
> Which also happens to be the word for 'bitter.'

Amour has led Shirley to a life of anesthetizing gin-and-bitters that is about to end in a coronary or stroke. In her last moments she dreams herself into a *New Yorker* ad for Drambuie. A grotesque vision of George Rose *redivivus* is the last thing she sees in this life.

The poem is stunning, memorable, richly convincing with sharp detail. The subject itself is important and too little known, deserving of attention. Hecht's depiction of Shirley at different moments in her life renders her decline moving. Yet the poem seems tawdry all the same. Part of the problem is that every screw is turned and turned again— that is Hecht's manner. All of the exactness in this 418-line poem is superficial. Hecht conveys milieu adroitly, even brilliantly, but the treatment of human motives is coarse and crudely schematic. Middle America is vulgar and debilitating in its influence; the society of men is crass; clever, sensitive, aspiring women have no opportunity to fulfill themselves in this America. Roughly put, these are the familiar "truths" upheld by the poem. If traveling salesmen have redeeming qualities, if male society is sometimes delicately polite, or if lower-middle-class American housewives take deserved satisfaction from their lives, the poem does not record the truth fully.[26] Hecht pretends to know intimately what he seems not to comprehend fully; in that sense, the poem is something of a cheat.

The distance between poets and popular cultural subjects is sometimes reconstructed as a gulf between the years on either side of World War II, for only in the aftermath of the war did popular culture achieve its full hegemony. Poets have written as though the problem were not with pop culture per se, that is, not a problem with the sensibilities of those people for whom such culture is reproduced, but

rather with the distinctive brand of pop culture that has exploded in
the last forty years. Here is a 1965 poem by Turner Cassity on an old-
style hero, "Period Piece."

> Leather helmet, lifted goggles,
> Out of the cockpit Lindbergh struggles—
>
> Henceforth, accident or plan,
> Anything but Everyman:
>
> Icarus intact, all Paris
> His, and, his to be, an heiress;
>
> While the honest press chants still
> "Ambition, self-reliance, will."
>
> Yet, goggles lowered, helmet fastened,
> Photographed, he so is chastened;
>
> Grown a skull, thus put upon,
> He must himself cry Jedermann;
>
> As though foreseeing loss, the Axis,
> Graduated income taxes;
>
> Seeing corporate, bland thoughts
> Which are the minds of astronauts,
>
> And how one hears an honest press
> Chant "Teamwork, peace, togetherness."[27]

The period Cassity has in mind is 1927–1941, the years between
Lindbergh's solo flight from New York to Paris and the entry of the
United States into World War II. The last lines indicate that an ideological shift occurred then, for by 1941 the proclaimed values had become dully collective.

Lindbergh was a culture hero in the prewar years exactly because
his individual accomplishment so nicely confirmed those American
ideals that were endangered and about to pass.[28] Lindbergh himself
was appalled by the renown he achieved, and paid for dearly; after his
flight he tried, without success, to maintain the simple privacy that everyone else took for granted. Cassity's reference to his crying of Jeder-
mann is exact but complicated. After a visit to Germany in 1936,
Lindbergh warned his government of Nazi aviation capability. Two
years later the Germans honored him with a medal, which aroused
suspicion in America. In 1940–41 Lindbergh spoke against American

intervention in the European war. (Once America declared war on Germany, he threw all of his energy into the war effort.) Everyman is summoned by Death and tries unsuccessfully to persuade Fellowship, Beauty, Worldly Goods, and others to join him. Lindbergh foresees the loss of the individualistic ethos that rendered him a hero. Part of what he sees as loss, though, is just what Everyman tried to promote, not forestall.

The complications of Cassity's attitude turn on this point: one can regret blandness and income taxes, but the collective spirit behind editorials of 1941 and later has often been seen accurately as a redemptive force—by Everyman (under the rubric of Fellowship), by Doctor Win-the-War. Before the war and after, the press was sufficiently honest in its way: the world, the ideological one, simply changed. The prosody of the poem adroitly analyzes the ideological struggle. In the first six couplets there are only two iambic lines, the eighth, spoken by the press, and the twelfth, referring to Lindbergh's attempts to propagandize against the war. The norm of trochaic tetrameter is firmly set out in the insistently regular, bisected first line. The bite and resistance (against the dominant iambic tradition) of the trochaic verse are meant to sound out the spirit of the prewar years. In the last three couplets that spirit fades. "Graduated income taxes": this clever snarl is the last firmly trochaic line. The next line shows the trochees literally dissolving into "bland thoughts." Thereafter all is smoothly iambic. The change, as Cassity suggests, can be termed "loss," but more generally one is entitled to feel no more than mild nostalgia for what the title indicates was just another "period."

In 1975 O'Hara's friend John Ashbery published in the *New York Review of Books* an unusually lucid poem about the continuity from that period to our own, "Mixed Feelings."

> A pleasant smell of frying sausages
> Attacks the sense, along with an old, mostly invisible
> Photograph of what seems to be girls lounging around
> An old fighter bomber, circa 1942 vintage.
> How to explain to these girls, if indeed that's what they are,
> These Ruths, Lindas, Pats and Sheilas
> About the vast change that's taken place
> In the fabric of our society, altering the texture
> Of all things in it? And yet
> They somehow look as if they knew, except
> That it's so hard to see them, it's hard to figure out
> Exactly what kind of expressions they're wearing.

What are your hobbies, girls? Aw nerts,
One of them might say, this guy's too much for me.
Let's go on and out, somewhere
Through the canyons of the garment center
To a small café and have a cup of coffee.
I am not offended that these creatures (that's the word)
Of my imagination seem to hold me in such light esteem,
Pay so little heed to me. It's part of a complicated
Flirtation routine, anyhow, no doubt. But this talk of
The garment center? Surely that's California sunlight
Belaboring them and the old crate on which they
Have draped themselves, fading its Donald Duck insignia
To the extreme point of legibility.
Maybe they were lying but more likely their
Tiny intelligences cannot retain much information.
Not even one fact, perhaps. That's why
They think they're in New York. I like the way
They look and act and feel. I wonder
How they got that way, but am not going to
Waste any more time thinking about them.
I have already forgotten them
Until some day in the not too distant future
When we meet possibly in the lounge of a modern airport,
They looking as astonishingly young and fresh as when this
   picture was made
But full of contradictory ideas, stupid ones as well as
Worthwhile ones, but all flooding the surface of our minds
As we babble about the sky and the weather and the forests of
   change.[29]

The "fabric of our society," as Ashbery banally puts it, is coarsely
varied: sausages along with old photos. Anything goes with anything
else, so evened out are expectations now. The rise and fall of idioms
through the poem seem to depict the cultural change from 1942 to
1975 as one involving qualities of mind. A person might register the
images before his senses freshly, as Ashbery does in the first line, but
the thoughts in his head stalely—"fabric," "texture." Yet the 1942
photo girl does no better: her language also oscillates through the
same scale, "nerts" to "a cup of coffee." Language is simply dated;
words might, like packages of food, be made to carry warnings about
expiration. The girls' names evoke an era, and so does his question.
"Hobbies," yes, this is how one might, in the leisured postwar years,

inquire like a pesonnel director about someone's personal life. But "it's so hard to see them," to gauge their attitudes, exactly because the language does not mesh with the subject—wrong question. And her language is off too: that dated figure "the canyons of the garment center" ("Down Wall, from girder into street noon leaks," Hart Crane wrote in 1926[30]) seems stuck to the wrong edge of the continent, as far off as an American can be.

No coherence emerges from his language or hers, which is part of the joke about the possibility of her lying. The incoherence is all his, freely accepted; further thought about the subject would be a waste of time. His feelings and thoughts, like theirs, are simply mixed—contradictory, stupid, and worthwhile. This fuss about the world being remade by fighter bombers is just portentous babble about stale figures, "the forests of change." For Ashbery, the challenge of accepting the loss of degree and coherence that is commonly spoken of as the special contribution of mass culture is rather a matter of facing the perennial confusion and superficiality of life, without any illusion of its having once been much different. Ashbery denies that a gap between popular culture and poetry exists, or ever did. Yet even if some truth to the claim be granted that life was always mostly superficial, whether poetry can be comparably superficial to anyone's benefit is still an open question, rendered all the more unavoidable by Ashbery's success.

Allen Ginsberg wrote a poem in 1955 imagining Whitman and Lorca in a California supermarket. "Will we stroll," he asks the good, gray one elegiacally, "dreaming of the lost America of love past blue automobiles in driveways, home to our silent cottage?" Whitman's hope for great audiences is part of that "lost America."[31] By 1955 the supermarket had become an outlet not just for frozen carrots and hair dye but also for the stuff of mass literacy. At the checkstands, one is beseeched by collections of crossword puzzles (for those who like to play with words), this month's romances, and, most obnoxious of all, this week's tabloid. "California Sex Killer Confesses"; "Woman Starves for 13 Years." They do so routinely, and how grim for the poets who want to appeal, as Whitman did, to the nation's imagination. A German poet passing displays for the *Bild* can feel no better: the limitations of mass literacy are not strictly national. The commonest readers are weekly fed stories that must debase the imagination and blunt the mind's desire for discriminations. In Munich one sees "Meinungs Mörder" spray-painted on the *Bild* vending machines.

Frank Bidart's first book began with these lines:

"When I hit her on the head, it was good,

and then I did it to her a couple of times,—
but it was funny,—afterwards,
it was as if somebody else did it . . .

Everything flat, without sharpness, richness or line.

Still, I liked to drive past the woods where she lay,
tell the old lady and the kids I had to take a piss,
hop out and do it to her . . .   *"Herbert White"*[32]

A poet for the *National Enquirer*? Probably not.

Bidart has taken up the challenge, neglected by most of his contemporaries, of finding depth and intelligence where others see only
cheap thrills. The first line, in two blunt clauses (twisting Genesis
1:3), sets up the problem of locating value in relation to violence. Bidart manages to provide rich answers to two questions that many of
his readers would not think worth asking. What can a homicidal nec-
rophiliac know of morality? What can a poet make of the most debased
imaginative material in America in 1973? Not much, one might say—
twice, too easily. Bidart does not try to plead the case of Herbert White;
technically, he is nearly as far out of the monologue as Browning was
out of his first monologues, "Porphyria's Lover" and "Johannes Agri-
cola in Meditation" (1836). Herbert White seems to speak for himself;
only his language makes those two questions ultimately compelling.

The accuracy of the idioms, solecisms and all, is acute, even when it
depends upon no more than the omission of a word or two: recalling a
motel meeting with his father, Herbert says, "and he started, / real
embarrassing, to cry." More consequential, though, is the way that
some of the blankest vulgarities are rendered exact, telling.

He was still a little drunk,
and asked me to forgive him for
all he hadn't done—; but, What the shit?
Who would have wanted to stay with Mom? with bastards
not even his own kids?   (ll. 30–34)

Shit, kids, and bastards turn out to be the crucial terms, not just the
coarse ones. Behind that self-protective, hard-boiled question, "What
the shit?", is Herbert's description of the decomposing body "in those
ordinary, shitty leaves." For him, the physical world is "just *there*, just

there, doing nothing!" Killing a little girl and necrophilia are, to his mind, ways of bringing that inert chancy world of shit to life.

> —Once, on the farm, when I was a kid,
> I was screwing a goat; and the rope around his neck
> when he tried to get away
> pulled tight;—and just when I came,
> he *died* . . .
>
> I came back the next day; jacked off over his body;
> but it didn't do any good . . .
>
> Mom once said:
> 'Man's spunk is the salt of the earth, and grows kids.'

"Kids" is a sick pun. Herbert is trying to breed baby goats out of the corpse of a dead goat. Giving life and taking it are confused for him, as they are in that Renaissance pun on "dying" that finds its way into classroom introductions to poetry. For a while Herbert denies responsibility for this confusion by covertly confessing: "somebody *else* did it, some bastard / had hurt a little girl." Anyone who did that to a little girl must be a bastard, in the loose sense, though Herbert earlier said (line 33) that in the literal sense he himself is a bastard.

Letting these words, especially *these* words, take on a life of their own, in Symbolist fashion, counts greatly for the poem because Bidart is out to find the common ground between the literary and the supermarket culture. He is trying to draw instruction from the sort of story that the *National Enquirer* would simply capitalize upon, and for poets the lessons are in the words. Why does Herbert have no more explicit, earthy word for intercourse in the second line ("I did it to her")? Is there some vulgar politesse, a shyness behind this common expression? And how does that evasive "it" come to stand for murder so easily two lines later? Is there something slyly predatory in the common expression "getting a girl"? Like Bidart and his readers, White is a user of words. In fact, his usage, however coarse, is conspicuously literary from moment to moment, and not just because Herbert is a latter-born lover of Porphyria. The fifth line of the poem—"Everything flat, without sharpness, richness or line"—is the sort of observation a poet might make of an experience or of a painting. Herbert's sense that the dead might be brought to life rests on a stock term of poetic description:

> As the seasons changed, and you saw more and more
> of the skull show through, the nights became clearer,
> and the buds,—erect, like nipples . . .

One cannot move far in the poem without surprise at the range of idiom and reflection open to Herbert. Bidart is determined to eliminate all the easy ways a reader might have of feeling superior or more sophisticated than Herbert or the lives represented in the *National Enquirer;* he makes the details of Herbert's narrative overlap with those of his own autobiography in a later poem in order to claim directly his connection to the murderer.[33] One of the tricks of the poem is to employ phrases that literate readers might feel are their own ("it was funny,—afterwards" [line 3]), without closing off access to those idioms that reflect Herbert's nasty streak (lines 9–10, 64–66). The chief weakness of the poem is not, as has been claimed, that the language is flat—these words are terrifically worked—but rather that Bidart pushes too hard, in the end, on Herbert's literary awareness, making the murderer allude to Milton and Marlowe, as if such a character were interesting insofar as he were literary.[34] Bidart might rather say that the allusions suggest that Herbert's imagination is somehow there too in Browning, in Frost, and in Milton and Marlowe. Certainly Bidart's accomplishment is there on the page, and it has a bearing on recent literary history, for this poem shows how far some of the best American poets have recently been willing to go in order to command the scope of the most popular culture. The alienation Ginsberg expressed in 1955 seems now, from Bidart's viewpoint, tediously predictable.

The 1950s critics of mass culture wrote as if the fate of western civilization were hanging in the balance—so powerful was the sense that television would abruptly change national taste and sensibility, as it surely did. The idea of a national taste is now itself almost anachronistic. Insofar as an American popular taste can be identified, it is imperious, exuberant, and, as is clear to Europeans, expansionist. Camels, Macdonalds, Levis, Joan Baez, J. R., and okay—an expression of acquiescence—are all props for an international stage, something for everyone. The success of American cultural imperialism on this level is indisputable and, however appalling to some, attractive to many poets.

Irving Howe saw in 1948 that writers need public experiences to which they can allude in order to gain some small common ground, however sandy.[35] If writers can no longer invoke shared beliefs as expeditiously as they once could, they can at least write about what Hollander said is "most believed in"—the Bijou culture.[36] The power, occasional freshness, and enforced exhilaration of popular culture are resources that recent poets have tried to tap, with varying success. They have not gone for this power greedily, but instead have tried to discriminate its respectable attractions and to understand its inevitability.

The techniques of registering discriminations that poets inherit as part of their craft, especially prosodic techniques, have a special function in poems about popular culture. Two of the free-verse poems discussed, "The Day Lady Died" and "Mixed Feelings," express attractive but blunt contentment with an absence of discrimination between high and low art, between the popular culture of the pre- and postwar years; these are levelers' poems. Those by Hecht, Hollander, and Cassity, on the contrary, use metrical resources to discriminate rather quietly but constantly the particular pleasures and corruptions of their subjects, for meter, like syntax, is a way of placing emphases. Bidart's free-verse "Herbert White" suggests that not only techniques of dissociation and emphasis but also the importance of literary tradition in a grander sense are at stake here. Since "Herbert White" does not employ traditional meters, Bidart must resort to allusion in order to measure contemporary popular culture by the standards of traditional high culture (this measure must be made if popular culture is to be discussed seriously), and just there the poem gets into trouble. Hecht, Hollander, and Cassity can take that measure with less fanfare because metrical allusions are less ostentatious than quotations. And certainly no particular judgment, no blushing or sneering, is necessarily entailed in metrical writing about pop culture, nor in bringing the intensity of high art to bear on the ordinary life of tabloids, magazine ads, and Saturday matinees, for "Movie-Going" along with "Period Piece," the very best of these poems, make their careful, qualified, but altogether good-tempered peace with the garishness of pop culture largely through prosody.

The social critics of the 1950s did not, as Howe noted, get very far with the pop-culture debate. Poets of the succeeding decades have managed to do a little better. Magnanimity for O'Hara, as for Whitman, came easily, by nature perhaps, but all the same affection for popular culture may well be a necessary first step toward accurate understanding of its energy and effect. O'Hara's affection is grounded, after all, in the considerable claim that the mass phase of cultural production entails a democratization of art that enriches life simply and without fuss. New York City is a little richer for having paperbacks everywhere (and Strega too); this concrete point the mass-culture critics did not appreciate fully. Nor would Philip Rahv and others admit, as Ashbery insists, that what Howe speaks of assuredly as the "heights of consciousness" come seldom and leave great plains and valleys unregarded. This terrain between the peaks, Ashbery suggests, has been a more or less permanent part of the mental landscape, despite cataclysmic cultural historical accounts of the effect of World War II. Cassity sees recent cultural history less along Ashbery's lines, but he dissociates different kinds of popular culture, and this simple step had not been made by the social critics. Nor did they see, as Bidart does, that the manipulation of language and the twists of mind in the popular imagination are compelling and beyond condescension. In 1975 Edward Dorn, perhaps the most astute observer of popular culture, managed to make a wonderful long poem out of just this language and imagination.

8 · Edward Dorn: "This Marvellous Accidentalism"

During the early 1950s, Edward Dorn was one of that vanishing species at Black Mountain College, the students. More precisely, in academic taxonomy, he was a transfer student from the state college at Charleston, Illinois, near the tractor factory where he worked, and before that from the University of Illinois. In 1951 he went to Black Mountain to study painting—and to get a draft deferment. About five years and one leave of absence later, he took a degree from Black Mountain; by then he considered himself a poet. Robert Creeley, his outside examiner for the B.A., thought him a passable student, and Dorn left to settle in Skagit Valley, Washington. Within a couple of years the college had folded, and Charles Olson, former rector of Black Mountain, was lecturing about Whitehead to a small group in San Francisco.[1]

Olson's influence, though, was abiding. More than a decade later, in 1968, Dorn dedicated *Geography*, then his most ambitious book, to his former teacher.[2] He took from Olson a commitment to didactic, discursive poetry.[3] In 1973, looking back twenty years, Dorn reflected that Olson's "whole passion for a scope of knowledge that I hadn't dreamed of gave me a clue to what the extent of the mind might be. I'm speaking now more in the poetic sense, as enthusiast, really more than in the scholarly sense." (I 37). Poems like "The Kingfishers," "The Praises," and "In Cold Hell, in Thicket" show how Olson's mind, fueled by enthusiasm, can range over a wide terrain which encompasses nothing that might be construed as inherently poetic. Olson extended the bounds of what is considered poetry, by his use both of flatly discursive language and of scholarly subject matter. In 1968 Dorn remarked to Olson: " [it] still gasses me that you can be the

most *poetic* worker alive while saying something, nearly anything."[4]
The extension of poetic subject matter counted heavily for Dorn because he knew that poetry that takes personal experience, domestic
and psychological, as its subject was out of his reach: Creeley could be
his examiner but never his mentor (I 23–24).[5] Yet Olson's enthusiasm for his subjects was still more important, for ultimately the subject itself matters little: "What I *admire* about all of you is that Ability
to start anywhere, Jesus, *that* must be *life*."[6] For Olson, that was more
than an ability: convention demanded that he always seem to start in
unfamiliar territory; his poems are meant to repeat what he called
"the first American story": exploration.[7] His discursive poems are
made to seem exploratory, even when their arguments have been
framed at the outset. Many of Dorn's poems too are exploratory, even
when their arguments have been framed at the outset. Many of his
poems are also exploratory in this discursive sense—"Idaho Out" is
the best example—and others directly concern the theme of exploration. But for Dorn, this first American story is a tangle. In 1961 he
spoke of yet another attractive aspect of his teacher: "It seems to me
that Olson is doing something I've never read before . . . I don't think
any previous work so attempts to tap the realities of a region in all its
economic and political and human aspects" (I 2). For Dorn, Olson
was a political poet—in a problematic way. The politics of exploration,
Dorn knew, were anything but clean; there is a further sense too in
which exploration (in land or words) is at odds with what is commonly
regarded as human. And whatever else political poetry ought to be, for
Dorn it must be humane.

The clearest study of this problem is a poem Dorn wrote in 1958,
"The Air of June Sings," a bright elegy in a country graveyard. A few
lines into the poem Dorn says,

> And now, the light noise of the children at play on the inscribed
>   stone
>
> jars my ear and they whisper and laugh covering their mouths.
>   "My Darling"
> my daughter reads, some of the markers
> reflect such lightness to her reading eyes, yea, as I rove
> among these polished and lime blocks I am moved to tears and
>   I hear
> the depth in "Darling, we love thee," and as in "Safe in
>   Heaven."   (CP 11)

Human sentiment is his subject: his daughter giggles with small embarrassment and Dorn is moved to tears before these stones that
triangulate three generations. To the little girl, the inscriptions speak

an abstract language of conventions whose proprieties she does not yet fully comprehend. Dorn represents her interpretation through his diction: "the markers reflect such lightness to her reading eyes"; he goes abstract just where she does, as the stones become texts for her. His own sense of the epitaphs is suggested by the solemnly archaic phrase that takes over that line—"yea, as I rove"—and by the frank declaration of sentiment in the next lines—"I am moved to tears and I hear / the depth." Declarative diction is fitting because what Dorn hears is the irreducible, inexplicable depth of common sentiment—to that, Olson's ear was never tuned. In the next lines he hypothesizes more fully articulated alternatives to these inscriptions, the "wisdom" of the dead:

> I am going off to heaven and I won't see you anymore. I am
> going back into the country and I won't be here anymore. I am
> going to die in 1937

But these "explanations" of mortal separations are light by comparison with the declarative inscriptions, "My Darling," "Darling, we love thee," "Safe in Heaven"; they do not serve the needs of the living.

As these explanations speak from beyond the grave, as though retrospectively, so frontierism tries to transcend the mortal limits of the simply human.

> My eyes avoid
> the largest stone, larger than the common large, Goodpole
>   Matthews,
> Pioneer, and that pioneer sticks in me like a wormed black
>   cherry
> in my throat, No Date, nothing but that zeal, that trekking
> and Business, that presumption in a sacred place, where chil-
>   dren
> are buried, and where peace, as it is in the fields and the coun-
>   try
> should reign. A wagon wheel is buried there.

That undated tombstone grossly violates the proprieties of the graveyard by its grasp beyond time and the common lot. Zeal for motion, the wagon wheel, did not fade away entirely in the nineteenth century:

> . . . exhausted it still moves
> across "the precious uncluttered
> land" as its will takes it
> plastic boats behind.   (CP 40)

Suburbs mark its wake, where "strange cowboys live / in ranch style houses" (CP 40). Dorn's response to frontier zealotry:

> Lead me away
> to the small quiet stones of the unpreposterous dead and leave
> me my tears for Darling we love thee, for Budded on earth and
>   blossomed
> in heaven, where the fieldbirds sing in the fence rows,
> and there is possibility, where there are not the loneliest of all.
> Oh, the stones not yet cut.

Sentimentality is a principle for Dorn, a disciplined unraveling of a tangled ideology; his word for straight is "unpreposterous." The genre he chooses in which to oppose that preposterous hunger for new beginnings is one of the most hackneyed and debased of lyric forms: the graveyard elegy. "The swallows twittering from the straw-built shed" (1751, from Gray's "Elegy"); "the fieldbirds sing in the fence rows" (1958)—then to now, no new sentiments. Inside the fenced enclosures "there is possibility," but not that timeless absolute of "No Date." The people whose inscriptions speak with such depth are tied to each other by simple, common sentiments and by the plainest of literary and funereal conventions; the pioneer is "the loneliest of all," for he is attracted by the landscapes that are "refusing / population" (CP 40).

The solitary, though, has its attractions—even for Dorn. The poem that celebrates pioneer loneliness most compellingly is "Death While Journeying," which first appeared in the summer of 1960.

> At Grinder's Stand
> in his sleep
> on the Natchez Trace,
> in the Chickasaw country
> Meriwether Lewis
> had what money
> and incidently his life
> stole. And I never read what time of year
>
> it was, Fall? when the papaws
> drop their yellow fruit,
> or Spring? and bear's grease.
> Enough now
> to write it down in celebration
> on first reading . . .

At Grinder's Stand
on the Natchez Trace
in the Chickasaw country
an exotic place
              to die
and to fit him.   (ll. 10–20, ellipsis in original; CP 49–50)

This is a poem about the ignoble end of a great beginner, Meriwether Lewis, who died mysteriously at thirty-five, a few years after his triumphant return with William Clark from the Pacific coast. From 1807 until his death, Lewis was governor of the upper Louisiana Territory. During the expedition to the Pacific, he had grown accustomed to the carte blanche Jefferson had permitted him. But the Washington government was later unwilling to allow him the same liberty in administering the Louisiana Territory: several of his vouchers were not honored by the federal government. Severely disappointed by what he took to be a reprimand, Lewis set out alone in September 1809 for Washington, where he intended to straighten out these financial matters. (He also planned to visit his mother, who was not dying, at Ivy Creek in Virginia on his return route.)

Dorn honors his subject as much by the form of his poem as by explicit statement. The poem is adamant about beginnings, but it cannot generate a principle of continuity. The first four lines initiate a set of beginnings, four prepositional clauses that each seem to start the sentence from scratch. Once the syntax has produced a subject ("Meriwether Lewis") and a verb ("had"), it forestalls completion by convoluting the object: "what money / and incidently his life / stole." Syntactically the sentence is complete; but semantically its conclusion is undisclosed and the sense aborted. Dorn then veers away from this subject with his digressive conjectures about the time of year, as if he did not want the poem to continue along any one path. (The seasonal conjectures punctuate the poem with unsettling reminders of the poem's inability to get beyond its very beginning.) And those conjectures are similarly dismissed, unresolved, with a half-sentence of "conclusion" (ll. 12–14). At this point (ll. 15–17) the poem can begin again with its initial formula—the poem goes through five such beginnings: ll. 1–4, 15–17, 33–34, 45–46, 58. The rhyme (ll. 16–18) suggests that what interests Dorn is the exoticism not of the location but of the sound of those place names: "Grinder's Stand," "Natchez Trace," "Chickasaw country." The fourth strophe indicates that Dorn is truly engaged by a single personal quality:

Going to see his dying mother
or was it summer,
the live oak waving
in the clear air,
but imagine,
trying to make a trip
like that alone.   (ll. 21–27)

Motive (l. 21), time (l. 22), place (ll. 23–24)—these finally matter little. What is wondrous is Lewis' solitariness (ll. 25–27)—that, the true heritage of the American frontier, transcends all the mundane details.

. . . imagine
along the Natchez Trace in loneliness
to Grinder's Stand, and the ferret
Grinder, eyeing you as you passed through
the door. And an entire continent had flapped
at your coattails.

But surrounding this death
Boone had just returned to Femme Osage
with sixty beaver skins 'still strong
in limb, unflinching in spirit'
standing there with a gaunt eye
watching the Astorians prepare their keel-boats,

his old ear bent
toward the Pacific tide.

But at Grinder's Stand,
which is south of Femme Osage
on the Trace, whom probably the Astorians
had nearly forgotten, a man rode in
to the final recognition
and who would have been there
          but money-eyed

Grinder,

while the Astorians prepared their keel-boats
and Boone watched.   (ll. 44–67)

What Daniel Boone is made to watch here is the erosion of the frontier heritage. Robert Grinder was the proprietor of Grinder's Stand, where Lewis died; he was said by his wife to be twenty miles away from home on 11 October 1809. About that, however, there is some doubt. Many years after Lewis' death, a friend of one of Grinder's servants stated that Grinder was present the night Lewis either killed himself or was killed by a robber. Lewis' watch and money (at least $200) were not with his body on the morning of the 12th; before long, Robert Grinder purchased more slaves and better property and moved away from the Natchez Trace. Dorn evidently takes the view, shared by others, that Grinder murdered Lewis for money. As an old man, Boone trapped furs to pay his debts. Dorn makes the point that more or less simultaneously with Lewis' death, John Jacob Astor chartered one of the first great trusts, the American Fur Company (1808), which established a post at Astoria, Oregon, near where Lewis and Clark had camped along the Columbia River. From Meriwether Lewis and Daniel Boone to Robert Grinder and John Jacob Astor, from lone explorers to weaseling capitalists—that is the decline of the West, as Dorn sees it.

A few months after "Death While Journeying" appeared, David Ignatow edited a special issue of *Chelsea* on political poetry that included "Los Mineros," one of Dorn's best political elegies.[8] During the two years since writing "The Air of June Sings," Dorn had learned to write cooler elegies addressed more to understanding than to sentiment. In "Los Mineros" he meditates on a mute group photo, as he had meditated two years earlier on the plain brevity of epitaphs:

> These men whom we will never know are ranged 14 in number
> in one of those pictures that are very long, you've seen them.

> And the wonder is five are smiling Mexicanos, the rest
> could be English or German, blown to New Mexico on another
> winter's snow. Hard to imagine Spanish as miners, their
> sense is good-naturedly above ground (and their cruelty).
> In a silly way they know their pictures are being taken,

> and know it isn't necessary honor standing in line with their
>   hands hiding
> in their pockets. I was looking to see if they are short
> as Orwell says miners must be, but they aren't save two
> little Mexican boys. What caught my eye at first was the way
> they were so finely dressed in old double-breasted suit coats,
>   ready for work.

> Then I looked into their faces and the races separated.
> The English or Germans wear a look which is mystic in its ex-
>   pectancy;

able men underground,
but the Spanish face carries no emergency
and one of the little boys, standing behind a post
looks right out of the picture faintly smiling: even today.

(ll. 15–32; CP 55)

The aspirations behind this casual style finally seem to be pretensions (ll. 28–30)—and for interesting reasons. Dorn seems to address his reader directly, without the stylistic apparatus that might turn such an address into a formal occasion: "you've seen them" (l. 16)—a common ground of experience can be easily assumed. And he takes conspicuous advantage of shortcutting colloquialisms, as if he were musing over the photo while he jotted this poem down: "Hard to imagine" (l. 19); "they know their pictures are being taken, / and know it isn't necessary [but rather an] honor standing in line" (ll. 21–22). That second ellipsis (with its faulty parallelism) suggests that Dorn is simply talking while he thinks. In 1964 Dorn praised LeRoi Jones's prose for its plainness: "There are no devices of thought, happily."[9] That year he wrote to Jones about his desire to talk openly to his readers: "I only mean that I consider the fight to tell other Men, just other Men, a little of what I know I've seen, in as straight a manner as possible, my only occupation. My only commitment. My only true duty. That's everything of course."[10] Yet a talking, didactic style is a complicated matter, for a too simply "straight" manner can be misleadingly casual: "It is that crucial talk that is so important, and indispensible, and phony. It's the only stuff there is to work with. The Western World hasn't yet come on to a language it can use to say something important, or, even, pertinent."[11] Casual talk is not the appropriate medium for what Dorn considers important subject matter; he'll have no cracker-barrel contrivance. Instead, after invoking a colloquial manner, he displaces his diction from spoken usage, using ungainly terms like "good-naturedly," which appear only in formal, written contexts. For Dorn is engaged here by a kind of cultural sociology that, though unprofessional, is directed toward the sort of understanding commonly conveyed through formal discourse, not casual chat. His motive is close to that of the expository prose writer: like an essayist, he tests (ll. 23–25) and posits (ll. 28–30) general propositions. Yet the "laws" Dorn formulates are not intended, as an essayist's customarily are, to be definitive. He wants to digress into his generalizations (ll. 19–20). And his terms and categories—"above ground," "mystic," "expectancy," "emergency"—are suggestive and exploratory rather than determinate. He looks for the telling not the definitive detail.

. . .

Between 1961 and 1965 Dorn's political poetry changed character. To show how distinct a change occurred I would like to look at a poem probably written in 1959 but never published. In late April and early May 1959, Fidel Castro visited Washington; his two-week stay received wide coverage in American newspapers. While he was trying to convince Washington politicians and newsmen that his intentions were not to be feared, the *New York Times* ran this item: "A military court sentenced Dr. Olga Herrara Marcos today to death by firing squad. She is believed to be the first woman to be sentenced to death in the history of the republic."[12] Dr. Marcos was found guilty of informing officials of the Batista regime as to the whereabouts of three rebels who were caught and executed in 1955. Her alleged motive: $200 and a better job.[13] On 11 May 1959 *Time* ran a particularly pathetic photo of her sitting, numbly terrified, in the courtroom. The skeptical press estimated that she would be at least number 550 on the list of those executed for war crimes by the Castro government, but her sentence was reduced by a higher court to thirty years' imprisonment.[14]

Dorn evidently saw the *Time* photo and read newspaper accounts of her trial, for two years later he sent to LeRoi Jones "An Address for the First Woman to Face Death in Havana—Olga Herrara Marcos":

> (Mrs. Marcos went to havana
> all on a summer's night
> she was caught in a plot, which
> side,
> she forgot
> but her face was the picture
> of fright)
> . . . . .
> . . . face of the bullet
> smashing
> against timber
> behind Mrs. Marcos
> whose practical crime was
> being on the wrong payroll, anybody's[15]

Dorn and Jones were close friends at the time. That year, 1961, Jones's Totem Press brought out Dorn's first collection of poems, *The Newly Fallen*. Dorn admired Jones's writing and, though from a distance, his political polemics as well: "Your social radicalism sounds very much to the point, as you'd know I'd feel, envious even, altho I know it is much more others' scene than mine. Keep slugging for whatever reason, and when you run out of reasons, the better."[16] It was natural for Dorn to send Jones this two-year-old poem because Jones had not long before published an essay about his 1960 visit to Cuba.[17] Jones, however, disapproved of the poem: "counter-revolutionary" was his phrase. He pointed out that the title itself was misleading: "If you say of the woman in the poem 'The first' woman to die in Habana . . . you know it is strictly 'poetic.' Not at all true. Batista killed 20,000 . . . I think Castro means to do better. It is some small thing I want. Some goodness I have to see."[18]

Dorn was troubled enough by Jones's response to articulate an explanation of topical verse that is worth quoting at length.

> Come on, back off. I'm not no fucking counter-anything. I'm as truly gassed as anyone, but much more embarrassed than others, at the poor prospect of fellow poets singing the praises of any thing so venal as a State. I am afraid I am not very interested in the "argument" aspects of a statement like the Herrara poem. It wasn't written "against" anything, and . . . aesthetics . . . aside, you ought to know the very word Batista makes me puke . . . I don't see the thing as "rational" at all, and perhaps you'd stick to the view that that's the trouble. Whatever the Cuban people are doing, God blesses them, and for however long they can make it. A statement in a poem such as I sent you is highly accidental, in the same way junk gathering sculpture is, and gratifying accidents are a really bigger part of the West than that aestheticism [?] you mention. If I had seen a picture of a Pre-Castro victim of the same system of organized horseshit, approximately the same thing wld have come out. This is one of the famous limitations of occasional writing. Its alignments are like the ligaments of a starved man, very clear.[19]

Dorn's response to the Herrara story was not political, he thought; his poem was an expression of sentiment, not ideology. He believed that he could easily write around the ideological encampments that are usually the governing forces, rhetorically and thematically, in political poetry; for him, ideological differences were "accidental" rather than essential. He could meditate on her photo as freely as he had meditated on gravestones in his earlier elegy.

The only point I ever had is that when a picture, namely of Mrs. Herrara Marcos, is printed, showing her puckered up babyface tears, brought forth by the lunatic braggart announcement of her death, it is a matter of *public shame. Sides,* are a bigassed drag. The biggest small-talk of all, like which one are you on? motherfucker. I think I know what kind of a stupid, scared, caught woman she was. But whatever she did, or what those who murdered her did, or their "reasons," my limited prospect of the thing is completely correct. And satisfying for everyone. Because there is no embarrassment in sympathy. Aside from the fact that "sympathizers" are always assholes.

Despite the title of this poem, Dorn had intended to write another elegy, not a polemic, not a discursive explanation of a political event. Jones seemed partly to have confused the genre of the Herrara poem, though he would not easily allow Dorn the propriety of an elegy on Dr. Marcos. He answered Dorn with back-handed apologies for the offense:

If my letter re your poem sounded crusadery and contentious I'm sorry. But I have gone deep, and gotten caught with images of the world, that exists, or that will be here even after WE go. I have not the exquisite objectivity of circumstance. Only we, on this earth, can talk of material existence as just another philosophical problem . . . "Moral earnestness" (if there be such a thing) ought [to] be transformed into action. (You name it.) I know we can think that to write a poem, and be Aristotle's God is sufficient. But I can't sleep. And I do not believe in all this relative shit. There is a right and a wrong. A good and a bad. And it's up to me, you, all of the so called minds, to find out. It is only knowledge of things that will bring this "moral earnestness."[20]

Jones's apology was halfhearted, but Dorn's faith in his defenses was not long-lasting anyway. For another year after this exchange, Dorn seemed to proceed with greater regard for particular situations than for the classes of events that anatomize ideologies. He has been highly praised for this sort of self-restraint. Donald Davie, in a discussion of Dorn's novel, *The Rites of Passage,* said,

What validates Dorn's lyric voice is, time and again, its humility, the instruction it looks for and gets from people and places and happenings. It reflects upon them, it moralizes on them; but the reflection and the moral are drawn not from some previously accumulated stock of wisdom, but (so the writing persuades us) immediately out of the shock of confronting each of them as it comes, unpredictably.[21]

In political terms, a stock of wisdom is an ideology; occasional poetry, in Dorn's understanding, challenges ideological certainties by pitting contingent events against the categories commonly used to hold political history in order. A more successful example of this technique than the Herrara "Address" is a poem Jones in fact wanted to publish in *Floating Bear,* "On the Debt My Mother Owed to Sears Roebuck" (1962).[22] After two strophes describing how his parents trudged their uneventful way on Sears' revolving track of debt, Dorn turns against his own conclusions:

> On the debt my mother owed to sears roebuck?
> I have nothing to say, it gave me clothes to
> wear to school,
> and my mother brooded
> in the rooms of the house, the kitchen, waiting
> for the men she knew, her husband, her son
> from work, from school, from the air of locusts
> and dust masking the hedges of fields she knew
> in her eye as a vague land where she lived,
> boundaries, whose tractors chugged pulling harrows
> pulling discs, pulling great yields from the earth
> pulse for the armies in two hemispheres, 1943
> and she was part of that *stay at home army* to keep
> things going, owing that debt.   (CP 46–47)

It was easy enough in the first two strophes to suggest that the company's promotion nibbled away at his mother's life the way mice nibbled at the corn in the crib, that Sears stripped his parents' dry, melancholy lives the way locusts stripped the rows of corn—too easy, too pat: the mind curls up to sleep in those metaphors. In this last strophe Dorn catches himself with the reminder that indirectly the debt helped him get to school, helped his family continue working their Illinois farm, even helped supply the allies in Europe and the Pacific and helped strengthen the American economy. Dorn wants to redeem even the tritest claims of the Sears catalogue ("clothes to wear to school") and the portentous propaganda of the war administration ("pulling great yields from the earth / pulse for the armies," "that *stay at home army*"). This reminder takes nothing away exactly from the first two strophes—but these indirect consequences of the debt are also part of the story. Finally, he lets these two sides of the story sit together, neither trouncing the other; Dorn will not subordinate either side.

By 1965, however, it was more difficult to see signs in Dorn's work of that sort of humility, for a number of his most engaging poems were then Juvenalian diatribes. Jones seems finally to have made his point convincingly. Yet Davie's explanation of Dorn's method still holds, even for such opinionated poems as "The Problem of the Poem for My Daughter, Left Unsolved." The poem opens with a description of a surgical scar on Dorn's daughter's neck:

> a thin line red with its own distinction
> some goiter
> of what she has been made to understand is civilization
> not the brand of the adventurous cutlass
>
> The misery is superficial now.
> I have dwelt on that quality in other poems
> without attention to the obvious
> drain
>
>   of social definition
> the oblivious process
> of a brutal economic calculus, where to
>   place the dark hair
> save above moist eyes   (ll. 10–22; CP 93)

One of Dorn's points here is that as human misery has been lessened, made "superficial," so the explanation of why misery exists at all has been obscured. When suffering was profound, it was endured by classes: misery defined the social structure responsible for much suffering. Now suffering is superficial and cuts across what remains of the class structure. What has been lost is clarity and access to understanding. Dorn's method struggles against that loss. He skips back and forth in this poem between his daughter's misery, her literally superficial suffering of this scar around her neck, and the diffuse misery of Americans who are incapable of deeply suffering, incapable of genuine culture; the poem might be entitled "On the Absence of True Culture."

Dorn's ease in moving from his daughter to Americans in general

makes the poem seem wayward, but a serious point is implicitly registered by this method: the ways in which an individual owes his or her
identity to the overall social structure ought to be at once too obvious
and too all-embracing to mention; such links between the individual
and the society should be taken for granted. For the purposes of this
poem, his daughter is one of the American Women:

<blockquote>

                                                    the women are
                                        set loose to walk spiritless
            their marks are deep cuts on the neck, moist eyes, sagging
                nylons
            eyes painted to dry everything, loose figures of despair
            or hard flesh prolonged by injections and tucks into an isolated
                youngness
            a manufactured Galateability
                                        The end
                                        of applied genetics will be
                                        the elimination of freely disposed
                                        intellection, via the rule
                                        that a science is oriented toward
                                            Use, some predictable
                                breed, is the end
            (Automation ends with a moral proposition), THE LESSON of
            one maximum factor of it
            will suggest all the correspondences. . . .   (CP 96)

</blockquote>

She is a member of a class identifiable by "an isolated youngness" and
"a manufactured Galateability."

Stiff phrasing is typical of Dorn's manner, in both his verse and
prose; he characteristically insists on abstractness, especially where it
might be resisted. For example, here is a descriptive paragraph from a
short story, "A Narrative with Scattered Nouns," about a wiener roast:

<blockquote>

Plum Island became one of our favorite haunts. The lightness
of its air, the fairness of its granulation and the extreme openness to the seas who run home there. The lightness of its air.
That is the way it is aspected. There is not a great amount of
driftwood. What driftwood there is scattered near the sea grass
is of a compelling nature. Its surface is possessed of a mild satin
glow, an encircling gestalt which seems independent of stock
solar light. It is otherwise farctate.   (SB 1–2)

</blockquote>

Description, Dorn regards as "mind killing" (SB 6). He prefers to translate qualities into abstract substances: "lightness," "fairness," "openness." In this manner, he will go a long, clumsy way to sound formal, antiseptic ("aspected," "farctate"). Of course, his tongue is in his cheek: he is toying with the corruptions of academic prose, especially as they are, one might say, manifest in the pretensions of college freshmen whose desire to sound authoritatively intellectual exposes some of the shabbier conventions of academic discourse. Clarity and concision, the mass-dispensed antidotes for freshmen, are not held in Dorn's esteem: they are the muses of those who wish simply to "understand." "Understanding, of course, is not the point. It is that you are not dancing with them, not chanting Tiwa with them. Which is much more important. Understanding is a device used to separate us."[23]

For Dorn, exploration and judgment are the proper goals of intellectual activity. Paradoxically, stony dogmatism is intended as a means of exploration. Courtesy, fair-mindedness, and comprehensiveness are some of the inhibiting virtues of intellectuals; those who are obviously coarse, rude, opinionated, and biased are not, by the academic code, on the humane road to truth. Dorn claims that just these inhibitions keep intellectuals from a penetrating explanation of contemporary politics. "There is always that compromising point beyond which you aren't allowed to go and beyond which there would lie the fullest explanation of a people [such as Native Americans] who have been so wholly maligned by crimes of omission . . . If you are an artist you have to live with your art, which is on every level total."[24] That Black Mountain high seriousness about art suggests why, in *Slinger*, the Poet plays an Abso Lute. A poet can deliberately violate canons of fair-mindedness in order to push explanation beyond certain inhibiting barriers—that is his act of exploration. Stubborn opinionatedness and even name calling are not, in Dorn's work, the consequences of crystallized conclusions but the technology of fantasy.

> More and more people are writing political poetry, and it's not politics they're writing, at all, it's a fantasy of certain things. It doesn't name, the way poetry in the past has named actual names or substituted names that were well known, for actual names. It isn't that kind of thing that I think is possible today, because, frankly, politics is carried on by literal men—so it's a schoolboy's interest . . . But the fantasy of politics, in terms of poetry, and the images and the ghosts of that kind of thing are very valuable in terms of the writing and getting of poetry fur-

> ther on a footing of meaning for a large mass of people . . . For
> one thing, I don't know a thing about politics, and I think
> that gives me the greatest right in the world to be a zealot
> about it.   (I 5–6)

Dorn's rough vulgarity is meant to be playful where others are serious, for play may generate possibilities that would otherwise remain locked behind the polite, conventional barriers to exploration. Rudeness is Dorn's version of literary frontierism: "The whole world of exploration where the object was not discovery but living in and playing with the great brutal elements of earth."[25] To stay within the bounds of polite discourse is stultifying: "The enclosure of the land / leads directly to / the enclosure of the mind."[26]

Dorn's discursiveness, his wandering and his explanatory motive, like Olson's, is an attempt to bring into poetry a frontier methodology. The poetry he values displays "freely disposed / intellection"; it is not satisfied, despite its didactic ambition, "with a moral proposition, THE LESSON of / one maximum factor." Instead, his generalizations, his conclusions, seem to be happened upon, casual; they crop up everywhere.[27] Dorn once expressed admiration of Jones's ability to get "surplus verities" in his writing; likewise Jones, after reading *Idaho Out,* wrote to Dorn: "That *discursiveness* I envy you so much for."[28] Despite their disagreements in 1961, in 1965 it was clear that these poets agreed that a writer deals in explanations, compelling ones.

That a poet's explanations might well be unreasonable is a proposition approved all too commonly now, with too little measure of what is given up with that assent. If it is proper, as I think it is, to ask of the very best political poets (Marvell would be a standard, but Lowell would serve too) that they offer guidance on particular political issues, that they be of abiding help in the determination of political policy (that we ask of political poetry at least as much as we do of political prose), then the poetic program that Dorn outlined should lead to a lesser order of political poetry. Dorn is didactic the way satirists often are. He tries to be fresh, unpredictable, severe; not wise or even right. He cannot be a faithful guide to the nation's political career, but a stunning maverick has his uses too. If we ask of political poetry only that it be surprising, opinionated, extreme, we would sell poetry short because along with such a notion goes the belief that prose, not poetry, bears the greatest intelligence and utility in regard to our collective public life. Yet satire is that one form of didactic writing that we go to mainly for vivacity. *The Dunciad,* not the *Essay on Man,* has that. Dorn's aspirations might best be measured, as Donald Wesling suggests, against the Augustan satiric tradition. Unlike Olson, he is more an ironist than an explainer; that, I think, means he is by design a more modest poet.

By 1967, when the first *Gunslinger* passage appeared, Dorn had determined that the most compelling explanations were, as he had said six years earlier, "a fantasy of certain things." In the late sixties he moved from the audacious political "explanations" of poems like "The Problem of the Poem for My Daughter" and "Inauguration Poem #2" to the less didactic but still outrageous mode of explicit fantasy. Yet aside from such abstract continuity, when the first book of *Gunslinger* appeared in 1968 it was clear that Dorn's writing had taken a sharp turn. *Gunslinger* was unpredictable: it owed little to Dorn's earlier manner and nothing at all to the prevailing poetic styles of the late sixties. Dorn's major effort looked like a kind of stunning mutant.

Like so many of this century's long poems, *Slinger* (as the completed poem is called) is one more quest poem, but this quest has less to do with recovery than with genesis. Gunslinger's quest is literally genetic: he goes in search of mutations. His weapon is the dreaded .44:

> Look, into each chamber
> goes one bit of my repertoire
> of pure information,
> into each gesture, what
> you call in your innocence
> "the draw"
> goes Some Dark Combination   (S 35)

He seems to be shy two chromosomes, but his mount carries that pair. Lil recollects her first encounter with Claude the talking horse:

> ... *he had the texan's hat on*
> *a stetson XX sorta cockwise*
> *on his head it was*
> *I tell you Slinger you would of*
> *split your levis and dropped your*
> *beads to seen it.*   (S 11)[29]

Claude's hat sits cockwise for a reason: he bears a mangled pair. "I" inquires about the horse's name, "Claude Lévi-Strauss is that— /

Yes, you guessed it / a homonym" (S 34). Actually, two homonyms are crossed with a pun: Clawed Lévi-Strauss / clawed jeans / clawed genes. Slinger's quest is to get beyond the mangling of genes—of memory ("The Horse is a wringer for memory" [S 117])—which was accomplished in the past. He seeks a change predicated on nothing in the past, a mutation.

Doctor Jean Flamboyant (flamboyant gene, of course) presents himself as the all-promising mutant—"I can fix anything" (S 79)—but there is the depressing possibility that all mutations, all unpredictable changes have occurred in the past, that evolution is obsolete; which is why the "Anti-Darwinian" Mogollones pose so serious a threat (S 181), and why too Doctor Jean Flamboyant may be confined to "Beenville" (S 133–35). Slinger describes his dispute with Howard Hughes as a genetic duel between cattlemen (S 4–5), though more than steer are involved. Howard Hughes, Dorn has said, "is a rather pure metaphor of a kind of primitive, entrepreneurial capitalist take of what America is, which is still embedded in the political and social instincts of a lot of American activity. He's a great singular—in a strange way like a dinosaur, but nevertheless his lineage goes back to the seventies and eighties of the last century and I do see him as an extension of the earlier, nonelectronic, financial geniuses like Fisk and Gould" (I 51). As Robart, he represents the internalization of capitalism, "the psychological condition of the United States of America" (I 31). The race of poets is endangered by Robart (read: rob art, a scrambled antithesis to "trobar" [S 59–60]), and even horses may not make it (S 62). The signs say that Western man's "Imprudential Behavior" (S 131) is catching up with him.

> The divisions of hunger
> 　　shut behind their Doors
> Pinned down by their Stars
> Kept going by their Rotors
> Waked up by their Alarms
> Attended by a Prose
> 　　which says how Dead they are
> Frozen by a Brine
> 　　which keeps them from Stinking
> It looks to me Jack
> 　　like The Whole Set is Sinking
> And theyre still talkin ecology
> Without even Blinking
>
> Ah Men, saith the Horse 　　　　　　　　　　(S 119)

The media ("Stars"), industrial technology ("Rotors"), the scheduled bourgeois routine ("Alarms"), marked by "the inertia of National Lunch" (S 78), the compliant literature ("Prose"), and even underarm deodorant ("Brine") collaborate to enforce the distribution of income and resources ("divisions of hunger") that will bring the race to its garrulous end. Universe City "looks like a rundown movie lot / a population waiting around to become / White Extras" (S 68).

The solution envisioned, and finally achieved, is suggested by some apostrophic lines of the Poet's song, "Cool Liquid Comes":

> oh people of the coming stage . . .
> Oh temptation of survival
> oh lusterless hope
> of victory in opposites   (S 49)

The "coming stage" is the approaching stagecoach bearing the poem's characters, but it also refers to the people of the future. Some small hope for the genetic survival of people rests on the possibility of a cosmic reversal of direction, "victory in opposites." The prevailing program, Robart's design, is set to the principle of "Auto-destruction" (S 17). To turn a single individual around is easy enough to be managed at the beginning of Book II:

> I is dead, the poet said.
> . . . . .
> Having plowed the ground
> I has turned at the end of the row
> a truly inherent *versus*
> . daeha sa kcab emas eht si I ecnis   (S 54)

LSD, which the troupe takes at the opening of Book II (to the accompaniment of "Cool Liquid Comes") can alter human perception so as to bring to life all the objects of the world; that adjustment of "the perceptual index" is marked in the narrative by the filling of "I"'s body with Kool Everything's five-gallon batch of LSD:

> What then, if we make I
> a receptacle of what
> Everything has,
> our gain will be twofold,
> we will have the thing
> we wish to keep

> as the container of the solution
> we wish to hold
> a gauge in other words
> in the form of man.   (S 58–59)

The larger task is the reversal of the "cultural collective" (S 146), and that, Slinger says, is the Poet's job:

> Turn the Great Cycle of the Enchanted Wallet
> of Robart the Valfather of this race
> turn the Cycle of Acquisition
> inside the Cobalt Heads of these
> otherwise lumpish listeners and make
> their azured senses warm *Make your norm*
> their own   (S 87)

Robart, or Howard Hughes, drives the cycle of acquisition through the heads of the citizenry; a mock-Lenin, "riding backward" in a sealed train to Las Vegas, he is ultimately turned around ("red-shifted"— deflected from this solar system) by his products, the Mogollones and the Single-Spacers, battling each other for supremacy in the mock-epic style of an STP television commercial. The cosmic reversal that resolves the genetic duel at the poem's conclusion (S 196) follows from a search for opposition. The Mogollones "got no vices / of course they got no virtues either" (S 181), and "the Single Spacers are Any-thing-arians / Ie, opposed to nothing" (S 182). (Like all the turning points in the poem, the resolution of this battle comes suddenly and inexplicably; there is aptly little causation behind the junctures of the narrative.) Robart's way is to eliminate contraries, to homogenize. His train gives out

> The scream of the Accomplished Present
> A conglomerate of Ends, The scream of Parallels
> All tied down with spikes
> Of the cold citizens made to run wheels upon
>
> Parallels are just two things
> going to the same place that's a bore   (S 95)

Against that steely cultural order, Dorn constructs a poem hungry for contradiction, especially on the level of style. The most obvious feature of this negative way is the pun, which generates signification out of not-meaning. The cleverest word play effectively seals the poem off as more a language game than a narrative. For instance, this is a quick, casual exchange between "I" and Claude the talking horse:

> Are you trying
> to "describe" me, boy?
> No, no, I hastened to add.
> And by the way boy
> if there's any addin
> to do around here
> *I'll* do it, that's my stick
> comprende?   (S 23)

Aside from the wonderful joke on "add," these lines succeed in subordinating the plot to the narration, the action to the language. Normally, the language of narration is subsequent to the events of the plot—first the events, then the telling of them. Yet in this poem the characters themselves are pronouns ("I") and puns (Claude Lévi-Strauss and Jean Flamboyant), and they respond to the narrator's language ("I hastened to add") as readily as to the actions of other characters; neither the plot nor the characters claim priority over the language of narration. For the poem is really seeking the unsystematic possibilities for meaning that inhere in language: "I'm trying to grasp what the words *can* mean" (I 47). Narrative poems are customarily committed to an action, often a realistic one; their language is meant to seem referential. In such poems, what the language *does* mean is confined in part by criteria of plausibility and consistency of character. All realistic possibility, in *Slinger*'s world, is controlled by Robart, and consistency is part of his technology. Dorn is looking for the unpredictable possibilities in language—the mutant puns; hence referentiality is a constraint which "I"—the "referee" (S 21)—must get rid of (S 30). As a system of connections and homologous structures, language is the métier of the poem; once Robart's death grip on political activity was firm, language became the only promising arena. *"The Art of poetry will choose to be born by the agent of the greatest syntactical density in the language, which we naturally call the world. And there is no other responsible definition of *the world*"* (V 121). Alternative conceptions of the world do not respond to desire, to the human sense of possibility, which keeps even Robart's city, Las Vegas, going night and day.

Dorn makes the language of this poem turn in on itself, rejecting obligations to ordinary signification. On its verbal surface, the poem is a weblike system of interconnections. Sometimes one phrase will clown about an earlier formulation, the way "I"'s description of the horse as "lathered . . . with abstract fatigue" (S 6) casts an arched eye back on Gunslinger's remark that his "mare lathers with tedium" (S 3). The point is not just that statements hook up to each other, but rather that their connections are made on some verbal ground—here, that abstracting figure, personification. The words have lives of their own; they can squirm free of a speaker's grip without warning. Metaphors refuse to stand still; they slyly, unpredictably insinuate themselves from the figurative to the literal level. Lil, impressed by the Horse's large joints, refers to them in passing as telescopes (S 21); a few pages later the narrator seems not to have noticed that she was speaking only figuratively:

> Umm, considered the Gunslinger
> taking the telescope
> from the Turned On Horse.   (S 27)

Not that the narrator is obtuse: literalizing is a convention of the poem, part of the *Slinger* manner. That convention prevails nicely over puns. Gunslinger refers to his adversary, a "plain, unassorted white citizen," as "this Stockholder" (S 25), which is literally correct because the citizen is holding the stock of a gun. Lil then identifies the citizen as an "investor" (S 26). The words of the poem play havoc with the conventions of narrative, character, plot; those greedy signs steal the whole show. Kool Everything responds even to the narrator's dead metaphors:

> Would you like a light
> I see yor roach has gone out
> continued the Doctor Catching his breath
>
> Slinger, did you flash how
> the PHD caught his breath,
> never saw anybody do it with their *hand*
>
> Yes agreed the Slinger, Brilliantly fast   (S 79)

High praise from a gunslinger.

Dorn wants possibility, "what the words can mean," to urge the poem on. Dead metaphors spring, one might say, to life, and hidden ones reveal themselves in the poem. Once the horses pulling the coach have been referred to as "driverless" (S 65), calling them "autocephalous" (S 159) seems to come naturally. The middle step in this literalizing process, the colloquial phrase that a driverless horse "has its own head," hardly needs to be stipulated; part of the fun of the poem is that such middle steps are typically elided. This process of literalization, kept going by puns, metaphors, live, dead, and merely implied, gathers enough momentum to absorb even what appear to be typographical errors. "An Idle Visitation" (1967), the short poem that gave birth to Gunslinger, now, revised, stands as the opening of the book. In this poem and in the first edition of Book I, Howard Hughes rents the second floor of "a hotel" in Boston; in *Slinger*, however, his domain is "ahotel." It seems that a copyist's error appealed to Dorn's imagination: in *The Cycle* (1971) Robart occupies "the blank hotel"—an apt abode for this phantom.

The systemic properties of language may assert themselves at any point, turning the narrative from action to grammar. Discussion of the object of Doctor Jean Flamboyant's dissertation, "The Tensile Strength of Last Winters Icicles," slips easily into a grammarian's colloquy on the third-person pronoun, "it," which does not change form when it is shifted from the nominative to the accusative or dative cases (S 80). The best example of this grammatical bent comes in the last book:

> Uh, I'm not sure I get your question Lil
> the Horse exhaled, but
> are you speaking of the need for horsepower?
>
> *Yes, I suppose I am, In Horses!*
> How would you like poco coito, Lil?
> Claude asked suddenly
>
> *My virtue is not presently on the market, fella*
> Lil glared, *which is bad timing of course*
> *because I might be amused*
> *to make it with a horse.*
>
> Make *It*, Claude frownd
> *It* aint nothing but a neuter pronoun.   (S 168)

The Horse turns the talk from flesh to grammar here because he has taken offense, as if Lil had called a stud a gelding. One of Elizabeth Sewell's remarks about nonsense literature provides a nice hold on the conventions of *Slinger:* "In Nonsense all the world is paper and all the seas are ink."[30] Dorn often acknowledges his lineage from Lewis Carroll. The Gunslinger wears a Queen of Hearts on his gauntlet (S 2), and his only song is a nonsense verse that specifically recalls a remark by Alice.[31] "I," the naif, is capable of sounding as confused and apologetic as Alice ("No . . . I mean I've never / seen his wife" [S 33]), and there are particular passages in Carroll that could have been models for this poem:

> "What do you mean by that?" said the Caterpillar, sternly. "Explain yourself!"
> "I can't explain *myself*, I'm afraid, Sir," said Alice, "because I'm not myself, you see."
> "I don't see," said the Caterpillar.[32]

Carroll would have been a useful model because he too was after conversions, "REVERSE SENSE," as "I" puts it (S 138); in the world of language, though not of men, the poet has the leverage to turn things upside down. From his new domain, as secretary to Parmenides, "I" sees the poem as an "ABSOLUTE LINGUATILT" (S 139). The words of the poem tilt in several directions: toward the scientists with offerings like "azimuthal" (S 56), "presyntactic metalinguistic urgency" (S 71), "organic radicals" (S 88), "epactos" (S 108), and "monotremata" (S 182); toward the hallowed past with such archaic formulations as "where will you now" (S 4) and "What meanst thou?" (S 169); and those tilts become formal bows with such contrivances as "a bed / will be my desire" (S 3). Yet the most severe inclination of Dorn's manner is colloquial. The night letter of "I" notes that "COLLOQUIAL LOCKS HOLD AGAINST ANY METHOD APPLIED OUTSIDE TIME" (S 139); Robart's mentality depends on the illusion that the present cultural order is timeless (one of his slogans—a nicely reversible one—is "EMIT NO TIME" [S 102]). *Slinger* is a hodgepodge of allusions: to Shakespeare and Keats, for example, but also to Grateful Dead song lyrics and Kay Kaiser's *Musical Question*. Almost any source may supply a phrase, any idiom may serve for a line or two. The *Slinger* manner is as absorbent as it is distinctive. Dorn has always been a mannered writer. The *Slinger* manner, however, is so peculiar a way of talking that Dorn can encompass competing idioms without endangering the coherence of his voice. In fact, the coherence of the poem rests more on that manner than on the plot or thematic structure.

Although the conventions of *Slinger* are taken over largely from nonsense literature, and Dorn's manner is above all jokey,[33] the ultimate seriousness of *Slinger* should not be in question; Lewis Carroll is one acknowledged master, but Parmenides is another. From the poet-

philosopher, Dorn takes details such as the topos of the driverless
horses, yet he also pursues Parmenides' ontological claim "that it *is*
and cannot not-be."[34] In *Slinger* the dimensions of being, of what is,
are plotted around a series of antitheses: language versus being,
meaning versus being, thinking versus being. Discourse *about* what
exists, like description, is deadly: "We'd all rather *be* there / than talk
about it" (S 22). Language clumsily gropes after being, and mean-
ing-mongers woodenly try to tug loose a lesson from being:

> What does the foregoing mean?
> I asked. Mean?
> My Gunslinger laughed
> *Mean?*
> Questioner, you got some strange
> obsessions, you want to know
> what something *means* after you've
> seen it, after you've *been* there
> or were you *out* during
> That time? No.
> And you want some *reason.*
> How fast are you
> by the way?   (S 26–27)

Dorn wants the poem to occupy *"the Very beginning of logic"* (S 21).
Before logic, before language, is a field of experience fresh enough to
generate mutant psyches. "Oh, yea, man I *never thot* I'd see this
place. / Then you'll have the privilege of seeing it / without having
thot it, prompted the Slinger" (S 63). That is the proper structure of
mental activity: first perception, then conception; the more common,
reverse procedure—*"askin so many questions / his eyes had already
answered"* (S 55)—is simply preposterous because it presumes that
sense experience is directed toward knowable ends.

Gunslinger sets himself against the teleological motive of experience, and he claims the sanction of Olson's Maximus on his side:

> When the act is
> so self contained
> and so dazzling in itself
> the target then
> can disappear
> in the heated tension
> which is an area between here

and formerly
In some parts of the western world
men have mistakenly
called that phenomenology—   (S 28–29)[35]

Such worthy acts come to transcend the ends they were intended to
serve, and the "conglomerate of Ends" (S 95) ordinarily envisaged is
just what Gunslinger and his companions plan to avoid. Gunslinger
means to challenge readers to "inhabit themselves" and "occupie
their instant" (S 91); put simply, the test is whether one is satisfied to
be oneself, without straining after distant goals.

There is your domain.
Is it the domicile it looks to be
or simply a retinal block
of seats in,
he will flip the phrase
the theater of impatience.

If it is where you are,
the footstep in the flat above
in a foreign land
or any shimmer the city
sends you
the prompt sounds
of a metropolitan nearness
he will unroll the map of locations.   (S 1–2)

The choice is between two sorts of consciousness: one, "the theater
of impatience," is a phantom consciousness tuned to the "perceptual
index" of television; this is Robart's mentality, and his lack of being is
indicated by the fact that "He aint never bin seen!" (S 91). The alternative is to make of one's consciousness a "domain" or "domicile"
where one can truly be present. Gunslinger's "map of locations," his
quest, can be of use only to those who seek such presence. The wittiest expression of Dorn's skepticism about motives and ends is the
"*Literate Projector, / which, when a 35 mm strip is put thru it / turns
it into a Script / Instantaneously! / and projects that*—the finished
script / onto the white virgin screen" (S 74). This parodic contraption
disassembles the apparatus of causation:

Yea,
it will Invent a whole new literachure
which was Already There

a lot of big novels will get restored
in fact Everything, uh, I mean
all of it can be run the other way—
some of the technikalities
havent been worked out for documentaries
but let's face it,
you could rerun I mean all of it
¡atencion!—Shoot a volcano, project it
and See the Idea behind it
sit down at the geologic conference
and hear the reasons Why
skip the rumble, move into the inference.
Eventually you could work your way back
to where it's still really dark
all the way back of the Brain?!   (S 74–75)

In the dark area, prior to all intentions, mental mutants lurk. Dorn
hopes that *Slinger*'s puns, paradoxes, palindromes, and gags lead
there, for that way lies beyond description.

Dorn now has behind him one of the most remarkable long poems of
the last thirty years. For a poet who is not yet ready to stop writing,
that can be a difficult position: witness how few long poems are
brought to conclusion by middle-aged writers. Perhaps Dorn is un-
comfortable, but among his contemporaries no one is more adept at
beginnings. His eye for contingent events is too sharp ever to allow
him the resting spot of a comprehensive achieved vision. That attention to circumstance makes him a hard poet to second-guess—which
is an odd thing to say of one whose principal concerns are political. Political poets, we tend to think, are programmatic, *if* they are sincere; a
political poet who publicly changes his mind (Dryden, say) is suspect.
Dorn has not shifted allegiances; allegiances have never been his concern. His political poetry either focuses elegiacally on individuals,
such as Dr. Herrara, Cleveland Thompson, Bigbear, and Reeta
Poonee, or improvises general propositions to account for the behavior
of social groups. His topics are either poignantly human or impersonal
and abstract; the middle ground of political parties and factions, or of
consistent application of policy lies barren for him.[36]

   . . . what is unmistakable is
that DeGaulle,
Ho Chi Minn, Chou en-Lai,

LeRoi Jones, Dean Rusk
are all doing the same bit:
pressing
        and they are
all correct—it is their thing
against anybody else's
                (there is no longer
        any *cause,* the fastest
    with the mostest is the rule   (CP 209–210)

Dorn's analytical cool can generate new groupings, but they are not directly political. There is nothing unusual about recent poets rising above ordinary political categories; rather rarely do they commit their writing to a politically working "side." This aloofness implies a generation's residual doubt about political poetry, as though to take sides (as Dryden did) were inappropriate, as though poetry can accommodate politics only on the level of abstraction above particular factions. However voguish political poetry has been in the last fifteen years (Dorn has been at it longer, of course), it has typically been a spectator art. Lowell's *History* is the grandest work of this political watching. Even Dorn, whose poetry is more intelligently political and more sensitive to wide complicity than that of almost any of his American contemporaries, has not written as a political participant, as a citizen. This general limitation may well descend from the Victorian sense—certainly not shared by Dorn—that the "worlds" of poetry and of politics are essentially at odds. Dorn's didacticism, however, invokes older sanctions that might seem capable of encouraging a more humane engagement of contemporary politics. Yet the danger of taking Dorn too strictly as a didactic political poet should be clear: "Such a thing as humanity seems very relative, the final abjuring of any vision" (CP 76).

Dorn seems now less than ever a poet of ideas. Since *Slinger* he has published two insistently small books, *Hello, La Jolla* (1978) and *Yellow Lola* (1980). He is using epigrams to break his narrative habits. But he remains committed to an acerbic, brittle manner:

A pontificatory use of the art
is both interesting & a lot of fun
the pope's got a really good role   (YL 31)

These books of sententiae are didactic for the fun of it, sarcastic and cutting, it seems, out of conviction that the pleasure of severe judgment is part of what poetry now needs. A poet, like the pontiff, can ex-

ercise the authority that comes of judgment almost at will, for his constituency is so vague as an institution that it imposes no unnegotiable
limits. Dorn roams like a tourist through American mass culture: with
allegiance to nothing local, an eye for the strange, and the desire to get
at the thinking or feeling behind the strangeness commonly taken as
normal. Often he comes up with just a quick gag:

> 1 Billion Chinese are telling me
> the gang of 4 are wrong?
> doesn't this seem out of proportion? (YL 103)

But his China Watch scans along some oddly independent angles:

> A protest against still another empty-minded choice
>
> I've acquired this political problem
> since I returned to North Beach
>
> Every day now, for a while,
> I've been handed a yellow piece of paper
> which tells me to normalize
> and just last week I saw
> a banner spanning Grant Street
> over in the China section
> which told me to *not* normalize
>
> I'm just a simple american*
> which means that I don't *object*
> to the normal, yet
> the *not* normal of course interests me more

> ———
>
> *I.e., a fate-torn traveller. (YL 97)

Normalization of U.S.–Chinese relations, recycling, Nadarism; Dorn
goes to some trouble to goad his readers—mainly liberal of course—
into examining their pieties skeptically. His trick is to write in a manner that makes his readers feel like insiders at the same time that their
sacred cows are rendered a little swinish.

In order to engage civic beliefs, Dorn keeps his poetry specific in its
reference. Of course much of his work has always been occasional, but
now it is tendentiously so.

In Defense of Pure Poetry

The guards can say what they want
And so can Vernon and so can NBC
But whatever it is they have to say
Nobody can fault the King
For squeezing the trigger on Robert Goulet.   (HLJ 30)

Than which, no verse is less pure. Elvis Presley, of course, was the
king of rock and roll. After his death, a number of stories, originating
with his father Vernon Presley, his bodyguards, and others, appeared
in the papers about the king's quirks. One story had it that he was
once so annoyed at watching Robert Goulet that he fired a pistol at the
television set. Dorn's joke has to do with the pop culture's appetite for
what seems suave: Goulet, Streisand, Barry Manilow. The programmatic point is that when such taste prevails, poets who try to write
purely surrender one of the traditional (and now urgent) offices of
their vocation—the correction of taste.

That correction, Dorn presumes, begins with attentiveness and
ends in judgment, not emotion. Goulet, Streisand, and Manilow sell
great swells of feeling to a culture that needs the lance.

The Word (20 January 1977)

Moved was a bit too classy
to be used to note an emotion
and I doubt that it occurred to him.
And who knows, it might
have seemed too Lowell-like
if it had crossed his mind

Sentimental, to be sure, cheap,
imported and ordinary   (YL 71)

20 January 1977 was Gerald Ford's last day in office. The *New York
Times* ran an article entitled "Farewells and Tears at the White
House," but Dorn is referring, with outrageous specificity, to a remark
by Henry Kissinger in an interview about his service as secretary of
state: "Finally I was terribly moved when President Kaunda [of An-
gola] got up at the end of my [1976] Lusaka [Zambia] speech and
embraced me. I thought that was a moving occasion." Dorn suggests
that perhaps the interviewer, not Kissinger, came up with that claim

to have been moved; Henry the world shaker is hard-nosed. For all of
Lowell's interest in the ways of the powerful, Dorn doubts that he
truly understood such people at all. Lowell, in Dorn's eyes, was the
Goulet of poets: he was always presenting the powerful in terms of
emotions that are reassuringly familiar. The powerful (even J. Edgar
Hoover), Dorn believes, are stranger than they get credit for; they'll
bear watching closely. That point is made, with these last two books,
in sentences that are rawly polemical and topical—and usually amusing.

> Environmental carcinogens
> and large bowel cancer
> go together like marble steps
> and fancy dancers   (YL 18)

"Go together like" is a formula made famous by Frank Sinatra ("Love
and Marriage") in the 1955 television version of Wilder's *Our Town*.
Dorn is a Juvenalian connoisseur of American mass culture.

Dorn shows rather little of Lowell's ambition. He has never attempted a summa, like *History*, and these last books suggest that he is
unlikely to do so soon. The case for Dorn as a major poet may one day
be strong; certainly his work cannot be adequately represented by a
small number of single poems. His accomplishment, however, will not
be properly assessed if his engagement with ideas becomes the main
measure. He himself has said expressly that his use of Heidegger and
Lévi-Strauss is playful, light (I 50–51); and the categorical discriminations that count heavily for didactic poets—between honorable and
pernicious behavior, say—double back on themselves and dissolve in
Slinger.[37] Judgment and understanding are not, for Dorn, ends in
themselves; they are vehicles of wit, which is his true muse. In *Slinger*
and these last two books, Dorn has become something of a note taker:
he watches the fantasies and distractions of American popular culture
from the sidelines. He has been "covering" the mass culture for the
last decade—as commentator, not teacher, surely not prophet. This is
a modest form of writing, always secondary, though his subject matter, the mind and manners of the nation, is major indeed. His poems
are not particularly deep or wise, and few are moving (in a pathetic
sense), however unsettling they are. Above all, they are spirited. And
that, especially now, is a fine thing for poetry to be.

Conclusion: Suburbs

I have tried to show that many of the best poets of the last forty years have written with fascination for the ideas, experiences, and even institutions that seemed central to the country. The notion that literature should judge and condemn the mainstream culture is not helpful in understanding the shape of recent literary history. Where poets have been most intent upon playing adversary to the dominant culture (and many of the poets I have overlooked are content with that role) the poetry has been blunt, rhetorical, and misleading. Much of what I take as the best recent poetry has not been written from an adversary perspective, and one of its distinguishing characteristics is a tendency to register fine distinctions where other poets and people see none. The poetry I admire from this period is fairly spoken of as one of accommodation rather than opposition. In the last decade, several important poets have tried in particular to accommodate the middle and lower-middle classes resident in the suburbs and represented through television, movies, and tabloids. In part this effort has been made in a spirit of concession to an audience, though the actual audience for poetry is suburban only insofar as college and university towns are suburban. Of course most American academic communities are by policy suburban, deliberately at no great remove from the central social institutions. To that extent, poets who have turned to the suburbs for subject matter are honestly engaging experiences that are indeed familiar, even to readers of poetry, and rather little explored by poets.

From just after the war through the 1950s, poets joined with influential intellectuals, like David Riesman and William H. Whyte, Jr., in criticizing suburban settlement.[1] The critique had its political motive: it was commonly said that the Republican suburbs elected Eisenhower, and Kennedy's success in the suburbs in 1960 did indeed contribute to his victory.[2] The 1950s were years of enormous growth for American suburbs. The greatest migration in the shortest time in the country's past occurred then, when Americans proudly occupied the suburbs.[3] Although some poets went too, they seem to have taken little pleasure in the move. In 1948 Richard Wilbur brought his elegy "To an American Poet Just Dead" to a close with these quatrains:

> Will the sprays weep wide for you their chaplet tears?
> For you will the deep-freeze units melt and mourn?
> For you will Studebakers shred their gears
> And sound from each garage a muted horn?

> They won't. In summer sunk and stupefied
> The suburbs deepen in their sleep of death.
> And though they sleep the sounder since you died
> It's just as well that now you save your breath.[4]

So far apart were American poets and suburbanites then. The wit of the penultimate quatrain is lost in the ponderous gloom of the last lines. It would be decades before the distance started to close. The 1970 census showed that for the first time more Americans lived in the suburbs than in the central cities.[5] In 1971 Mona Van Duyn, who makes no secret of being a suburban housewife and also a poet ("I weed and plant or write poems in the backyard garden"),[6] was given the National Book Award (she had received the Bollingen prize a year earlier), and a controversy between Allen Ginsberg and Richard Howard ensued. Ginsberg felt that Van Duyn represented little beyond "domesticated mediocrity."[7] And Howard observed that Ginsberg's avant-gardism had calcified all too early. Howard and the majority of the NBA committee were correct in gauging the migration of literary taste—though they would not have admitted doing this—toward greater sympathy with suburban subjects. During the next decade a number of excellent suburban poems appeared.

In 1982 Mona Van Duyn published *Letters from a Father, and Other Poems*, a book dedicated to her aged parents who both died in 1980. The two best poems in this uneven collection each concern one of her parents. The impressive success of "The Stream," written for her mother, clarifies the difficulties facing poets who have come to acceptable terms with the culture that offers row houses to young-marrieds, backyard gardens and New England vacation homes to the middle-aged, Oil of Olay and nursing homes to the elderly—something special for everyone. These are the closing lines (69–90) of this poem about Van Duyn's last visit with her mother:

> I see your loving look wherever I go.
> What is love? Truly I do not know.
>
> Sometimes, perhaps, instead of a great sea,
> it is a narrow stream running urgently
>
> far below ground, held down by rocky layers,
> the deeds of mother and father, helpless sooth-sayers
>
> of how our life is to be, weighted by clay,
> the dense pressure of thwarted needs, the replay
>
> of old misreadings, by hundreds of feet of soil,
> the gifts and wounds of the genes, the short or tall
>
> shape of our possibilities, seeking
> and seeking a way to the top, while above, running
>
> and stumbling this way and that on the clueless ground,
> another seeker clutches a dowsing-wand
>
> which bends, then lifts, dips, then straightens, everywhere,
> saying to the dowser, it is there, it is not there,
>
> and the untaught dowser believes, does not believe,
> and finally simply stands on the ground above,
> till a sliver of stream finds a crack and makes its way,
> slowly, too slowly, through rock and earth and clay.
>
> Here at my feet I see, after sixty years,
> the welling water—to which I add these tears.[8]

The preceding 68 lines develop out of the conventions set in the first line—direct address and reportage: "Four days with you, my father three months dead." These are practically the least appropriate procedures, for her mother presumably needs no narrative of events she herself witnessed. Yet this sense of a gap between artifice and simple, human subjects is at the heart of this poem and of much of Van Duyn's often roughed-up work. Van Duyn pretends to speak to the person she can now only speak about. The syntax moves blithely past the line breaks, without regard for the mainly offrhymed couplets;

only for the eye do the rhymes hold the words in place. Much of this poem is meant to seem pushed, offtarget, wrongly displaced (as when her mother calls her "Jane," or when the daughter patronizingly lies to her mother, "We'll do it again"). Van Duyn recounts how

> With a girl's grace you sat up
> and, as if you'd done it lifelong, reached out to cup
>
> my face in both your hands, and, as easily
> as if you'd said it lifelong, you said, "Don't cry,
>
> don't cry. You'll never know how much I love you."
> I kissed you and left, crying. It felt true.

Only one naturally skeptical of simple feelings needs to acknowledge the surprising sense that "It felt true." In this, her most direct book, Van Duyn seems consistently to mistrust her own poems, for at just the moment when her utterances must leave her and stand as artifacts she rushes to enrich them with resonant conclusions, as though the preceding lines were just not enough, at least for poetry. Poems seem to need some quantum of elevation at the last:

> So the world woos its children back for an evening kiss.
> *"Letters from a Father,"* L 6

> I close the box. Somewhere a telephone
> has made the appointment—a flower-scented pose
> where they wait with patience for one witnessing heart
> to snap its picture of their final faces. *"Photographs,"* L 15

The close of "The Stream" is rather an exception. In those 22 lines she takes up, altogether masterfully, the traditional figurative language of poetry, content to use allegory openly for so basic a subject as the death of her mother and the recovery of affection. Most of the poems that snap closed with a quick injection of meaning or metaphor seem flawed by a fear of writing plainly. That fear, I think, arises most predictably when a poet feels that his or her audience expects something visionary rather than a plain pleasure in things as they are. Insofar as critics select visionary moments in the poems they praise, they help to shape not only a limited, easy taste for poetry, but a special kind of corruption in the writing of those poets like Van Duyn whose inclination is always to resist the visionary, even at the cost of being known as a writer of reportage or a complacent representative of "domesticated mediocrity."

Among recent poets, probably Elizabeth Bishop and Robert Pinsky know their audiences best. One reward for that awareness is the ability to play easily and deftly upon preconceptions, a facility for making self-deprecatory jokes. Pinsky, for instance, says to his daughter:

> . . . if I felt the need
> To make some smart, professor-ish crack about
> Walt Whitman, the Internment Camps, or *Playboy*
> I could, if necessary, explain it to you . . .[10]

That combination of possible subjects needs no explanation; the range is embarrassingly familiar to the academic sensibility, I know. To be able just in passing to let the air out of his own pretensions, and those of like-minded readers, with more simple self-awareness than malice, is a useful resource to a poet who wants to talk with his audience. The cost of this rapport can also be calculated, however, as Pinsky knows well. A poet who knows his or her audience so well may too often be tempted to pull on those stops that give just the desired effect; the rhetorician gets facile admiration and quick acceptance.

Pinsky, in successfully maneuvering around this pitfall, sometimes strains a bit to defy his audience's expectations, in ways that can seem willful. His syntax, usually supple, dwells unusually on adversatives and alternatives, as if the art of elaboration were governed by a search for contraries. The first sentence of *An Explanation of America* pushes this syntax—and establishes its priority in the poem—about as far as it can reasonably go.

> As though explaining the idea of dancing
> Or the idea of some other thing
> Which everyone has known a little about
> Since they were children, which children learn themselves
> With no explaining, but which children like
> Sometimes to hear the explanations of,
> I want to tell you something about our country,
> Or my idea of it: explaining it
> If not to you, to my idea of you.   (p. 5)

Pinsky at times exploits the discursive resources of the language and thus rightly deals in sharp distinctions, in categories that sit still and erect, with the result that his verse is lucid, discriminating, and exact. At the same time, the categories of this poem—the love of death, the emptiness of the country, its great potential—genuinely develop from section to section and provide the poem with rich thematic coherence. But, wanting neither to fit too snugly a chair for the discursive poet nor to play always to his audience's known preconceptions, he occasionally undermines the clarity of his own verse with proliferating alternatives and complicating contingencies. There is a virtue to this procedure, that of avoiding simplifications, but a vice as well: undue self-consciousness.

Before looking further at this underside of self-consciousness, I want to state briefly some of the admirable qualities of the poem, though these could be demonstrated best by lengthy quotation and analysis. The clarity and coherence of the poem will strike any reader, admiring or not, but the book has dignity and warmth as well. If warmth comes easily to a father writing to his daughter, so much more reason to appreciate the rhetorical frame in which this explanation of a nation is set. The dignity of the book is plainest in terms of technique.

> In a way, every stranger must imagine
> The place where he finds himself—as shrewd Odysseus
> Was able to imagine, as he wandered,
> The ways and perils of a foreign place:
> Making his goal, not knowing the real place,
> But his survival, and his progress home.
> And everyone has felt it—foreign ground,
> With its demand on the imagination
> Like the strange gaze of the cattle of the Sun—
> Unless one is an angel, or a hick,
> A tribesman who never made his wander-year.   (p. 25)

The diction derives from a range of experience at once worldly, mental, and literary; one thinks that one has seen the eyes of the cattle of the Sun. Most of this experience can be referred to with conventional language: "shrewd Odysseus," "The ways and perils of a foreign place." Pinsky writes with confidence that not every perception needs to be rendered striking in order to count as poetry; the importance of much of life rests on its being understood in common with others, live as well as dead.[11] That too is richness, though it is bare of braveries. Pinsky quietly tries to purify the language already well known to his readers, making newly clear those linguistic trends that have moved around some of the most stable human experiences. At the tail end of an eleven-line sentence, he writes, "whether sinister / Or bland as a Christmas card from 'Unicef' " (p. 10), reminding his mainly liberal-minded readers of the obtuseness of American political discriminations and enthusiasms; for while support for Unicef has long been a liberal piety, to the American right this arm of the UN has been denounced as sinister, that is, leftist.[12] Pinsky can employ stately as well as colloquial language, speaking of hicks along with angels, because of the assurance that comes from knowing one's listeners well. The style is under no pressure to demonstrate coherence, as Merrill's is, because it rests soundly on the coherence of the audience—its known tastes, beliefs, experiences, opinions.

This is not to say that he is constrained by merely conventional wisdom; the book is arranged, explicitly, around three clichés about America—it is fragmented, empty, and all-potential—that are picked apart and examined, tested, and qualified in the poem. The praise one can employ most fairly here is that the book displays freshness of conception. Many passages are compelling as thought, certainly a rare quality in recent poetry.

A country is the things it wants to see.
If so, some part of me, though I do not,
Must want to see these things—as if to say:

"I want to see the calf with two heads suckle;
I want to see the image of a woman
In rapid sequence of transparencies
Projected on a bright flat surface, conveying
The full illusion and effect of motion,
In vast, varying scale, with varying focus,
Swallow the image of her partner's penis.
I want to see enormous colored pictures
Of people with impossible complexions,
Dressed, often, in flamboyant clothes, along
The roads and fastened to the larger buildings.
I want to see men playing games with balls.
I want to see new cars; I want to see
Faces of people, famous, or in times
Of great emotion, or both; and above all,
It seems, I want to see the anthropomorphic
Animals drawn for children, as represented
By people in smiling masks and huge costumes.
I want to shake their hands. I want to see

Cars crashing; cards with a collie or a pipe
And slippers, dry flies, mallards and tennis rackets—
Two people kissing for Valentine, and then
A nicky-nacky design, a little puppy
Begging for me to like the person who mailed it."

In Mexico, I suppose they want to see
The Eyes of God, and dogs and ponies coupling
With women, skeletons in hats and skirts,
Dishwashers, plutocrats humiliated,
Clark Gable, flashy bauhaus buildings, pistols.
It always is disturbing, what a country
Of people want to see. . . . In England once,
A country that I like, between two Terms,
In Oxford, I saw a traveling carnival
And fair with Morris dancers, and a woman
Down in a shallow pit—bored-looking, with bored
And overfed, drugged-looking brown rats lolling
Around her white bare body where it was chained
Among them: sluggish, in a furtive tent.

And that was something, like the Morris dance,
Which an American would neither want
To see, nor think of hiding, which helps to prove
That after all these countries do exist,
All of us sensing what we want to see
Whether we want it separately, or not.   (pp. 8-9)

The section begins altogether straightforwardly with a proposition that, once stated plainly, is entertained as a hypothesis in order to determine what can be made to follow from it. The question governing the section is not so much what America is, as how he, a frankly educated and discriminating person, can define his own identity in relation to the vulgarity of American mass culture. The part of him that is involved with the national identity, he conjectures (line 2), bears some responsibility for the corruptions of public imagination so plentiful in America. That one does not individually consent to pornography, or for that matter Disneyland, is not enough to dissolve the bond between the mass culture and any American, even a poet or an intellectual. "The plural-headed Empire," he tells his daughter, is "Beyond my outrage or my admiration" (p. 15). His strikingly abstract diction ("rapid sequence of transparencies," "anthropomorphic / Animals drawn for children") holds this subject at a genuine enough distance, for these are not the objects of his imagination (an earlier draft read: "Apparently, people want to see / a woman swallow a man's prick").[13] But how much effort is made to restrain judgment, a facile conclusion, is plain when one recalls how Olson, in 1953, referred to the billboarding of America:

> colored pictures
> of all things to eat: dirty
> postcards
>   And words, words, words
> all over everything
>   No eyes or ears left
> to do their own doings . . .[14]

Twenty-five years later, Pinsky writes with a sense of how even these impossible images may, in time, become naturalized in the imagination (lines 11–13). He can write, as Olson could not, with flexibility of attitude, a fair-mindedness that one cannot expect from avant-gardists like Olson.

Still, as I have suggested, Pinsky does pay a price for this peace with his audience. At the center of *An Explanation of America* is a turbulence of categories. In "A Love of Death" (Part Two, section I) he takes up terms of analysis (shadow, sod) that he used in *The Situation of Poetry* to criticize poets who have been obviously influenced by Roethke, Merwin, Bly, and Strand. This particular section of *An Explanation* is written as though to demonstrate (where no demonstration should be necessary) sensitivity to the genuine attractions of a way of thinking and writing that this poet had elsewhere, as critic, censured.[15] The subsequent section, "Bad Dreams," takes this subject a step further and edges the analytical categories toward obscurity. At first, Pinsky describes one way of life, wholly honorable.

> People who must, like immigrants or nomads,
> Live always in imaginary places
> Think of some past or word to fill a blank—
> The encampment at the Pole or at the Summit;
> Comanches in Los Angeles; the Jews
> Of Russia or Roumania, who lived
> In Israel before it was a place or thought,
> But a pure, memorized word which they knew better
> Than their own hands.   (p. 25)

They clearly live as poets do, "always in vision." The danger of this life is that the blank may enlarge until the actual scene of the senses fades entirely.

> In place of settled customs,
> Such a man might set up a brazen calf,
> Or join a movement, fanatical, to spite
> The spirit of assembly, or of words—
> To drown that chatter and gossip, and become
> Sure, like machines and animals and the earth.
>
> Such a man—neither a Greek adventurer
> With his pragmatic gods, nor an Indian,
> Nor Jew—would worship, not an earth or past
> Or word, but something immanent, like a shadow . . .   (p. 27)

The dichotomy here might at first be taken as clear, especially by those who know Pinsky's critical discussion of his contemporaries: good poets, like tribesmen (Indians or Jews), hold on to their games, jokes, gossip, and love of skill, for their lives are committed to communities. But poor poets, in their loneliness, become enamoured of a word, say "shadow," and worship that like a brazen calf. The brazen calf, however, is a debased icon of Jewish history, and Pinsky says plainly that the type of the poor poet, "Such a man," is not a Jew. Pinsky emphasizes this embryo of a contradiction a few lines later by saying that this representative "of a sentimental fascism," as an earlier version had it, wants to "lose himself / Among a brazen crowd, as in a calf." The man of corrupted imagination is and is not Jewish, is and is not Pinsky himself; he is a symbol (in a particularly literal poem) of a rejected alternative, but also of a repressed and abiding desire. His place in the poem is not that of an example because the proposition he might illustrate is too dark and contradictory for formulation; rather the confusion that surrounds the brazen calf marks Pinsky's uneasiness about the clarity of his own judgment, his status as an observer of the corruptions of imagination, and the depth of his own commitment to communities. These mixed feelings are not unpacked in the poem, yet the pressure on that epithet brazen calf makes these buried complications seem deliberate, if not programmatic.

The strengths of *An Explanation,* I'm sure, will become increasingly evident in the next decade. This book will probably serve as one of the markers by which the literary history of this period will be known, and so its weaknesses are important to discover now. The rougher parts of the poem serve to illuminate some of the special difficulties of the culture poetry I have been describing. Pinsky is most in trouble not, as others would have it, when he is most discursive, most explanatory, but rather when he is too aware of himself and his relation to his audience, for then he strains to be surprising, zany, unpredictable. And this too is a mannerism that can eventually corrupt the contract between writer and reader.

The third section of Part Two develops this problem in a fresh direction with a translation of Horace's epistle to Quinctius; "I should be more Horatian about my man," earlier drafts of "Bad Dreams" read. Horace elaborates the advantages of living on his farm "just out of Rome," as Pinsky says. (Actually, the Sabine farm was about forty kilometers, a long afternoon's ride, from Rome; Pinsky is intent on preserving the notion of easy access to the imperial city.) The danger of living in Rome, as Quinctius does, is

> Of course, that one might listen too much to others,
> Think what they see, and strive to be that thing,
> And lose by slow degrees that inward man
> Other first noticed— . . .   (p. 32)

Quinctius' immersion in the affairs of the metropolitan center brings the risk of a kind of corruption that a poet like Pinsky must consider. To participate in the affairs of Rome is noble and invigorating, but to lose oneself in the consensus of one's contemporaries is a special kind of death for a poet.

>   I like to be told I'm right,
> And brilliant, as much as any other man.
> The trouble is, the people who give out
> The recognition, compliments, degrees
> Can take them back tomorrow, if they choose;
> The committee or electorate decide
> You can't sit in the Senate, or have the Prize—
> 'Sorry, but isn't that ours, that you nearly took?'   (p. 33)

Horace's protection against this danger is in part his removal to a suburb of Rome—and this is Pinksy's hedge too.

This long poem is devoted to an extraordinary ambition: to explain America. It delivers well, as I've indicated. One of the surprises of the poem is that the explanation proceeds from a suburban perspective:

the first narrative passage, fifteen lines into the poem, concerns a Brownies' dancing lesson. That a poet in 1979 should manage to survey the nation with generous yet unblinkered urbanity from a suburb of Boston is an indication of how poetry has migrated in the last few decades. Pinsky constructs a compelling account of his nation with very little reference to the chief metropolis, and without a touch of embarrassment at being surburban.

In 1980, the end of the period under discussion here, James McMichael published *Four Good Things,* which I take to be the best book of poetry for that year.

> From the McMichaels',
> Florence. She passed the Silvers', the Johnsons'.
> She was walking to Martello and the bus. She was
> the woman who took care of me, and she was going
> shopping.[16]

The book opens like a novel ("Martello you call it?"): with a character moving through a social territory, performing the sort of simple act that may come to seem consequential in some larger series, a plot. Florence is the housekeeper (almost no one but domestic workers ride the buses of southern California); her role is a confusing mix of economics and intimacy. The social terrain is suburban; people collect in (at least) pairs, the McMichaels, the Silvers, the Johnsons, and inhabit houses. (McMichael refers always to plural nouns when what truly interests him is the typical: people are representative, we have come to believe, only as their numbers add up.) But the houses only seem to be separate:

> Where the money for a house had
> come from, what the Mayor had in mind, or
> Public Works, or how the street would look with lights—
> affairs like these beyond the garden stayed
> accessible, a movement to and from the house
> implicit in its horizontal lines. The roof was
> long and relatively flat. Beams above the frames of
> doors and windows were much broader than the
> frames themselves and paralleled the covered
> entryways and porches. Even the stairs inside
> were less than vertical, each section of the railing

carved from a single piece of teak and joined to
all the other teak—the notched and interlocking
kickplates . . .
Everything showed you how it went together.   (pp. 14–15)

Four Good Things is about Pasadena, once a small city but after
1950 a quaint suburb of the city of suburbs (only the Pasadena free-
way, the nation's oldest, has four lanes of traffic winding under a rail-
road trestle). McMichael works on a number of questions about
American suburban life: What does it feel like to live in a suburb? How
do social relations become distinctly suburban? What sort of economy
and technology foster suburban settlement? Where did this form of
social organization originate? Is there a psychology, a set of personality traits, that develops easily in the suburbs? These are not questions
that poets commonly ask. Novelists, essayists, yes, but not poets: poetry, the conventions that comprise that term for a generation, has
more or less given up on many subjects (especially social ones) and
shies away from discursive explanations. Great poems often break the
conventions of one generation, only to reestablish others for a succeeding generation: McMichael is one of those poets (Olson, Ashbery,
Ammons, and Pinsky are others) whose writing reclaims for poetry
some of the prerogatives ceded to prose, fictional and expository.
McMichael gives answers to these questions, but more important he
feels his way around answers, as an essayist would not. Although
there are remarkable independent passages in this long poem (such
as that about trying to fall asleep), McMichael's achievement is less
there than in the constant thoughtfulness brought to bear on questions that, in the last thirty years, have become peculiarly questions of
our time. McMichael begins with the architecture because this medium puts social questions directly to the senses, and because his father was a real-estate developer. Those horizontal lines of California
architecture express a reach beyond the surveyor's boundaries to the
systematic organization of the community—bankers, mayors, engi-
neers. What one hears much more often is that suburbanites want to
live by themselves, everyone a cowboy on his own ranch. McMichael's
observation is quite the reverse.

But the connection between suburban social units is quite distinct.
Pound's *Cantos* were designed to focus on the "repeat in history," a
moment when something permanent breaks through to the quotidian
world.[17] McMichael imagines a thoroughly different repeat: suburban
"lots that for several blocks each way / repeated themselves with
slightly different houses" (p. 16). Why that conformity, so plain to

anyone with eyes? McMichael suggests that the source goes back to the mechanics of eighteenth-century manufacture. The British textile industry was once domestic, "looms and jennies in the kitchens of the / small freeholders and the farmers who would / sell their cloth to merchants." A breakthrough came with technical innovation: "Arkwright's water-frame replaced the hand's inexpert / pulling and pushing, movements that begin and end / and can't repeat themselves exactly" (p. 27). The mercantile goal is to reduce variation to the point where one can speak of processes being repeatable; once that objective is met, the future is controllable, and not just economically. Nineteenth-century entrepreneurs

> were looking for those samenesses that make us feel we've
> broken through to something, through those
> unsure things that happen in a place in time to
> something like our safe impalpable and self-sustaining
> plans that are always future. (pp. 35–36)

Mechanical engineering, as a way of thinking, shaped McMichael's own sensibility. The comfort of a repeatable act is familiar and convincing, as when a boy dismantles and reassembles a kitchen appliance while casually talking with the housekeeper; or when travelers, after their first meal in a foreign city, return to the hotel room, somehow assured by its new familiarity. And if the stakes are raised, that comfort can be deeply sustaining. McMichael's father knew that his wife would

> live five years. She wouldn't
> think about it, would be in and out of
> wheelchairs, hospitals, assuming to the end
> that she was getting better. That made it
> tolerable for her, and covered him to work
> so thoroughly at what he did all day
> that coming home was easy. Dinner. Florence
> leaving. Me in bed, asleep. Alone, it was
> their time, unless the phone would ring. (p. 3)

So long as the variations (whatever their magnitude) can be predicted—a telephone call, death from cancer—life is manageable. McMichael is a worrier, and that sometimes damages the poem, when his language becomes too vague, fretful, and hypothetical ("as what might happen to us / happens or doesn't" [p. 27]), and distinctions dissolve. But the excesses are remarkably rare: with enormous equanimity, the book attends to a wide range of subjects. McMichael's astonishing achievement is to show how the apparently limitless worrying of a psychiatric patient—

> He'll put it in his
> suitcase, on the top, his shirts are last. He'll pull the
> zippers all the way until it's closed and then he'll
> lift it by its handles, carry it across the rug. The
> door will be there, he'll open it. He'll go on through the
> hallway to the door and open it and come inside toward that
> other door.   (p. 52)

—differs only by degree from the charting of maps, the programing of a computer that achieves comprehensiveness by adding one digit to another, worrying over a single distinction at a time. This is not to say that we are tied to our technology only by our neuroses, though that is what we are accustomed to hearing. McMichael thinks (about making love, for example) and writes (about the organ in his stepmother's house) along the same channels as Antony, the psychiatric patient, with the same goal (prediction) that moved the scientists George Cayley, Theodore von Karman, and Fritz Zwicky.

McMichael would rather understand than condemn suburban America. How could he condemn those whose inventions set the terms for his own thought, for his character? We are within those terms still and will get outside only after some innovation sets us working in a different direction. The recent historical pivot was the resolution of World War II. Before 1945 the suburban boom was a mere pop. Pasadena's

> one industry,
> the Novelty Works of Mr. Wakeley went on stuffing
> scorpions and trapdoor spiders, horny toads,
> small animals and birds. The balance of trade was
> not in Pasadena's favor.   (p. 13)

After the war, though, military contracts permitted the growth of an electronics industry: "The beams of cathode-ray / electrons through a vacuum tube would synchronize each / thirtieth of a second. Successively, in league, / they looked like something" (p. 22). Close enough together, dots on a screen form a continuous line, or seem to, such is the power of repetition. So people, living close enough together, in houses sufficiently similar, need not be known individually; the variations are slight enough to ignore. Families can then flow through one house after another, as they do in California, keeping developers in business, and the configurations hold constant; to a cartographer's eye, those houses lose nothing by being vacant.

Robert Hass has called *Four Good Things* a classic, and with good reason.[18] This book seems a fulfillment of McMichael's intentions on several levels—that, more than a staking out of area for future development. The prosody is kept mainly iambic and assured (though someone might speak of it as vague), never more than a digit or two from a blank-verse norm; McMichael exploits the systematic repetitions of pentameter only when some rhetorical emphasis is appropriate. His themes are amply developed and brought to satisfying conclusion, largely by a meditative method: subjects are scrutinized with all the usual resources of meditation, introspection, and association, but also with coherent discursive analysis. McMichael brings together a broad range of subjects not by juxtaposing striking images, as his contemporaries often do, but with the techniques of narrative and expository art. The result is a book rich enough to demand many readings, and candid enough to terrify—not with revelations so much as with patient examination of the excesses of a way of thinking and worrying that is hard to get around. I can imagine no greater justification of the line of culture poetry during the last four decades than that it led to a book of such range of feeling and delicate intelligence.

The historical argument that the spirit of the time has forcefully and productively engaged the imaginations of recent poets is meant to characterize not the largest number of writers but, like most literary-historical explanations, only the poetry that comes to matter most, a small selection from all that is written. Ezra Pound once said that critics are "To be judged far more by their selections than by their palaver."[19] I have quoted many of the poems of the last thirty-five years that seem to me worthy of attention and admiration. If these passages are an incitement to further reading, perhaps the historical explanation rests on the proper cases. But my selection of poets is meant to make a secondary point as well. Two of the poets, Lowell and Dorn, are, on the face of it, culture poets, but at least two others, Creeley and Merrill, certainly are not. Yet so forceful has the spirit of the times been that even a miniaturist, like Creeley, and a decisively unpolitical poet, like Merrill, have been moved to write about the cultural life of their era. One more line, a crossing one, needs to be drawn clearly too.

Lowell and Merrill have mainly kept their meters, while Creeley, Ashbery, and Dorn, who associated themselves with avant-garde circles of the 1950s, have written resolutely in free verse. Whether poets have thought of themselves as avant-garde or traditional, whether they have been by inclination and talent public, rhetorical poets or insistently private, still the intellectual and ideological excitement of American public life since World War II has made itself felt in their work. More particularly, many of the best recent poets have done what they could to benefit as writers from that excitement, to make a profitable peace with the nation. If some readers and critics persist in the belief that American poets have made themselves cultural outlaws, they must do so in spite of a very distinguished group of poets who, it seems to me, have looked more searchingly and fairly at the national culture.

· *Notes*
· *Credits*
· *Index*

· Notes

Introduction: Centers

1. Karl Shapiro, *In Defense of Ignorance* (New York: Random House, 1960), p. 22.

2. Matthew Arnold, "The Function of Criticism at the Present Time," in *Complete Prose Works,* ed. R. H. Super, 11 vols. (Ann Arbor: University of Michigan Press, 1960–1977), III, 261.

3. *Goethe's Literary Essays,* ed. J. E. Spingarn (New York: Frederick Ungar, 1921), p. 88.

4. Ibid., pp. 83–84.

5. Arnold, "The Literary Influence of Academies," *Complete Prose,* III, 247.

6. Edward Shils, *The Intellectuals and the Powers* (Chicago: University of Chicago Press, 1972), p. 171.

7. Stephen E. Ambrose, *Rise to Globalism: American Foreign Policy, 1938–1976* (Harmondsworth: Penguin, 1976), p. 11.

8. See Ronald Steel, *Pax Americana* (New York: Viking, 1967).

9. Arnold, *Culture and Anarchy,* in *Complete Prose,* V, 103–104, 134.

10. Arnold, "The Literary Influence of Academies," III, 249.

11. Ibid., pp. 241–242.

12. Johnson, "Preface to Shakespeare," in *The Yale Edition of the Works of Samuel Johnson,* vols. 7–8, *Johnson on Shakespeare,* ed. Arthur Sherbo (New Haven: Yale University Press, 1968), VII, 61.

13. William Wordsworth, "Preface" to *Lyrical Ballads, The Prose Works,* W. J. B. Owen and Jane Worthington Smyser, 3 vols. (Oxford: Clarendon Press, 1974), I, 159.

14. Arnold, "The Study of Poetry," in *Complete Prose,* IX, 168–171.

15. Arnold, "Preface to First Edition of *Poems* (1853)," *Complete Prose,* I, 3, 13.

16. George Saintsbury, *A History of Criticism and Literary Taste in Europe,* 3 vols. (Edinburgh: William Blackwood, 1949), III, 516–517.

17. Arnold, "On the Modern Element in Literature," *Complete Prose,* I, 20, 33.

18. Arnold, "Dr. Stanley's Lectures on the Jewish Church," *Complete Prose*, III, 69.

19. Arnold, "The Bishop and the Philosopher," *Complete Prose*, III, 40.

20. Arnold, *Culture and Anarchy, Complete Prose*, V, 126.

21. Arnold, *Schools and Universities on the Continent, Complete Prose*, IV, 147.

22. Arnold, *Culture and Anarchy*, V, 178, 251.

23. Arnold, "On the Modern Element," I, 17, 28, 36.

24. Arnold, "The Bishop and the Philosopher," p. 41.

25. Arnold, *On Translating Homer, Complete Prose*, I, 174.

26. Lionel Trilling, "Preface," *Beyond Culture* (New York: Harcourt, Brace, Jovanovich, 1965).

1. Audience, Canon

1. John Crowe Ransom, "Poets Without Laurels," *The World's Body* (1938; Baton Rouge: Louisiana State University Press, 1968), p. 62.

2. T. S. Eliot, *Selected Essays* (New York: Harcourt, Brace and World, 1960), p. 248.

3. Christopher Clausen, "The Decline of American Poetry," *Virginia Quarterly Review*, 54 (Winter 1978), 76–77.

4. James Atlas, "The Appetite May Sicken and So Die," *Poetry*, 119 (December 1971), 169. Herbert Leibowitz, quoted in James Atlas, "New Voices in American Poetry," *New York Times Magazine*, 3 February 1980, p. 52. Joseph Epstein, "Is American Literature an Equal-Opportunity Employer?," *Commentary*, 64 (June 1980), 34. Charles Molesworth, *The Fierce Embrace* (Columbia: University of Missouri Press, 1979), p. 5. Wendell Berry, "The Specialization of Poetry," *Hudson Review*, 28 (Spring 1975), 12. Delmore Schwartz, *Selected Essays*, Donald A. Dike and David H. Zucker, eds. (Chicago: University of Chicago Press, 1970), pp. 15, 19. Karl Shapiro, *In Defense of Ignorance*, p. 26.

5. T. S. Eliot, *On Poetry and Poets* (New York: Farrar, Straus and Cudahy, 1957), p. 49.

6. Shelley, quoted in Levin L. Schücking, *The Sociology of Literary Taste*, trans. Brian Battershaw (1966; Chicago: University of Chicago Press, 1974), p. 47.

7. Clausen says that in England, where modernism was less triumphant than it was in America, the audience for poetry has not fallen off so sharply. I do not have comparable figures for British and American book sales. If one were to compare book sales and overall population, Britain might well seem more literate than the United States.

8. William Wasserstrom, ed., *A Dial Miscellany* (Syracuse: Syracuse University Press, 1963), p. 1.

9. *Letters of Wallace Stevens*, ed. Holly Stevens (London: Faber, 1967), p. 243.

10. Robert Creeley, "Introduction," *Black Mountain Review*, 3 vols. (New York: AMS Press, 1969).

11. On the weakening of American political consensus, see Morris Janowitz, *The Last Half-Century: Societal Change and Politics in America* (Chicago: University of Chicago Press, 1978), esp. chs. 4, 6.

12. I have argued for this assessment of Olson's career at length in *Charles Olson: The Scholar's Art* (Cambridge: Harvard University Press, 1978). In Chapter 2, here, I make a similar point about Creeley's development.

13. When book salesmen have to market a large number of titles on their employers' lists, they may regard some of those titles as "skip-books," the ones they will not bother to promote to booksellers. Anticipating the booksellers' thinking of poetry volumes as skip-books, editors may increase the size of a printing in order to increase pressure on the salesmen not to overlook the poetry books.

14. It should be noted that narrative poems, such as *Slinger*, seem to have a special appeal to contemporary poetry readers.

15. Dorn's *Slinger* costs $5; Merrill's *Scripts for the Pageant,* from Atheneum, $8.95.

16. Karl Shapiro, "Creative Glut," *Poetry,* 135 (October 1979), 36–49.

17. Robert Pinsky, *The Situation of Poetry* (Princeton: Princeton University Press, 1976), pp. 162–169; Paul Breslin, "How To Read the New Contemporary Poem," *American Scholar,* 47 (Summer 1978), 357–370.

18. Atheneum and especially Harry Ford, who edits the poetry series, enjoy well-deserved high regard among poetry editors. Ford has demonstrated an unusual ability to recognize poetic talent, and his taste has anticipated, to a surprising degree, the taste of the national audience.

19. Wordsworth, "Preface" to *Lyrical Ballads,* p. 122.

20. *The Cantos of Ezra Pound* (New York: New Directions, 1970), pp. 518, 506.

21. Frank Kermode, "Institutional Control of Interpretation," *Salmagundi,* 43 (Winter 1979), 81–82; reprinted in *The Art of Telling* (Cambridge: Harvard University Press, 1983).

22. Ezra Pound, *ABC of Reading* (1934; New York: New Directions, 1960), p. 39. Pound was more concerned to distinguish the inventors from the dilutors than the major from the minor poets.

23. Eliot, *On Poetry and Poets,* pp. 44, 47.

24. See Walter Cahn, *Masterpieces: Chapters on the History of an Idea* (Princeton: Princeton University Press, 1979).

25. W. H. Auden, *The Dyer's Hand* (New York: Vintage, 1968), pp. 21–22. See also W. H. Auden, "Introduction," *19th Century British Minor Poets* (New York: Delacorte, 1966), pp. 15–16, where Auden says that in order to acquire the status of "major" a poet first "must write a lot."

26. *American Poetry Review,* 9 (April 1980), 20.

27. Robert Lowell, *History* (New York: Farrar, Straus and Giroux, 1973), pp. 193, 194.

28. "News Note," *Poetry,* 135 (November 1979), 115.

29. See Richard McKeon, "Canonic Books and Prohibited Books: Orthodoxy and Heresy in Religion and Culture," *Critical Inquiry,* 2 (Summer 1976), 781–806.

30. Hugh Kenner, "Louis Zukofsky: All the Words," *New York Times Book Review,* 18 June 1978, p. 11. See also Marjorie Perloff, "Pound/Stevens: Whose Era?" *New Literary History,* 13 (Spring 1982), 485–514.

31. Ernst Robert Curtius, *European Literature and the Latin Middle Ages,* trans. Willard R. Trask (1953; New York: Harper, 1963), p. 259. Frank Kermode, *The Classic* (New York: Vintage, 1975).

32. T. S. Eliot, "Poetry and Propaganda," *The Bookman,* 70 (February 1930), 601.

33. On the absence of a political center, see Janowitz, *Last Half-Century,* esp. pp. 95–96; on the absence of a literary center, see Ishmael Reed, "American Poetry: Looking for a Center," *The Pushcart Prize, IV: Best of the Small Presses,* ed. Bill Henderson (Yonkers: Pushcart Press, 1979), pp. 524–544.

34. David Riesman and Nathan Glazer, "The Intellectuals and the Discontented Classes (1955)," in *The Radical Right,* ed. Daniel Bell (Garden City: Doubleday, 1963), p. 128.

35. Walt Whitman, *Leaves of Grass,* ed. Sculley Bradley and Harold W. Blodgett (New York: Norton, 1973), p. 196.

36. *New York Times,* 15 May 1959, p. 1:14.

37. Ibid., 20 May 1959, pp. 8:4; 5 June 1960, p. 16:1.

38. John Hollander, *Town and Country Matters* (Boston: Godine, 1972), p. 61.

39. John Hollander, *A Crackling of Thorns* (New Haven: Yale University Press, 1958), p. 32.

40. John Hollander, *Blue Wine and Other Poems* (Baltimore: Johns Hopkins, 1979), pp. 37, 41.

41. Robert von Hallberg, "The Poets' Politics: A View from the Archive," *Chicago Review,* 28 (Summer 1976), 147–152, 156.

42. Arthur M. Schlesinger, Jr., *The Vital Center* (Boston: Houghton Mifflin, 1949), pp. 255–256.

43. Russell W. Davenport, in collaboration with the editors of *Fortune, U.S.A.: The Permanent Revolution* (New York: Prentice-Hall, 1951), pp. vii–viii.

44. *Goals for Americans: The Report of the President's Commission on National Goals* (New York: Prentice-Hall, 1960), p. xi.

45. Godfrey Hodgson, *America in Our Time* (Garden City: Doubleday, 1976), p. 96.

46. *Goals for Americans,* p. 137.

2. Robert Creeley and John Ashbery

1. *Goals for Americans,* p. 3; *Prospect for America: The Rockefeller Panel Reports* (Garden City: Doubleday, 1961), pp. 340, 402.

2. Peter F. Drucker, *The New Society: The Anatomy of the Industrial Order* (New York: Harper and Row, 1950), pp. 6, 265–266, 1.

3. Gregory Bateson, *Steps to an Ecology of Mind* (New York: Ballantine, 1972), p. 476.

4. Norbert Wiener, *Cybernetics* (New York: Wiley, 1948), p. 55.

5. Charles Olson, *Archaeologist of Morning* (New York: Cape Goliard/Grossman, 1970), p. 47.

6. Daniel Bell, *The End of Ideology* (Glencoe: Free Press, 1960), pp. 16, 370. For a full account of the development of systems analysis and a critical analysis of its ideological claims, see Robert Lilienfeld, *The Rise of Systems Theory: An Ideological Analysis* (New York: Wiley, 1978), esp. ch. 9; and James W. Carey and John J. Quirk, "The Mythos of the Electronic Revolution," *American Scholar,* 39 (Spring and Summer 1970), 219–241, 395–424.

7. Talcott Parsons, "Systems Analysis: Social Systems," in *International*

Encyclopedia of the Social Sciences, ed. David L. Sills, 18 vols. (New York: Macmillan and Free Press, 1968), XV, 469.

8. Zbigniew Brzezinski, *Between Two Ages: America's Role in the Technotronic Era* (New York: Viking, 1970), p. 55.

9. Anatol Rapoport, "Systems Analysis: General Systems Theory," in *Encyclopedia of the Social Sciences,* XV, 454.

10. Parsons, "Systems Analysis," p. 460.

11. Wiener, *Cybernetics,* p. 9.

12. See Bell, *End of Ideology,* p. 244.

13. Robert Creeley, *Contexts of Poetry: Interviews, 1961–1971,* ed. Donald Allen (Bolinas: Four Seasons, 1973), p. 97; subsequent references to this book will be abbreviated CP. References to Creeley's *A Quick Graph: Collected Notes and Essays,* ed. Donald Allen (San Francisco: Four Seasons, 1970), will be abbreviated QG. The following abbreviations will also be used for Creeley's works: CH—*The Charm* (San Francisco: Four Seasons, 1969); DB—*A Day Book* (New York: Scribner's, 1972); FL—*For Love* (New York: Scribner's, 1962); P—*Pieces* (New York: Scribner's, 1969); TT—*Thirty Things* (Santa Barbara: Black Sparrow, 1974); W—*Words* (New York: Scribner's, 1967).

14. See also CP 40, 74.

15. The distinction I am making between a *systematic poet* (Creeley) and *poets with systems* (Olson, Duncan, Ginsberg) resembles a distinction discussed by Ernst Cassirer between the Enlightenment *esprit systématique* and the seventeenth-century *esprit de système,* in *The Philosophy of the Enlightenment,* trans. Fritz C. A. Koelln and James P. Pettegrove (Princeton: Princeton University Press, 1951), p. 8.

16. James Merrill, *Nights and Days* (New York: Atheneum, 1966), p. 46.

17. This desire later allowed Creeley remarkable optimism concerning the counter-culture apoliticism of the late 1960s; see CP 181–182.

18. For Creeley's remark to Robert Duncan that he is not interested in history, see CP 156.

19. Creeley discusses Ashbery's work in some detail in Robert Creeley and Robert Sheppard, "Stories: Being an Information, an Interview," *Sagetrieb,* 1 (Winter 1982), 46–48.

20. John Ashbery, *The Double Dream of Spring* (New York: Dutton, 1970), p. 18; subsequent references to this book will be abbreviated DD. The abbreviation TP will refer to Ashbery's *Three Poems* (New York: Viking, 1972).

21. The fullest commentary on this poem, however, interprets this phrase somewhat differently: "Whatever 'block' may mean, from building metaphor to cell block, the overt sense in the line moves toward grim, monosyllabic finality." Charles Berger, "Vision in the Form of a Task: *The Double Dream of Spring,*" in *Beyond Amazement: New Essays on John Ashbery,* ed. David Lehman (Ithaca: Cornell University Press, 1980), p. 191. Such are the differences among Ashbery's interpreters.

22. John Ashbery, *Some Trees* (1956; New York: Corinth, 1970), p. 51.

23. Yvor Winters, *In Defense of Reason* (Denver: Swallow, 1947), p. 87.

24. The passage from Baudelaire is quoted from Patrick F. Quinn, *The French Face of Edgar Poe* (Carbondale: Southern Illinois University Press, 1954), pp. 147–148. The quotation of Mallarmé comes from his letter to Cazalis, March 1866, *Mallarmé: Selected Prose, Poems, Essays, and Letters,* trans. Bradford Cook (Baltimore: Johns Hopkins University Press, 1956), p. 93.

3. Tourists

1. Charles Olson, *Letters for Origin, 1950–1956,* ed. Albert Glover (New York: Cape Goliard/Grossman, 1970), p. 9; see also James Dickey, *Babel to Byzantium* (New York: Farrar, Straus and Giroux, 1968), pp. 98–99.

2. Henry James, quoted by Morton Dauwen Zabel, "Introduction," *The Art of Travel,* by Henry James, ed. Zabel (Garden City: Doubleday, 1958), p. 32.

3. Ibid., p. 14.

4. Melville, quoted in Merton M. Sealts, Jr., *Melville as Lecturer* (Cambridge: Harvard University Press, 1957), p. 182.

5. W. H. Auden, *The Dyer's Hand* (New York: Vintage, 1962), pp. 309–310.

6. Hollander, *Town and Country Matters,* p. 9.

7. Anthony Hecht, *A Summoning of Stones* (New York: Macmillan, 1954), p. 41.

8. Adrienne Rich, *A Change of World* (New Haven: Yale University Press, 1951), p. 24.

9. Charles Gullans, *Arrivals and Departures* (Minneapolis: University of Minnesota Press, 1962), p. 18.

10. For a few examples of this subgenre, see Edgar Bowers, "Wandering 2," *Living Together* (Manchester, Eng.: Carcanet, 1977), p. 77; Thom Gunn, "Elvis Presley," *The Sense of Movement* (London: Faber, 1957), p. 31; and Gunn, "Modes of Pleasure," *My Sad Captains* (London: Faber, 1961), p. 24.

11. W. S. Merwin, *Green with Beasts* (London: Rupert Hart-Davis, 1956), pp. 71–72.

12. Ashbery, *Some Trees,* p. 14.

13. Richard Wilbur, *Poems* (New York: Harcourt, Brace and World, 1963), p. 104.

14. Ibid., p. 142.

15. Richard Howard, *Findings* (New York: Atheneum, 1971), p. 19.

16. Gullans, *Arrivals and Departures,* p. 5.

17. Turner Cassity, *Watchboy, What of the Night?* (Middletown: Wesleyan University Press, 1966), p. 34.

18. Elizabeth Bishop, *Complete Poems* (New York: Farrar, Straus and Giroux, 1969), p. 107.

19. U.S. Department of Commerce figures showed that American visitors to Europe and the Mediterranean area increased by 12 percent between 1953 and 1954 alone. *Tourism in Europe* (Paris: Organization for European Economic Co-operation, 1956), p. 15. Spokespersons for the tourist industry attributed this increase largely to decreased airfares. *U.S. Tourist Travel Abroad to 1975,* Economist Intelligence Unit (May 1971), p. 37.

Daniel Boorstin writes: "After allowing for the increase in population, there is about five times as much foreign travel by Americans nowadays as there was a hundred years ago. As a nation we are probably the most traveled people of our time, or of any time . . . In 1957, for example, about ten million American residents spent over two billion dollars on international travel." Boorstin, *The Image* (New York: Atheneum, 1961), pp. 79, 90. On the family background of American tourists, see John B. Lansing, *Interim Report on the 1960 National Travel Survey* (Ann Arbor: University of Michigan, Survey Research Center, 1960). Of those American families with incomes of $15,000 or above, 8 percent took an overseas trip in 1959 (ibid., p. 2). See also Charles C. Tillinghast, Jr., "The International Air Travel Industry," *Travel Market Yearbook*, 9th ed. (Manchester, Vt., 1974), which shows that 395,000 international flights were taken by nonwhite Americans, as compared to nearly 10 million by white Americans (p. 118).

20. See Harry Magdoff, *The Age of Imperialism: The Economics of United States Foreign Policy* (New York: Monthly Review, 1969), pp. 54–62, on America's replacement of Britain as the largest exporter of capital after World War II; and the same author's *Imperialism: From the Colonial Age to the Present* (New York: Monthly Review, 1978), pp. 171–172, on the shift of international finance and banking from London to New York following the Bretton Woods agreement of 1944. Magdoff also notes that America followed the withdrawing colonial powers largely by establishing a large number of military bases in the former colonial countries (*Imperialism*, p. 74). The clearest example of America's filling in the vacuum left by the retreat of a colonial power is, of course, Vietnam.

Two excellent books that trace the roots of American expansionism well beyond World War II are William Appleman Williams, *The Tragedy of American Diplomacy* (Cleveland: World, 1959), and Walter Lafeber, *America, Russia, and the Cold War, 1945–1971,* 2nd ed. (New York: Wiley, 1972). As Ronald Steel puts it: "With Russian troops on the Elbe and with the governments of Western Europe tottering under the strain of reconstruction, it seemed that only American power could halt the spread of communism" (*Pax Americana*, p. 21). A week after the second atomic bomb was dropped, on Nagasaki, Winston Churchill told the House of Commons: "America stands at this moment at the summit of the world" (quoted in Hodgson, p. 18). The following year he gave the famous speech in Fulton, Missouri, in which he said that God had willed that America should possess atomic weapons; responsibility for containment of the USSR rested with America (quoted in Lafeber, p. 30). Four years later Dean Acheson said, "Unity in Europe requires the continuing association and support of the United States. Without it free Europe would split apart" (quoted in Lafeber, p. 78).

21. Hodgson, *America in Our Time*, p. 19.

22. Ambrose, *Rise to Globalism*, p. 335.

23. *The Poems of John Keats*, ed. Jack Stillinger (Cambridge: Harvard University Press, 1978), p. 93.

24. *Selected Poems of Rainer Maria Rilke*, trans. Robert Bly (New York: Harper and Row, 1979), pp. 146–147.

25. Allen Tate to Frederick A. Colwell, 30 July 1959, in the Allen Tate Collection, Princeton University Library.

26. James Merrill, *The Country of a Thousand Years of Peace*, rev. ed. (New York: Atheneum, 1970), p. 82.

27. Adrienne Rich, *The Diamond Cutters* (New York: Harper, 1955), p. 36.

28. Merwin, *Green with Beasts*, p. 60.

29. Wilbur, *Poems*, p. 151.

30. Rich, *The Diamond Cutters*, p. 27.

31. Wilbur, *Poems*, p. 103.

32. Merrill, *The Country*, p. 47.

33. Anthony Hecht, *The Hard Hours* (New York: Atheneum, 1967), p. 94.

34. Gullans, *Arrivals and Departures*, p. 53.

35. Rich, *The Diamond Cutters,* p. 21.

36. John Hollander, *Movie-Going and Other Poems* (New York: Atheneum, 1962), p. 15.

37. I have discussed the use of Third Reich subject matter in a review of books by W. D. Snodgrass and William Heyen, in *Chicago Review,* 31 (Winter 1980), 116–121. See also Denis Donaghue, "Of Self and Society," *New York Times Book Review,* 20 January 1980, p. 9.

38. Rich, *The Diamond Cutters,* p. 110; Anthony Hecht, *Millions of Strange Shadows* (New York: Atheneum, 1977), p. 32.

39. Richard Howard, *Fellow Feelings* (New York: Atheneum, 1976), pp. 45–46.

40. See Steel, *Pax Americana,* and George Steiner, "The Archives of Eden," *Salmagundi,* 50–51 (Fall 1980–Winter 1981), 71.

41. Hollander, *A Crackling of Thorns,* p. 44.

42. Merrill, *The Country,* p. 48.

43. Rich, *The Diamond Cutters,* p. 43.

44. Edgar Bowers, *Living Together* (Manchester, Eng.: Carcanet, 1977), p. 15.

45. Bishop, *Complete Poems,* p. 106.

46. Ibid., p. 65.

47. Cassity, *Watchboy,* p. 33.

48. *Poems, 1928–1978* (Boston: Atlantic/Little Brown, 1979), p. 116.

49. Bishop, *Complete Poems,* p. 207.

50. Wilbur, *Poems,* p. 129.

51. Wilbur, *Poems,* p. 165; Merwin, *Green with Beasts,* p. 50.

52. Merrill, *Nights and Days,* p. 25.

53. The sort of viewpoint I mean can be seen much later in Robert Pinsky's "Poem About People," *Sadness And Happiness* (Princeton: Princeton University Press, 1975), p. 3; other similarly sympathetic poems are cited in my Conclusion.

54. Paul Blackburn, *The Cities* (New York: Grove Press, 1967), pp. 108, 93–95.

55. Merwin, *Green with Beasts,* p. 59.

56. Gullans, *Arrivals and Departures,* p. 53.

57. Blackburn, *The Cities,* pp. 93–95.

58. Bishop, *Complete Poems,* p. 103.

59. James Merrill, *The Fire Screen* (New York: Atheneum, 1969), p. 12.

60. For discussions of British tourist poetry of the 1950s, see John Press, *Rule and Energy* (London: Oxford University Press, 1963), ch. 7; and Robert von Hallberg, "Donald Davie and 'The Moral Shape of Politics,' " *Critical Inquiry,* 8 (Spring 1982), 415–436.

4. James Merrill

1. For an example of how the term has been inflated, see Robert Phillips, *The Confessional Poets* (Carbondale and Edwardsville: Southern Illinois University Press, 1973), esp. pp. 16–17.

2. James Merrill, *The Contemporary Writer,* ed. L. S. Dembo and Cyrena N. Pondrom (Madison: University of Wisconsin Press, 1972), pp. 139–140; subsequent references to this book will be abbreviated CW. The following ab-

breviations will also be used for Merrill's works: FP—*First Poems* (New York: Knopf, 1951); CT—*The Country of a Thousand Years of Peace* (New York: Atheneum, 1959; enlarged edition, 1970); WS—*Water Street* (New York: Atheneum, 1962); ND—*Nights and Days* (New York: Atheneum, 1966); FS—*The Fire Screen* (New York: Atheneum, 1969); BE—*Braving the Elements* (New York: Atheneum, 1972); DC—*Divine Comedies* (New York: Atheneum, 1976); M—*Mirabell: Books of Number* (New York: Atheneum, 1978); SP—*Scripts for the Pageant* (New York: Atheneum, 1980). The quotation in my chapter title is taken from "Little Fanfare for Felix Magowan" (ND 31).

3.   James Merrill, *The Seraglio* (New York: Knopf, 1957), pp. 107–108.

4.   In a review of *Nights and Days* David Kalstone discusses Merrill as a master of the confessional mode. *Partisan Review,* 34 (Winter 1967), 146–150. However, in a later discussion of Merrill, Kalstone prefers to emphasize the ways in which Merrill departs from confessional practices. *Five Temperaments* (New York: Oxford University Press, 1977), p. 79.

5.   Ashley Brown, "An Interview with James Merrill," *Shenandoah,* 19 (Summer 1968), 10.

6.   A comparable poem, thematically, is "The Friend of the Fourth Decade" (1968). In this later poem Merrill still feels the lure of an aesthetic experience without any referential sense, a poetic of surfaces, but he is unable to slip free of human ties to the past—"Certain things die only with oneself" (FS 7).

7.   Cox actually said: " 'The Thousand and Second Night' describes a breakdown in his identity in middle age, the end of purposive union between mind, soul and body or perhaps between himself and his Muse." *The Spectator,* 21 October 1966, p. 523.

8.   Brown, "Interview with Merrill," p. 13.

9.   "Germaine Nahman" and "A. H. Clarendon," so far as I can determine, are phantom authors, absences to which Merrill ascribes meaning.

10.   Brown, "Interview with Merrill," pp. 12–13.

11.   Henry A. Grubbs, *Paul Valéry* (New York: Twayne, 1968), p. 61.

12.   Judith Moffett has discussed this connection to the Aphrodite palm of *From the Cupola* in her review of *Divine Comedies,* in *Poetry,* 129 (October 1976), 42–43.

13.   For an excellent discussion of Merrill's syntax, see Richard Howard's essay on Merrill in *Alone with America* (New York: Atheneum, 1969), p. 329.

14.   A later instance of Merrill's condescension is a little more comic than snide: "Another memory of Mademoiselle. / We're in a Pullman going South for Christmas, / She in the lower berth, I in the upper / As befits whatever station we pass through" (DC 15).

15.   Ezra Pound, *Literary Essays,* ed. T. S. Eliot (Norfolk: New Directions, 1954), p. 25. Pound goes on to say that the roots of logopoeia lie in seventeenth- and eighteenth-century satire (p. 30); Laforgue, however, is the modern exemplar and true master of logopoeia (p. 33).

16.   Susan Sontag, *Against Interpretation* (New York: Farrar, Straus and Giroux, 1966), p. 288. My discussion of camp style is deeply indebted to her "Notes on Camp." The only other discussion of camp I know is mentioned by Sontag: Christopher Isherwood, *The World in the Evening* (London: Methuen, 1954), pp. 125–126.

17.   See, e.g., CW 148; and *The Seraglio,* pp. 48–49, 217.

18. Sontag, *Against Interpretation*, p. 290.

19. It should be clear, though, that Merrill wants to preserve his ironic access to this level of colloquial usage; the wittiest example of his delight in that language comes in "Days of 1935" (BE 13).

20. Pound, *Literary Essays*, p. 75.

21. Alvin W. Gouldner, *The Future of Intellectuals and the Rise of the New Class* (New York: Oxford University Press, 1979), p. 28.

22. Lawrence Lipking, *The Life of the Poet* (Chicago: University of Chicago Press, 1981), ch. 2.

23. Stephen Spender, "Heaven Can't Wait," *New York Review of Books*, 35 (21 December 1978), 36.

24. Helen Vendler, "James Merrill's Myth: An Interview," *New York Review of Books*, 36 (3 May 1979), 12.

25. Peter Stitt, "Knowledge, Belief, and Bubblegum," *Georgia Review*, 33 (Fall 1979), 706.

26. Calvin Bedient, review of Merrill's *Divine Comedies*, in *New Republic*, 174 (5 June 1976), 22.

27. Merrill oddly attributes brilliance to several rather ordinary remarks by Auden in this poem; see M 81, 146, and SP 47, 111.

28. David Bromwich, "Answer, Heavenly Muse, Yes or No," *Hudson Review*, 32 (Autumn 1979), 457.

29. Helen Vendler, *Part of Nature, Part of Us* (Cambridge: Harvard University Press, 1980), p. 222.

30. James Merrill, "The Art of Poetry, XXXI," *Paris Review*, 24 (Summer 1982), 189.

31. W. H. Auden, "Yeats as an Example,"* *Kenyon Review*, 10 (Spring 1948), 189.

5. Politics

1. Morris Dickstein, *Gates of Eden: American Culture in the Sixties* (New York: Basic Books, 1977), pp. 17, 75.

2. James F. Mersmann, *Out of the Vietnam Vortex: A Study of Poets and Poetry against the War* (Lawrence: University Press of Kansas, 1974); Walter Lowenfels, ed., *Where Is Vietnam?* (New York: Doubleday, 1967). See "List of Works Consulted" in Mersmann, pp. 269–274.

3. Although I have benefited from the work of those scholars who have attempted to retain the Marxist sense of the term "class," my own use of the term is not exact in the sense of predicting the outcome of class rivalry. Moreover, I have not relied on a single determinant—such as capital, birth, social background, education, occupation, or income—in order to define class standing. For discussion of the difficulties of employing this term in analysis of advanced societies, see especially Anthony Giddens, *The Class Structure of the Advanced Societies* (London: Hutchinson, 1973); Nicos Poulantzas, *Classes in Contemporary Capitalism*, trans. David Fernbach (London: Verso, 1975); and the work of Alvin Gouldner and Everett Carll Ladd, Jr., cited below. I prefer to follow the historian Arthur Marwick in employing "class" in a descriptive sense, referring to the ways in which class distinctions are commonly perceived. Marwick, *Class: Image and Reality in Britain, France and the USA since 1930* (New York: Oxford University Press, 1980), pp. 14, 19.

4. On the political importance of the flow of information, see Herbert I. Schiller, *Mass Communications and American Empire* (Boston: Beacon Press, 1971), and *The Mind Managers* (Boston: Beacon Press, 1973), esp. ch. 8.

5. The best discussion of the new class, however, derives from a Hegelian left perspective: Alvin W. Gouldner, *The Future of Intellectuals and the Rise of the New Class* (New York: Oxford University Press, 1979).

6. Garry Wills, *Nixon Agonistes: The Crisis of the Self-Made Man* (Boston: Houghton Mifflin, 1970), p. 508. Louis Hartz quotes Elbert Hubbard on this theme: "All attempts to build up class hatred in this country must fail. We stand for cooperation, reciprocity, mutuality." Hartz, *The Liberal Tradition in America* (New York: Harcourt, Brace and World, 1955), p. 224.

7. Edward A. Shils, *The Torment of Secrecy: The Background and Consequences of American Security Policies* (New York: Free Press, 1956), p. 40.

8. Peter Viereck, "The Revolt against the Elite (1955)," in *The Radical Right,* ed. Daniel Bell (Garden City: Doubleday, 1963), p. 179; Talcott Parsons, "Social Strains in America (1955)," in *The Radical Right,* p. 212.

9. Janowitz, *Last Half-Century,* pp. 130, 131.

10. Hodgson, *America in Our Time,* pp. 51, 81–82, 83–86. *Statistical Abstract of the United States* (Washington, D.C.: Department of Commerce, 1961), p. 768.

11. Carl Kaysen, quoted in Hodgson, p. 463.

12. See George Butterick, *A Guide to the Maximus Poems of Charles Olson* (Berkeley: University of California Press, 1978), p. 86.

13. Seymour Martin Lipset, *Political Man: The Social Bases of Politics* (New York: Doubleday, 1960), p. 359; Shils, *The Intellectuals and the Powers,* pp. 174, 201.

14. Quoted in Lafeber, *America, Russia,* p. 183.

15. Among the participants in the Rockefeller Fund study that produced *Prospect for America* were Theodore M. Hesburgh (president of Notre Dame), John S. Dickey (president of Dartmouth), Richard McKeon, Robert Heilbroner, Walt Rostow, and Robert Scalapino, as well as Henry Kissinger, General Lucius Clay, Dean Rusk, David Sarnoff, and Henry Luce. Clinton Rossiter, John W. Gardner, Warren Weaver, and Clark Kerr worked on the *Goals for Americans* project.

16. Richard Hofstadter begins *Anti-Intellectualism in American Life* (New York: Knopf, 1963) by saying that the book "was conceived in response to the political and intellectual conditions of the 1950s" (p. 3).

17. Quoted in Hodgson, *America in Our Time,* p. 43.

18. "The Army-McCarthy Hearings," in *America since 1945,* ed. Robert D. Marcus and David Burner (New York: St. Martin's, 1972), p. 89.

19. Quoted in Wills, *Nixon,* p. 90.

20. This is not to say that the full significance of McCarthyism is accounted for by class analysis, but only that the phenomenon had a special bearing for intellectuals. Part of McCarthy's support plainly came from those who, once isolationist, were disappointed that the American war effort focused first on Europe and only later on the Pacific. Mao's success five months before McCarthy's West Virginia speech confirmed their sense that the American government had wrongly assessed its priorities in 1941. Their misgivings were strengthened by American military restraint during the Korean War. Anti-

intellectualism does not fully explain McCarthy's successes in the early 1950s, though it does clarify a great deal. The best discussion of McCarthy's sources of support is Michael Paul Rogin, *The Intellectuals and McCarthy: The Radical Specter* (Cambridge: MIT Press, 1967), esp. ch. 8.

21. Shils, *Torment,* p. 13. Richard Hofstadter, "The Pseudo-Conservative Revolt (1955)," in *The Radical Right,* p. 92.

22. Viereck, "The Revolt against the Elite," p. 162.

23. For example: "We have spoken," Riesman and Glazer say, "of the xenophobia and slowness in altering opinions characteristic of the lower classes. If in a survey people are asked, 'Do you think it wise to trust others?' the less educated are always the more suspicious; they have in the course of life gained a peasant-like guile, the sort of sloganized cynicism so beautifully described by Richard Wright in *Black Boy"* ("The Intellectuals," in *The Radical Right,* p. 118). These are the last two sentences of their essay: "Of course, to suppose that the intellectuals can do very much to guide the discontented classes by winning friends and influencing people among them is as ridiculous as supposing that Jews can do much to combat political anti-Semitism by amiability to non-Jews. Nevertheless, there is only one side from which understanding is likely to come, and that is their own" (p. 135). I quote these sentences merely as a reminder that there was ugliness on both sides of this antagonism.

24. The monumental effort along this line was *The Authoritarian Personality,* by T. W. Adorno and others (New York: Harper, 1950). This psychoanalytical bent can also be seen in the essays in *The Radical Right* by Bell (pp. 13–14), Viereck (pp. 162, 217–218), Parsons (p. 235), Riesman and Glazer (p. 118).

25. Hodgson, *America in Our Time,* p. 290.

26. B. Bruce-Briggs, "Enumerating the New Class," in *The New Class?,* ed. B. Bruce-Briggs (New York: McGraw-Hill, 1979), p. 221. Hodgson, *America in Our Time,* p. 54. Everett Carll Ladd, Jr., "Pursuing the New Class: Social Theory and Survey Data," in *The New Class?,* pp. 102–103. Daniel Bell, "The New Class: A Muddled Concept," in *The New Class?,* p. 178.

27. Wills, *Nixon,* p. 215.

28. See Paul Fussell's witty essay, "A Dirge for Social Climbers," *The New Republic,* 183 (19 July 1980), 18–21.

29. B. Bruce-Briggs, "An Introduction to the Idea of the New Class," in *The New Class?,* p. 2.

30. Jeane J. Kirkpatrick, "Politics and the New Class," in *The New Class?,* p. 35.

31. Ibid., p. 37; Robert L. Bartley, "Business and the New Class," in *The New Class?,* pp. 58–59. Bell, "The New Class," p. 181. See also, on the increasing authority of managers, Janowitz, *Last Half-Century,* p. 245.

32. Ladd, "Pursuing the New Class," pp. 101–103. I do not mean to suggest, however, that the recent victories of the Republican Party can be explained by reference to class distinctions alone. Kevin P. Phillips shows that regional and ethnic groupings make the most sense of recent voting patterns—*The Emerging Republican Majority* (New Rochelle: Arlington House, 1969), esp. ch. 2. He speaks of the current Republican hegemony as emerging from the increased political power of middle and lower-middle class suburbs (pp. 467–468, 474). More than two decades ago, Seymour Martin Lipset spoke

of the upper class as Republican in its party allegiance—*Political Man* (Garden City: Doubleday, 1960), ch. 9; and more recently Richard Hamilton has shown that, especially outside the South, "the white Protestant upper-middle class constitutes *the* Republican stronghold"—*Class and Politics in the United States* (New York: Wiley, 1972), p. 195. Hamilton goes on to show that "the biggest 'break' in the class structure is not between manuals and non-manuals but rather is between the lower-middle and upper-middle classes" (p. 218).

33. See Norman Podhoretz, "The Adversary Culture and the New Class," in *The New Class?*, p. 28, and Ladd, "Pursuing the New Class," p. 102.

34. Wilbur, *Poems,* p. 101.

35. See Allan H. Ryskind, *Hubert: An Unauthorized Biography of the Vice-President* (New Rochelle: Arlington House, 1968), pp. 188–196.

36. Gullans, *Arrivals and Departures,* p. 34.

37. Robert Bly, *Silence in the Snowy Fields* (Middletown: Wesleyan University Press, 1962), p. 27.

38. Wilbur, *Poems,* pp. 213–214.

39. For a discussion of Williams' political viewpoint in this poem, see Robert von Hallberg, "The Politics of Description: W. C. Williams in the 'Thirties," *ELH,* 45 (Spring 1978), 131–151.

40. Wilbur, *Poems,* p. 14.

41. Bishop, *Complete Poems,* p. 112.

42. Quoted in Lafeber, *America, Russia,* p. 79.

43. Wilbur, *Poems,* p. 220.

44. Rich, *A Change of World,* pp. 44–45.

45. Robert Lowell, *For the Union Dead* (New York: Farrar, Straus and Giroux, 1964), p. 11.

46. Gullans, *Arrivals and Departures,* p. 36.

47. Mark Strand, *Selected Poems* (New York: Atheneum, 1980), p. 5.

48. Cassity, *Watchboy,* p. 41.

49. Information on these ocean liners can be found in C. R. Vernon Gibbs, *Passenger Liners of the Western Ocean* (New York: Staples Press, 1952).

50. Robert Bly, *The Light around the Body* (New York: Harper and Row, 1967), p. 25.

51. Denise Levertov, *To Stay Alive* (New York: New Directions, 1971), p. 18.

52. George Oppen, *Collected Poems* (New York: New Directions, 1975), p. 113.

53. James Wright, *Collected Poems* (Middletown: Wesleyan University Press, 1971), p. 113.

54. Ibid., p. 177.

55. Dave Smith, "James Wright: The Pure Clear Word, an Interview," in *The Pure Clear Word* (Urbana: University of Illinois Press, 1982), pp. 3–4.

56. Robert Bly, *Sleepers Joining Hands* (New York: Harper and Row, 1973), p. 23.

57. Ezra Pound, *The Spirit of Romance* (1910; New York: New Directions, 1952), p. 218.

58. See Clark Kerr, *The Uses of the University* (New York: Harper, 1966).

59. Robert Lowell, *Life Studies* (New York: Farrar, Straus and Grioux, 1959), p. 7.

60. Letter, Lowell to Allen Tate, 5 November 1952, in the Tate Collection, Princeton University Library.

61. But see James Wright, "American Twilights, 1957," for another early instance of this death-wish poem, *Collected Poems,* pp. 79–80.

62. Robert Hass, *Field Guide* (New Haven: Yale University Press, 1973), p. 15.

63. Wright, *Collected Poems,* p. 117.

64. Bly, *Sleepers,* p. 26.

65. Bly, *The Light,* pp. 34, 21; Bly, *Sleepers,* pp. 18, 15; Wright, *Collected Poems,* pp. 117, 131; Bly, *The Light,* p. 33; Hass, *Field Guide,* pp. 6, 57; Wright, *Collected Poems,* p. 116.

66. Hass, *Field Guide,* p. 50

67. Lafeber, *America, Russia,* p. 259.

68. Robert Duncan, *Bending the Bow* (New York: New Directions, 1968), p. 114.

69. Bly, *Sleepers,* p. 21.

70. Bly takes up the old charge of hypocrisy (professed Christians who make war) in "Johnson's Cabinet Watched by Ants," *The Light,* p. 5. Duncan makes a similar point more interestingly by reminding his audience that it was the intellectuals' candidate, Adlai Stevenson, who knowingly lied in the UN (*Bending,* p. 71).

71. Duncan, *Bending,* p. 81.

72. Bly, *The Light,* p. 30. Duncan, *Bending,* pp. 82–83.

73. Anthony Hecht, "An Overview," in *The Venetian Vespers* (New York: Atheneum, 1979), p. 27. On the treatment of bomber pilots see also Bly, *Sleepers,* pp. 18–19, 22–23, and Duncan, *Bending,* pp. 95–96.

74. Ambrose, *Rise to Globalism,* p. 331.

75. Bly, *Sleepers,* p. 21.

76. The circulation of *Poetry* magazine is instructive in this regard: by December 1970 it had achieved a total distribution of 9312; at the end of 1962 the figure was 6000.

77. Duncan, *Bending,* p. 93. Levertov, *To Stay Alive,* p. 29; a note identifies Dennis Riordan and others as "young active war-resisters."

78. Wordsworth, "Preface" to *Lyrical Ballads,* p. 129.

6. *Robert Lowell's* History

1. See Reed Whittemore, *William Carlos Williams: Poet from Jersey* (Boston: Houghton Mifflin, 1975), pp. 309–313.

2. Calvin Bedient, for example, said that "the volume comes to seem uncertain of its aim, like most of the poems"—*New York Time Book Review,* 29 July 1973, p. 15. Douglas Dunn spoke of the volume as "self-indulgent on a grand scale"—"The Big Race: Lowell's Visions and Revisions," *Encounter,* 41 (October 1973), 108.

3. Norman Mailer, *The Armies of the Night* (New York: New American Library, 1968), pp. 89, 32. See also Lowell's reference to Mailer's ambitiousness: "Et in America Ego," *The Listener,* 4 September 1969, p. 303.

4. More accurately, Cupcake says this of Lac: John Hollander, *Reflections on Espionage* (New York: Atheneum, 1976), p. 34.

5. Robert Lowell, *History* (New York: Farrar, Straus and Giroux, 1973), p. 135; subsequent quotations from this book will be identified simply by page number.

6. Ian Hamilton speaks of Lowell's shrewd ambitiousness in *Robert Lowell: A Biography* (New York: Random House, 1982), pp. 112, 334, 336–337.

7. For an excellent discussion of the crafting of poetic careers, see Lipking, *The Life of the Poet.*

8. Lowell's sense of writing for posterity was encouraged by his early teacher, Allen Tate. Tate disapproved of some of the poems that would later go into *Life Studies* when they were shown to him in manuscript in 1957. These poems made him write to Perry Miller with anxiety about Lowell's mental state. Later he suggested to Elizabeth Hardwick that she not encourage Lowell to publish the poems, "which would do great harm in the long run . . . It is not a question of a little poetic disagreement, as you put it; it concerns his eventual reputation as a poet and his immediate public *persona*" (letter, Tate to Elizabeth Hardwick, 18 December 1957, Allen Tate Collection, Princeton University Library). Tate was entirely serious. When, some years later, he prepared his papers for deposit at Princeton, he thoughtfully labeled the various letters and manuscripts in his possession. On the typescript of "A Mad Negro Soldier," he wrote, "author unknown."

9. Donald Hall, "Robert Lowell and the Literature Industry," *Georgia Review,* 32 (Spring 1978), 7–12.

10. *Plutarch's Lives,* trans. Bernadotte Perrin, 11 vols. (London: Heinemann, 1914–1926), VII, *Alexander.*

11. Mailer says that Lowell claimed to have written 800 lines during the month following the march (*Armies,* p. 295).

12. Letter, Lowell to Tate, 28 November 1952, Tate Collection, Princeton University Library.

13. Mailer, describing the same event, gives a different explanation. He suggests that the peaceful advance of the first wave of troops was strategic, not accidental: the objective was to position troops on two sides of the demonstrators before moving against them—a squeeze play. Lowell characteristically prefers to represent the difference between the first and second waves as arbitrary. *Armies,* pp. 294–295.

14. Lowell gave the same sort of toast years earlier in "The Old Flame," *For the Union Dead,* p. 6.

15. Vendler, *Part of Nature, Part of Us,* p. 165.

16. Lowell, *Life Studies,* p. 50. Ford himself had doubted the uses to which Lowell might put him: "That boy will write something terrible about me one day" (Hamilton, *Lowell,* p. 50). Actually Lowell recognized that his poem for Ford, first published in the spring of 1954, was a turning point in the development of his style (ibid., p. 234).

17. Ms. Am 1905 2433, Houghton Library, Harvard University.

18. Ms. Am 1905 2565, Houghton Library.

19. Ms. Am 1905 2628, Houghton Library.

20. Robert Lowell, "Liberalism and Activism," *Commentary,* 47 (April 1969), 19.

21. Robert Lowell, "What's Happening to America," *Partisan Review,* 34 (Winter 1967), 14, 37–38.

22. Letter, Lowell to Tate, 5 November 1952, Tate Collection, Princeton University Library.

23. Ms. Am 1905 2834, Houghton Library.

24. J. Glenn Gray, *The Warriors: Reflections on Men in Battle* (New York: Harcourt, Brace, 1959), pp. 59–60.

25. Unpublished draft of "Election Night," Ms Am 1905 2661, Houghton Library.

26. I realize that one might want to interpret those raised hands as the solidarity salute. However, had Lowell meant to indicate the salute, he probably would have said "fists" rather than "hands." The early drafts also support the pedagogical suggestion: "the only gun that will not kill the owners / is the people's language, insight made wise with anger" (Ms. Am 1905 2586, Houghton Library).

27. Ms. Am 1905 2760, Houghton Library.

28. Early draft of a long poem, later called "On the Steps of the Harvard Gym," Ms Am 1905 2240, Houghton Library.

29. These lines about sidesteppings and obliquities now open "On the End of the Phone," *The Dophin* (New York: Farrar, Straus and Giroux, 1973), p. 70.

30. Ms. Am 1905 2423, Houghton Library.

31. I have discussed the relation between liberalism and skepticism about general laws in "Donald Davie and 'The Moral Shape of Politics,' " pp. 415–436.

32. *Plutarch's Lives:* IV, *Sulla;* IX, *Caius Marius.*

33. See "New York," *The Dolphin,* p. 76.

34. Lowell met Jacqueline Kennedy in 1964. Periodically he would leave off books for her at her apartment on the East Side. Thanking him for one of these books, she wrote: "I will always be your friend across the park." Letter, Jacqueline Kennedy to Lowell, 16 June 1969, Houghton Library.

35. Lowell, "What's Happening to America," p. 38.

36. The drafts of these letters are in the Houghton Library.

37. In letters to Otto A. Bird, Pound expressed contempt for Mortimer Adler and the Great Books project; these letters are now owned by the University of Arkansas Library.

38. In 1959 Lowell wrote about the visit as occurring in April 1937. "Visiting the Tates," *Sewanee Review,* 67 (Autumn 1959), 557–559.

39. Ms. Am 1905 2492, Houghton Library.

40. Lowell, "Liberalism and Activism," p. 19.

7. Pop Culture

1. "Our Country and Our Culture," *Partisan Review,* 19 (May–June 1952), 282, 284; see also Charles C. Alexander, *Here the Country Lies: Nationalism and the Arts in 20th Century America* (Bloomington: Indiana University Press, 1980), for the claim that this intellectual satisfaction goes back to the 1930s (p. 259). Patrick Brantlinger's *Bread and Circuses* (Ithaca: Cornell University Press, 1984) provides an excellent overview of critiques of mass culture.

2. Ernest van den Haag, "Of Happiness and of Despair We Have No Mea-

sure," in *Mass Culture: The Popular Arts in America,* ed. Bernard Rosenberg and David Manning White (Glencoe: Free Press, 1957), p. 520.

3. Dwight Macdonald, "A Theory of Mass Culture," in *Mass Culture,* p. 62.

4. Ernest van den Haag, "A Dissent from the Consensual Society," *Daedalus,* 89 (Spring 1960), 316.

5. Leslie A. Fiedler, "The Middle against Both Ends," in *Mass Culture,* p. 546.

6. Herbert J. Gans, *Popular Culture and High Culture* (New York: Basic Books, 1974), p. 3.

7. Fiedler speaks of the petty-bourgeoisie ("The Middle," p. 546) and Gans of the lower middle class (*Popular Culture,* p. 131) as the powers behind pop culture.

8. Rahv, "Our Country and Our Culture," p. 310.

9. Irving Howe, "Notes on Mass Culture," in *Mass Culture,* p. 496.

10. Delmore Schwartz, "Our Country and Our Culture," p. 595.

11. The one distinguished exception is Robert Warshow, *The Immediate Experience* (New York: Atheneum, 1970).

12. Irving Howe, "The New York Intellectuals," in *The Decline of the New* (New York: Harcourt, Brace and World, 1970), p. 226.

13. Ibid., p. 227.

14. Gans, *Popular Culture,* p. 7.

15. Frank O'Hara, *Collected Poems,* ed. Donald Allen (New York: Knopf, 1972), p. 325.

16. Marjorie Perloff, *Frank O'Hara: Poet among Painters* (New York: Braziller, 1977), observes that Patsy Southgate and Mike Kanemitsu, O'Hara's good friends, are in fact referred to in the poem (pp. 181, 213n2).

17. O'Hara, *Poems,* p. 449.

18. Ibid., pp. 232–233.

19. Howe, "Notes on Mass Culture," pp. 497–498.

20. Hollander, *Movie-Going,* p. 2.

21. Wordsworth, "Preface" to *Lyrical Ballads,* p. 129.

22. Kenneth Burke, *Attitudes toward History* (1937; Boston: Beacon Press, 1961), p. 225.

23. Bishop, *Complete Poems,* p. 149.

24. Hecht, *The Venetian Vespers,* p. 10.

25. Over thirty years ago Hecht's mentor, Auden, complained of an "excess of detail" in Hecht's poems. Letter, Hecht to Allen Tate, 16 October 1951, Tate Collection, Princeton University Library.

26. A convenient point of comparison is Robert Pinsky's treatment of the polite young working men in "Poem about People," *Sadness and Happiness* (Princeton: Princeton University Press, 1975), p. 3.

27. Cassity, *Watchboy,* p. 51.

28. John William Ward, *Red, White, and Blue* (New York: Oxford University Press, 1969), pp. 21–37.

29. John Ashbery, *Self-Portrait in a Convex Mirror* (New York: Viking, 1975), pp. 42–43.

30. Hart Crane, "To Brooklyn Bridge," *Complete Poems and Selected Letters and Prose,* ed. Brom Weber (Garden City: Doubleday, 1966), p. 45.

31. Allen Ginsberg, "A Supermarket in California," *Howl and Other Poems*

(San Francisco: City Lights, 1956), p. 24. In an essay written a few years later, "A Sad Heart at the Supermarket," Randall Jarrell said, "Poetry disappeared long ago, even for most intellectuals; each year fiction is a little less important." *Daedalus,* 89 (Spring 1960), 368.

32. Frank Bidart, *Golden State* (New York: Braziller, 1973), p. 3.

33. One of the wives of Bidart's father, for example, was also twenty-five years younger than her husband (p. 34).

34. See Sharon Mayer Libera, "Bartholomew Fair," *Parnassus,* 3 (Spring-Summer 1975), 262, on the alleged flatness of Bidart's language.

35. Howe, "Notes on Mass Culture," p. 496.

36. Hollander, *Movie-Going,* p. 6.

8. Edward Dorn

1. This biographical information is taken from Dorn's 1972 interview with Barry Alpert, in Edward Dorn, *Interviews,* ed. Donald Allen (Bolinas: Four Seasons, 1980), pp. 7–35; subsequent references to this book will be abbreviated I. The following abbreviations will also be used for Dorn's works: CP—*Collected Poems, 1956–1974* (Bolinas: Four Seasons, 1975); S—*Slinger* (Berkeley: Wingbow, 1975); SB—*Some Business Recently Transacted in the White World* (West Newbury, Mass.: Frontier, 1971).

2. Edward Dorn, "Report from the Front: The First Films of Don Lloyd," *Wild Dog,* 2 (22 March 1965), 3.

3. For a good definition and discussion of discursiveness in poetry, see Robert Pinsky, *The Situation of Poetry* (Princeton: Princeton University Press, 1976), pp. 134ff.

4. Letter to Olson, 24 January 1968, in the University of Connecticut Library; subsequent references to this archive will be abbreviated CtU.

5. In a letter to Olson, 1 December 1968, Dorn indicated his sense that Creeley is limited by a domestic subject matter: "I don't, also, find *The Finger* any indication, in itself, of an alteration of perception. It seems the same domestic inflexibility as ever" (CtU).

6. Dorn to Olson, 14 December 1967, CtU.

7. Charles Olson, *Call Me Ishmael* (San Francisco: City Lights, 1967), p. 11.

8. The version in *Chelsea,* 8 (October 1960), pp. 66–68, includes about thirty lines omitted from the text of "Los Mineros" printed in *Collected Poems.*

9. "The Camp—LeRoi Jones' *Blues People,*" in Edward Dorn, Michael Rumaker, and Warren Tallman, *Prose 1* (San Francisco: Four Seasons, 1964), p. 33.

10. Dorn to LeRoi Jones, July 1964, Library of the University of California, Los Angeles.

11. Edward Dorn, "Dutchman and The Slave," *Wild Dog,* 2 (28 October 1964), 6.

12. *New York Times,* 30 April 1959, p. 12.

13. *Newsweek,* 11 May 1959, p. 62.

14. *Time,* 11 May 1959, p. 46.

15. The manuscript of this poem, which is undated, was apparently sent by Dorn to Jones in late September or early October 1961; it is now in the UCLA Library.

16. Dorn to Jones, 21 September 1969, UCLA Library.

17. LeRoi Jones, "Cuba Libre," *Evergreen Review,* 4 (November–December 1960), 139–159.

18. Jones to Dorn, October 1961, Lilly Library, Indiana University; the letter can be dated to the week following October 14 because of a reference to the death of Maya Deren.

19. Dorn to Jones, 10 October 1961, UCLA Library. The unidentified quotation in the next paragraph is taken from the same letter.

20. Jones to Dorn, [14–21] October 1961, Lilly Library.

21. Donald Davie, review of Dorn's *The Rites of Passage,* in *Wivenhoe Park Review,* 1 (Winter 1965), 116.

22. Jones to Dorn, undated, Lilly Library.

23. Edward Dorn, "Beauty," in *The Moderns,* ed. LeRoi Jones (New York: Corinth, 1963), p. 66.

24. Edward Dorn, *The Shoshoneans: The People of the Basin-Plateau* (New York: William Morrow, 1966), p. 77.

25. In Jones, *The Moderns,* p. 56. As early as February 1961 Dorn knew that his writing was to take this rough turn: "It interests me . . . to make a political statement as hot as I can . . . I think probably I'll also get over a fear of being vulgar and rough about it. I hope so, because I think that might be beautiful too, and it's time for it, it seems to me" (I 3–4).

26. Edward Dorn, "The Day Report," *Caterpillar,* 15–16 (April–June 1971), 186.

27. For one small example of how Dorn likes to come across general laws, see his description of Ramona's car in *By the Sound* (Mount Vernon, Wash.: Frontier, 1971), p. 18.

28. Dorn to Jones, 12 October 1961 [?], UCLA Library. Jones to Dorn, undated, Lilly Library.

29. The fact that the Horse bears the XX pair helps explain why he is once (S 5) referred to as a mare; part of the mangling of his genes is that he carries the female chromosomes instead of the XY pair.

30. Elizabeth Sewell, *The Field of Nonsense* (London: Chatto and Windus, 1952), p. 17.

31. Gunslinger's phrase, "the name of the name of her feet" (S 14), alludes to Alice's fantasy of sending presents to her feet—"'Alice's Right Foot, esq." Lewis Carroll, *Alice's Adventures in Wonderland,* in *The Annotated Alice,* ed. Martin Gardner (New York: Clarkson N. Potter, 1960), p. 36.

32. Ibid., p. 67.

33. This is Donald Davie's point in "Ed Dorn and the Treasures of Comedy," *Vort,* 1 (1972), 24–35.

34. G. S. Kirk and J. E. Raven, *The Presocratic Philosophers: A Critical History with a Selection of Texts* (Cambridge, Eng.: Cambridge University Press, 1966), p. 269.

35. Dorn is alluding to Olson's discussion of "self-acts": "these things / which don't carry their end any further than / their reality in / themselves." Olson, *The Maximus Poems,* p. 42.

36. For a good discussion of Dorn as a political poet, see Donald Wesling, "A Bibliography on Edward Dorn for America," *Parnassus* 5 (Spring–Summer 1977), 142–160.

37. For an excellent discussion of how crucial categories in *Slinger* break down, see Michael Davidson, " 'To eliminate the draw': Narrative and Language in *Slinger,*" in *Internal Resistances: The Poetry of Edward Dorn,* ed. Donald Wesling (Berkeley: University of California Press, 1984).

Conclusion: Suburbs

1. William H. Whyte, Jr., *The Organization Man* (New York: Simon and Schuster, 1956), part 7.

2. Mark Gelfand, *A Nation of Cities: The Federal Government and Urban America, 1933–1965* (New York: Oxford University Press, 1975), pp. 306, 437n23, 440n66.

3. Ibid., chs. 5 and 6.

4. Wilbur, *Poems,* 161. See also Josephine Miles, "Housewife," in *Local Measures* (New York: Reynal and Hitchcock, 1946), p. 5.

5. Dennis P. Sobin, *The Future of the American Suburbs* (Port Washington: Kennikat Press, 1971), p. 24.

6. Mona Van Duyn, *Merciful Disguises* (New York: Atheneum, 1973), p. 39.

7. Ginsberg, in *New York Times Book Review,* 4 April 1971, p. 18.

8. Mona Van Duyn, *Letters from a Father, and Other Poems* (New York: Atheneum, 1982), pp. 18–19; subsequent references to this book are abbreviated L.

9. Only one poem, "Open Letter, Personal," from her earlier books is comparable in this final push (*Merciful Disguises,* p. 81).

10. Robert Pinsky, *An Explanation of America* (Princeton: Princeton University Press, 1979), p. 6; subsequent references in text to this book will be indicated simply by page number.

11. The apt explanation of this conventional aspect of Pinsky's language can be found in the work of Pinsky's teacher, Yvor Winters, *In Defense of Reason,* pp. 75–89.

12. On the relationship between etymology and the poetic impulse to purify the common language, see Donald Davie, *Purity of Diction in English Verse* (London: Routledge, 1952), esp. part 1, ch. 3.

13. Manuscripts of early drafts of *An Explanation* are part of the Robert Pinsky Papers on deposit in the Joseph Regenstein Library, University of Chicago.

14. Olson, *The Maximum Poems,* p. 13.

15. Pinsky, *The Situation of Poetry,* pp. 52, 55.

16. James McMichael, *Four Good Things* (Boston: Houghton Mifflin, 1980), p. 1; subsequent references in text to this book will be indicated simply by page number.

17. Ezra Pound, *Selected Letters, 1907–1941,* ed. D. D. Paige (New York: New Directions, 1971), p. 210.

18. Robert Hass, "An American Epic," *The New Republic,* 185 (4 November 1981), 23–27.

19. Ezra Pound, *Selected Prose, 1909–1965,* ed. William Cookson (New York: New Directions, 1973), p. 354.

· Credits

Given the list of friends, students, and colleagues who have offered criticism of the views expressed in the preceding pages, this should be a better book. The limitations evident here are my own, truly. William Chace, James Chandler, Donald Davie, Wendy Griswold, Jerome McGann, W. J. T. Mitchell, Richard Strier, Helen Vendler, and, above all, Alan Shapiro have helped me to improve individual chapters or to see clearly where improvements are needed. I am grateful to them, and to the many graduate students with whom I have discussed contemporary poetry over the last eleven years. I remember fondly discovering the subject of Chapter 3 with Edith Brinkel, discussing that of Chapter 5 with William Chace, and talking about the shape of the book with Margaretta Fulton, whose patient encouragement has been a blessing. Steven Axelrod, Edith Jarolim, Charles Gullans, James Merrill, and Mark Schwehn have answered particular inquiries. My analysis of the audience for poetry derives from conversations with Harry Ford, Jonathan Galassi, Alice Quinn, and Elisabeth Sifton, who were generous with their time as well as with their information. I am grateful too for the generosity of the National Endowment for the Humanities: the fellowship given me to write another book made the writing of this one seem a stolen pleasure. Thanks are due to the editors of *Contemporary Literature* and *Boundary 2* for giving space in their journals to some of the material in this book. After I thought the writing of the book was complete, Joyce Backman showed me how it might be better written, and she was right. With constant good humor, Dorothy Pesch produced the typescript and secured permissions for quotations. It was my good fortune to get the help of all these people.

· Index